The Recognition of Edgar Allan Poe

Edgar Allan Poe
From a daguerreotype, in 1848

The
Recognition
of
EDGAR
ALLAN
POE

Selected Criticism Since 1829

Edited by
ERIC W. CARLSON

Ann Arbor Paperbacks
THE UNIVERSITY OF MICHIGAN PRESS

First edition as an Ann Arbor Paperback 1970
Copyright © by The University of Michigan 1966
All rights reserved
ISBN 0-472-06168-2 (paperback)
ISBN 0-472-19700-2 (clothbound)

Published in the United States of America by
The University of Michigan Press and
in Don Mills, Canada, by Longmans Canada Limited

Manufactured in the United States of America

Permissions

The Johns Hopkins Press
Georges Poulet, "Poe," *Studies in Human Time,* translated by E. Coleman, 1956.

Laurence Pollinger Limited and the Estate of the late Frieda Lawrence
D. H. Lawrence, "Edgar Allan Poe," reprinted from *Studies in Classic American Literature* by D. H. Lawrence, 1923. Published by William Heinemann Limited.

Literary Estate of Marie Bonaparte and Imago Publishing Company
Marie Bonaparte, "Morella," from *The Life and Works of Edgar Allan Poe.*

Liveright Publishing Corporation
Hart Crane, from "The Bridge," from *The Collected Poems of Hart Crane.* By permission of Liveright Publishers, New York. Copyright © Renewed 1961, by Liveright Publishing Corporation.

Macmillan and Co. Ltd.
George Saintsbury, "Edgar Allan Poe," *Prefaces and Essays, 1933.*

The Macmillan Company
Vachel Lindsay, "The Wizard in the Street," reprinted with permission of The Macmillan Company from *Collected Poems* by Vachel Lindsay. Copyright 1913 by The Macmillan Company.
William Butler Yeats, letter to W. T. Horton, reprinted with permission of The Macmillan Company from *The Letters of W. B. Yeats* edited by Allan Wade. Copyright © 1953, 1954, Anne Butler Yeats.

Stephen L. Mooney
Stephen L. Mooney, "Poe's Gothic Waste Land."

New Directions
William Carlos Williams, "Edgar Allan Poe," from *In the American Grain* by William Carlos Williams. Copyright 1925 by James Laughlin, copyright 1933 by William Carlos Williams. Reprinted with permission of the publisher, New Directions Publishing Corporation.

Routledge & Kegan Paul Ltd.
Yvor Winters, "Edgar Allan Poe: A Crisis in the History of American Obscurantism," from *In Defense of Reason.*

Rupert Hart-Davis Limited
The Letters of W. B. Yeats, edited by Allan Wade.

Charles L. Sanford
Charles L. Sanford, "Edgar Allan Poe," *Rives,* No. 18, Paris, Spring 1962, pp. 1–9.

The Society of Authors and The Public Trustee
George Bernard Shaw, "Edgar Allan Poe."

The Viking Press, Inc.
D. H. Lawrence, "Edgar Allan Poe," from *Studies in Classic American Literature* by D. H. Lawrence. Copyright 1923, 1950, by Frieda Lawrence, © 1961 by the Estate of the late Mrs. Frieda Lawrence. All rights reserved. Reprinted by permission of The Viking Press, Inc.

Richard Wilbur
Richard Wilbur, "The House of Poe."

Edmund Wilson
Edmund Wilson, "Poe at Home and Abroad," from *The Shores of Light.* New York, Farrar, Straus and Young, 1952.

Yale University Press
The Letters of Algernon C. Swinburne, edited by Cecil Y. Lang.

Preface

This selection of essays and appreciations is drawn almost entirely from American, English, and French writers. In the words of a recent book on Poe, there is "an embarrassment of critics" in English alone. And if one were to include selections from memoirists, biographers, editors, and literary historians, the resulting anthology would run to several volumes. So much ink has been spilled over questions that are at best secondary—questions concerning Poe's character, personal conduct, family and sexual history, social and business experience, career as editor and "magazinist"—that the student of literary criticism, as well as the general reader interested in useful evaluations of Poe as poet and fiction writer, finds himself overwhelmed and confused. However, since the end of World War II such a wealth of significant criticism and commentary has accumulated that the process of selection for this book has been a difficult one.

The response of the creative writer, the professional critic, and the painter, or the artist generally, to Poe has been enthusiastic and unqualified, often taking the form of a personal identification with him. Baudelaire's initial reaction was one of "an unbelievable sympathy." Fifty-seven years later, in 1909, George Bernard Shaw extolled Poe as "the finest of fine artists," defending him as a great cultural rebel-hero in revolt against a crassly materialistic America. And fifty-six years later still, in 1965, Dwight Macdonald testified to his feeling of "closeness" to the Poe who defied the literary Establishment of his day. As for Poe's influence on modern painting, one recalls that on his first visit to New York in 1966, René Magritte expressed a special wish to see the Fordham cottage because of Poe's great influence on his whole career as artist.

From the beginning, also, Poe has been an "enigma," "a stumbling block for the critic," as T. S. Eliot repeatedly emphasized. But this inscrutability of Poe, man as well as artist, only partly explains the critical disagreement over his stature and achievement through World War I or even World War II. Most damaging of all—a legacy of the Griswold defamation and controversy—was the lingering suspicion that Poe was a man of weak if not of bad character, obsessed in his writing with morbidly unwholesome themes and situations. Whatever the full explanation may be for Poe's being "so curiously misjudged" in his own country by professors of literature, his work did encounter an early moralistic reaction, especially in the United States, a reaction which only in recent years has ceased to be a major obstacle to a just appreciation of his work. Seldom distinguishing subject matter from theme or artistic intent, the nineteenth-century reader and critic tended to confuse Poe's biography with his books, reading "The Black Cat," "The Fall of the House of Usher," and "The Raven" as expressions of the personality of the notorious Mr. Poe, rumored to be an alcoholic and drug addict, a legend reinforced by the baleful, asymmetrical countenance of some of his portraits. Even among Poe's admirers the moralistic strain manifests itself, as in John Neal's wish for "something loftier and more generous."

In contrast to such moralizing, a few of Poe's contemporaries sensed that his Gothic tales represented "a penetration into the causes of things," that Poe was an "ideologist" or abstractionist, not a realist. Also implicitly aesthetic were Baudelaire's appreciation of Poe as a precursor of the Decadence and Dostoevski's praise of Poe's insight as well as his fantasy.

By 1874, twenty-five years after Poe's death, it may be supposed that the more personal slanders of Griswold had been generally forgotten. At the 1875 memorial Swinburne and Mallarmé were joined by others in recognition of the genius and the spreading fame of Poe in England and Europe. But at home Henry James was far from holding the same opinion, and Higginson and Walt Whitman, though impressed by Poe's poetic music and imagination, deplored his preference for the "abstract," "nocturnal," and "demonic" over the moral and healthy norm. The unfavorable judgments of Henry James and Yeats, though twenty years apart and later modified, represented a dissatisfaction with what seemed provincial, meretricious, or aesthetically vulgar in the poems and criticism. The image of the Poe-hero, seen as vulgarly Gothic and Decadent, tended to confirm the moralistic view that deplored lack of "humanity" and "heart" in Poe.

The belief that Poe lacked "humanity" stuck even to Brander Matthews' essay on the superior qualities of "the true detective story" created by Poe. E. A. Robinson's poetic glimpse of Poe as the lonely "wild stranger" lost in the night resembles closely Whitman's Gothic figure on the storm-tossed ship and Vachel Lindsay's street "wizard," but in the mass of biographical sketches, generalizations, descriptions, and personal opinions that passed for literary criticism, new aesthetic insights were rare. Of the voices heard during the 1909 centenary, here and abroad, the most ringing and challenging came from George Bernard Shaw, who berated England and the United States for their smug indifference to art.

After World War I, Poe specialists developed a substantial body of fact and judgment about Poe's background, life, thought, and career. These investigations prepared the way for a spate of new biographies of Poe during the 1920's and later. This outburst of biography was matched by an even more significant series of critical essays in the 1920's and 1930's. Whereas criticism of Poe up to World War I had been mainly moralistic and otherwise had been preoccupied with isolated segments of his work—for example, his poems, and of them chiefly "The Raven," "The Haunted Palace," and "The Bells"—the postwar period produced studies of greater depth and originality. Valéry's essay on *Eureka* gave new significance to that neglected work, both as a form of literature and as scientific intuition; this was followed by Lawrence's germinal essay on Poe's psychic dramas. During the 1930's the very diverse forms of recognition expressed by Hart Crane, Constance Rourke, and Marie Bonaparte added to an already impressive number of high appreciations of Poe as artist. Then, in 1937 Yvor Winters, in the most comprehensive brief against Poe ever written, alleged that while he and others slept, the Poe scholars had entered into a conspiracy to build up Poe as an author of the first rank. Winters' essay, as much as Princess Bonaparte's biography, illustrates the fallacy of critical extremism, in his instance the belated absurdity of reading Poe from a literal rationalist-moralist viewpoint, and of concluding that Poe's work is wholly without truth, theme, and moral values.

In 1949, with the lectures of T. S. Eliot and Allen Tate highlighting the centenary year, Poe's influence and stature received recognition from two of the foremost critics and poets of our time. Eliot credited the French (Baudelaire, Mallarmé, and Valéry) with sensing the variety and the unity of Poe's work as a whole. In 1950 the essays by Auden and Poulet identified new patterns of rhetoric and function, particularly in style, hero, and time. Of major importance were the lectures of Allen Tate and Richard Wilbur redefining Poe's philosophic and artistic perspective, with special attention to Poe's symbology, and reinterpreting his poems and tales in the light of that perspective. These pioneering critiques were followed, in 1962, by the equally original and sophisticated essays by Stephen Mooney and Charles Sanford, one seeing the Gothic tales of Poe as "dramas of cognition," the other placing Poe's work in the context of the quest for paradise. Viewing Poe's work in the neo-Gothic and the American contexts respectively, these appreciations are welcome correctives of the old notion that Poe belongs to no tradition and is unrelated to the spirit of any age.

Insisting on Poe's narrators as *personae,* whose style and state of mind are not to be confused with Poe's own, James Gargano clarified the dramatic use of irony, structure, and rhetoric, thus disposing of several further fallacies about Poe's fiction.

The criticism and appreciation of Poe has come of age only in the last forty-five years, and then rather slowly. The Romantic-Gothic view of Poe is no longer acceptable: as the symbolic depths and the impressionistic power of his best tales and poems have been disclosed, he can no longer be dismissed as a peddler of mystification for children, as a purveyor of thrills for adolescents, or as a "wizard" simply creating wondrous effects with words, for adults. Under Poe's Gothic flummery, there is genuine power and seriousness. To call Poe a "heroic psychic pioneer" in the "neo-Gothic" tradition, as Leslie Fiedler does, is to recognize Poe as a major formulator of the "dark tradition" of Brown, Hawthorne, Melville, Hemingway, and Faulkner. Because that tradition is not limited to the American Gothic, there will undoubtedly be more studies in "comparatist criticism," such as those which have recently traced the influence of Poe on Gide and Joyce, and the parallels in Poe and Kafka.

The great postwar efflorescence of existentialism in literature, with its exploitation of the irrational, the grotesque, the fantastic, the psychotic, and the sadistic, has brought to many readers of Poe the "shock of recognition": the discovery of Poe as a great forerunner exploring the real horrors and self-realizations of modern man.

Simultaneously, the further discovery that Poe's dramas of psychic conflict are supported by a definite perspective—a coherent pattern of ideas about art, nature, man, and culture—has encouraged a more confident and disciplined criticism. The charge of moral unconcern, of lack of "heart" and "humanity," in Poe's character and writing, which dominated and distorted Poe criticism before World War I, seems in retrospect, knowing what we do about Poe himself and his stated artistic purposes, incredibly obtuse and moralistic. Allen Tate has made clear that there is no moral indifference in Poe, but "rather a compulsive, even profound interest in a moral problem of universal concern," the problem of "spiritual vampirism." If Poe's writing has become recognized as "the proving ground for the modern consciousness," as Stephen Mooney insists, and for the modern conscience, as others maintain, then perhaps the ghost of Poe's artist-self, no longer echoing the cry "Reynolds! Reynolds!" dares murmur, "At last! At last!"

Contents

I. 1829–99

I. 1829-99

JOHN NEAL [1793–1876], a native of Maine, was a novelist, poet, critic, historian, and editor of *The Yankee*. When Poe submitted some stanzas from "Fairyland," apparently entitled "Heaven," they were published in the September 1829 *Yankee and Boston Literary Gazette*.

Comments on Poe's Poems

JOHN NEAL

If E. A. P. of Baltimore—whose lines about "Heaven," though he professes to regard them as altogether superior to anything in the whole range of American poetry, save two or three trifles referred to, are, though nonsense, rather exquisite nonsense— would but do himself justice [he] might make a beautiful and perhaps a magnificent poem. There is a good deal here to justify such a hope.

/ Here a dozen lines were quoted from "Fairyland." /

Poe later described Neal's response as "The very first words of encouragement I ever remember to have heard."

In the November *American Monthly Magazine* (1:586–87), N. P. Willis rejected "Fairyland," describing the poem as "these sickly rhymes." In the *Yankee*'s December issue, Neal prefaced a letter from Poe (containing excerpts from "Al Aaraaf," "Tamerlane," and "To — —") with a paragraph of praise and advice.

The following passages are from the manuscript works of a young author, about to be published in Baltimore. He is entirely a stranger to us, but with all their faults, if the remainder of "Al Aaraaf" and "Tamerlane" are as good as the body of the extracts here given, to say nothing of the more extraordinary parts, he will deserve to stand high—very high—in the estimation of the shining brotherhood. Whether he *will* do so, however, must depend, not so much upon his worth in mere poetry, as upon his worth hereafter in something loftier and more generous —we allude to the stronger properties of the mind, to the magnanimous determination that enables a youth to endure the present, whatever the present may be, in the hope, or rather in the belief, the fixed unwavering belief, that in the future he will find his reward.

From *Yankee and Boston Literary Gazette*, September and December 1829.

/ Here Neal quoted Poe's letter and the extracts of his poems and adds the following statement: /

Having allowed our youthful writer to be heard in his own be-half,—what more could we do for lovers of genuine poetry? Nothing. They who are judges will not need more; and they who are not—why waste words upon them? We shall not.

————————

In the New York *Mirror* for December 28, 1839, there appeared a notice praising highly the style and the power of intellect and imagination mani-fest in *Tales of the Grotesque and Arabesque*. The notice was by LOUIS FITZGERALD TASISTRO [1807–68], abolitionist, editor, critic, actor, trans-lator, and author. His *Random Shots and Southern Breezes* was published in 1842.

A Notice of Poe's Tales

LOUIS FITZGERALD TASISTRO

Had Mr. Poe written nothing else but "Morella," "William Wil-son," "The House of Usher," and the "MS. Found in a Bottle," he would deserve a high place among imaginative writers, for there is fine poetic feeling, much brightness of fancy, an excel-lent taste, a ready eye for the picturesque, much quickness of observation, and great truth of sentiment and character in all of these works. But there is scarcely one of the tales published in the two volumes before us, in which we do not find the devel-opment of great intellectual capacity, with a power for vivid description, an opulence of imagination, a fecundity of inven-tion, and a command over the elegance of diction which have seldom been displayed, even by writers who have acquired the greatest distinction in the republic of letters.

From New York *Mirror*, December 28, 1839.

In *A Fable for Critics* [1848], JAMES RUSSELL LOWELL [1819–91] dealt
harshly with Poe. But reprinted below is an earlier and more favorable
opinion—the first, 1845, version of his "Edgar Allan Poe." When Griswold
reprinted this article in his 1850 edition of Poe's works, he omitted one
third of the original, including Lowell's praise of Poe as "the most discriminating, philosophical and fearless critic upon imaginative works who
has written in America." In place of the original concluding paragraphs,
Griswold substituted three which praised Poe's skill but not his subject
matter in the tales of mystery and terror, and described Poe's criticism as
analytically precise but lacking in the warmth of ethical feeling.

Edgar Allan Poe

JAMES RUSSELL LOWELL

The situation of American literature is anomalous. It has no
center, or, if it have, it is like that of the sphere of Hermes.
It is divided into many systems, each revolving round its several suns, and often presenting to the rest only the faint glim-
mer of a milk-and-watery way. Our capital city, unlike London
or Paris, is not a great central heart, from which life and vigor
radiate to the extremities, but resembles more an isolated um-
bilicus, stuck down as near as may be to the center of the land,
and seeming rather to tell a legend of former usefulness than
to serve any present need. Boston, New York, Philadelphia,
each has its literature almost more distinct than those of the
different dialects of Germany; and the Young Queen of the West
has also one of her own, of which some articulate rumor barely
has reached us dwellers by the Atlantic. [Meanwhile, a great
babble is kept up concerning a national literature, and the country, having delivered itself of the ugly likeness of a paint-
bedaubed, filthy savage, smilingly dandles the rag baby upon
her maternal knee, as if it were veritable flesh and blood, and
would grow timely to bone and sinew.] [1]

[But, before we have an American literature, we must have
an American criticism. We have, it is true, some scores of
"American Macaulays," the faint echoes of defunct originalities,
who will discourse learnedly at an hour's notice upon matters,

From *Graham's Magazine*, February 1845.
[1] Passages in brackets were omitted by Griswold.—Editor's note.

to be even a sciolist in which would ask the patient study and self-denial of years—but, with a few rare exceptions, America is still to seek a profound, original, and aesthetic criticism. Our criticism, which from its nature might be expected to pass most erudite judgment upon the merit of thistles, undertakes to decide upon

The plant and flower of light.

There is little life in it, little conscientiousness, little reverence; nay, it has seldom the mere physical merit of fearlessness. It may be best likened to an intellectual gathering of chips to keep the critical pot of potatoes or reputation a-boiling. Too often, indeed, with the cast garments of some pigmy Gifford, or other foreign notoriety, which he has picked up at the ragfair of literature, our critic sallies forth, a self-dubbed Amadis, armed with a pen, which, more wonderful even than the fairy-gifts in an old ballad, becomes at will either the lance couched terribly at defiant windmills, or the trumpet for a halfpenny pæan.]

Perhaps there is no task more difficult than the just criticism of contemporary literature. It is even more grateful to give praise where it is needed than where it is deserved, and friendship so often seduces the iron stylus of justice into a vague flourish, that she writes what seems rather like an epitaph than a criticism. Yet if praise be given as an alms, we could not drop so poisonous a one into any man's hat. The critic's ink may suffer equally from too large an infusion of nutgalls or of sugar. But it is easier to be generous than to be just [though there are some who find it equally hard to be either], and we might readily put faith in that fabulous direction to the hiding-place of truth, did we judge from the amount of water which we usually find mixed with it.

[We were very naturally led into some remarks on American criticism by the subject of the present sketch. Mr. Poe is at once the most discriminating, philosophical, and fearless critic upon imaginative works who has written in America. It may be that we should qualify our remark a little, and say that he *might be*, rather than that he always *is*, for he seems sometimes to mistake his phial of prussic-acid for his inkstand. If we do not always agree with him in his premises, we are, at least, satisfied that his deductions are logical, and that we are reading the thoughts of a man who thinks for himself, and says what he thinks, and knows well what he is talking about. His analytic power would furnish forth bravely some score of ordinary critics. We do not know him personally, but we suspect him for a man who has one or two pet prejudices on which he prides himself. These sometimes allure him out of the strict path of criticism,[2] but, where they do not interfere, we would put almost entire confidence in his judgments. Had Mr. Poe had the control of a magazine of his own, in which to display his critical abilities, he would have been as autocratic, ere this, in America, as Professor Wilson has been in England; and his criticisms, we are sure, would have been far more profound and philosophical than those of the Scotsman. As it is, he has squared out blocks enough to build an enduring pyramid, but has left them lying carelessly and unclaimed in many different quarries.]

Remarkable experiences are usually confined to the inner life of imaginative men, but Mr. Poe's biography displays a vicissitude and peculiarity of interest such as is rarely met with. The offspring of a romantic marriage, and left an orphan at an early age, he was adopted by Mr. Allan, a wealthy Virginian, whose barren marriage bed seemed the warranty of a large estate to the young poet. Having received a classical education in England, he returned home and entered the University of Virginia, where, after an extravagant course, followed by reformation at the last extremity, he was graduated with the highest honors of his class. Then came a boyish attempt to join the fortunes of the insurgent Greeks, which ended at St. Petersburg, where he got into difficulties through want of a passport, from which he was rescued by the American consul and sent home.[3] He now entered the military academy at West Point, from which he obtained a dismissal on hearing of the birth of a son to his adopted father, by a second marriage, an event which cut off his expectations as an heir. The death of Mr. Allan, in

---

[2] We cannot but think that this was the case in his review of W. E. Channing's poems, in which we are sure that there is much which must otherwise have challenged Mr. Poe's hearty liking.—J. R. L.

[3] Lowell is not responsible for this misstatement of fact. It appeared both in Poe's autobiographical sketch to Griswold (Poe's letter of May 29, 1841) and in the Philadelphia *Saturday Museum* sketch (March 4, 1843) for which Poe supplied the notes. Both accounts were sheer fabrication.—Editor's note.

whose will his name was not mentioned, soon after relieved
him of all doubt in this regard, and he committed himself at
once to authorship for a support. Previously to this, however,
he had published (in 1827) a small volume of poems, which
soon ran through three editions, and excited high expectations
of its author's future distinction in the minds of many competent judges.

That no certain augury can be drawn from a poet's earliest
lispings there are instances enough to prove. Shakespeare's first
poems, though brimful of vigor and youth and picturesqueness,
give but a very faint promise of the directness, condensation,
and overflowing moral of his maturer works. Perhaps, however,
Shakespeare is hardly a case in point, his *Venus and Adonis*
having been published, we believe, in his twenty-sixth year.
Milton's Latin verses show tenderness, a fine eye for nature, and
a delicate appreciation of classic models, but give no hint of the
author of a new style in poetry. Pope's youthful pieces have all
the sing-song, wholly unrelieved by the glittering malignity and
eloquent irreligion of his later productions. Collins' callow
namby-pamby died and gave no sign of the vigorous and original
genius which he afterward displayed. We have never thought
that the world lost more in the "marvelous boy," Chatterton,
than a very ingenious imitator of obscure and antiquated dullness. Where he becomes original (as it is called) the interest of
ingenuity ceases and he becomes stupid. Kirke White's prom-
ises were endorsed by the respectable name of Mr. Southey, but
surely with no authority from Apollo. They have the merit of
a traditional piety, which, to our mind, if uttered at all, had
been less objectionable in the retired closet of a diary, and in
the sober raiment of prose. They do not clutch hold of the
memory with the drowning pertinacity of Watts'; neither have
they the interest of his occasional simple, lucky beauty. Burns,
having fortunately been rescued by his humble station from the
contaminating society of the "best models," wrote well and naturally from the first. Had he been unfortunate enough to have
had an educated taste, we should have had a series of poems
from which, as from his letters, we could sift here and there a
kernel from the mass of chaff. Coleridge's youthful efforts give
no promise whatever of that poetical genius which produced
at once the wildest, tenderest, most original and most purely

imaginative poems of modern times. Byron's *Hours of Idleness* would never find a reader except from an intrepid and indefatigable curiosity. In Wordsworth's first preludings there is but a dim foreboding of the creator of an era. From Southey's early poems, a safer augury might have been drawn. They show the patient investigator, the close student of history, and the unwearied explorer of the beauties of predecessors, but they give no assurances of a man who should add aught to [the] stock of household words, or to the rarer and more sacred delights of the fireside or the arbor. The earliest specimens of Shelley's poetic mind already, also, give tokens of that ethereal sublimation in which the spirit seems to soar above the region of words, but leaves its body, the verse, to be entombed, without hope of resurrection, in a mass of them. Cowley is generally instanced as a wonder of precocity. But his early insipidities show only a capacity for rhyming and for the metrical arrangement of certain conventional combinations of words, a capacity wholly dependent on a delicate physical organization, and an unhappy memory. An early poem is only remarkable when it displays an effort of *reason,* and the rudest verses in which we can trace some conception of the ends of poetry are worth all the miracles of smooth juvenile versification. A schoolboy, one would say, might acquire the regular seesaw of Pope merely by an association with the motion of the playground tilt.

Mr. Poe's early productions show that he could see through the verse to the spirit beneath, and that he already had a feeling that all the life and grace of the one must depend on and be modulated by the will of the other. We call them the most remarkable boyish poems that we have ever read. We know of none that can compare with them for maturity of purpose, and a nice understanding of the effects of language and meter. Such pieces are only valuable when they display what we can only express by the contradictory phrase of *innate experience.* We copy one of the shorter poems written when the author was only *fourteen!* [4] There is a little dimness in the filling up, but the grace and symmetry of the outline are such as few poets ever attain. There is a smack of ambrosia about it.

---

[4] Actually "To Helen" was not published until 1831, and then in a form inferior to the final version printed here, which did not appear until 1843.—Editor's note.

To Helen

Helen, thy beauty is to me
    Like those Nicéan barks of yore,
That gently, o'er a perfumed sea,
    The weary, way-worn wanderer bore
    To his own native shore.

On desperate seas long wont to roam,
    Thy hyacinth hair, thy classic face,
Thy Naiad airs have brought me home
    To the glory that was Greece
    And the grandeur that was Rome.

Lo! in yon brilliant window-niche
    How statue-like I see thee stand!
The agate lamp within thy hand,
        Ah. Psyche, from the regions which
        Are Holy Land!

It is the *tendency* of the young poet that impresses us. Here is
no "withering scorn," no heart "blighted" ere it has safely got
into its teens, none of the drawing-room sansculottism which
Byron had brought into vogue. All is limpid and serene, with
a pleasant dash of the Greek Helicon in it. The melody of the
whole, too, is remarkable. It is not of that kind which can be
demonstrated arithmetically upon the tips of the fingers. It is
of that finer sort which the inner ear alone can estimate. It
seems simple, like a Greek column, because of its perfection.
In a poem named *Ligeia*, under which title he intended to per-
sonify the music of nature, our boy-poet gives us the following
exquisite picture:

Ligeia! Ligeia!
    My beautiful one,
Whose harshest idea
    Will to melody run,
Say, is it thy will
    On the breezes to toss,
Or, capriciously still,
    Like the lone albatross,

Incumbent on night,
As she on the air,
To keep watch with delight
On the harmony there?

John Neal, himself a man of genius, and whose lyre has been too long capriciously silent, appreciated the high merit of these and similar passages, and drew a proud horoscope for their author. [The extracts which we shall presently make from Mr. Poe's later poems fully justify his predictions.]

Mr. Poe has that indescribable something which men have agreed to call *genius*. No man could ever tell us precisely what it is, and yet there is none who is not inevitably aware of its presence and its power. Let talent writhe and contort itself as it may, it has no such magnetism. Larger of bone and sinew it may be, but the wings are wanting. Talent sticks fast to earth, and its most perfect works have still one foot of clay. Genius claims kindred with the very workings of Nature herself, so that a sunset shall seem like a quotation from Dante or Milton, and if Shakespeare be read in the very presence of the sea itself, his verses shall but seem nobler for the sublime criticism of ocean. Talent may make friends for itself, but only genius can give to its creations the divine power of winning love and veneration. Enthusiasm cannot cling to what itself is unenthusiastic, nor will he ever have disciples who has not himself impulsive zeal enough to be a disciple. Great wits are allied to madness only inasmuch as they are possessed and carried away by their demon, while talent keeps him, as Paracelsus did, securely prisoned in the pommel of its sword. To the eye of genius, the veil of the spiritual world is ever rent asunder, that it may perceive the ministers of good and evil who throng continually around it. No man of mere talent ever flung his inkstand at the devil.

When we say that Mr. Poe has genius, we do not mean to say that he has produced evidence of the highest. But to say that he possesses it at all is to say that he needs only zeal, industry, and a reverence for the trust reposed in him, to achieve the proudest triumphs and the greenest laurels. If we may believe the Longinuses and Aristotles of our newspapers, we have quite too many geniuses of the loftiest order to render a place among them at all desirable, whether for its hardness of attainment or its seclusion. The highest peak of our Parnassus is, according to these gentlemen, by far the most thickly settled portion of the country, a circumstance which must make it an uncomfortable residence for individuals of a poetical temperament, if love of solitude be, as immemorial tradition asserts, a necessary part of their idiosyncrasy. [There is scarce a gentleman or lady of respectable moral character to whom these liberal dispensers of the laurel have not given a ticket to that once sacred privacy, where they may elbow Shakespeare and Milton at leisure. A transient visitor, such as a critic must necessarily be, sees these legitimate proprietors in common, parading their sacred enclosure as thick and buzzing as flies, each with "Entered according to act of Congress" labeled securely to his back. Formerly one Phœbus, a foreigner, we believe, had the monopoly of transporting all passengers thither, a service for which he provided no other conveyance than a vicious horse, named Pegasus, who could, of course, carry but one at a time, and even that but seldom, his back being a ticklish seat, and one fall proving generally enough to damp the ardor of the most zealous aspirant. The charges, however, were moderate, as the poet's pocket formerly occupied that position in regard to the rest of his outfit which is now more usually conceded to his head. But we must return from our little historical digression.]

Mr. Poe has two of the prime qualities of genius, a faculty of vigorous yet minute analysis, and a wonderful fecundity of imagination. The first of these faculties is as needful to the artist in words, as a knowledge of anatomy is to the artist in colors or in stone. This enables him to conceive truly, to maintain a proper relation of parts, and to draw a correct outline, while the second groups, fills up, and colors. Both of these Mr. Poe has displayed with singular distinctness in his prose works, the last predominating in his earlier tales, and the first in his later ones. In judging of the merit of an author, and assigning him his niche among our household gods, we have a right to regard him from our own point of view, and to measure him by our own standard. But, in estimating his works, we must be governed by his own design, and, placing them by the side of his own ideal, find how much is wanting. We differ with Mr. Poe in his opinions of the objects of art. He esteems that object to be the creation of Beauty,[5] and perhaps it is only in the definition of that word that we disagree with him. But in what we shall say of his writings we shall take his own standard as our guide. The temple of the god of song is equally accessible from every side, and there is room enough in it for all who bring offerings, or seek an oracle.

In his tales, Mr. Poe has chosen to exhibit his power chiefly in that dim region which stretches from the very utmost limits of the probable into the weird confines of superstition and unreality. He combines in a very remarkable manner two faculties which are seldom found united: a power of influencing the mind of the reader by the impalpable shadows of mystery, and a minuteness of detail which does not leave a pin or a button unnoticed. Both are, in truth, the natural results of the predominating quality of his mind, to which we have before alluded, analysis. It is this which distinguishes the artist. His mind at once reaches forward to the effect to be produced. Having resolved to bring about certain emotions in the reader, he makes all subordinate parts tend strictly to the common center. Even his mystery is mathematical to his own mind. To him x is a known quantity all along. In any picture that he paints, he understands the chemical properties of all his colors. However vague some of his figures may seem, however formless the shadows, to him the outline is as clear and distinct as that of a geometrical diagram. For this reason Mr. Poe has no sympathy with *Mysticism*. The Mystic dwells *in* the mystery, is enveloped with it; it colors all his thoughts; it affects his optic nerve especially, and the commonest things get a rainbow edging from it. Mr. Poe, on the other hand, is a spectator *ab extra*. He analyzes, he dissects, he watches.

———with an eye serene,
The very pulse of the machine,

for such it practically is to him, with wheels and cogs and piston rods all working to produce a certain end. [It is this that makes him so good a critic. Nothing balks him, or throws him off the scent, *except now and then a prejudice*.]

[5] Mr. P.'s proposition is here perhaps somewhat too *generally* stated.—Editor, *Graham's Magazine*.

This analyzing tendency of his mind balances the poetical, and, by giving him the patience to be minute, enables him to throw a wonderful reality into his most unreal fancies. A mono-mania he paints with great power. He loves to dissect one of these cancers of the mind, and to trace all the subtle ramifications of its roots. In raising images of horror, also, he has a strange success; conveying to us sometimes by a dusky hint some terrible *doubt* which is the secret of all horror. He leaves to imagination the task of finishing the picture, a task to which only she is competent.

> For much imaginary work was there;
> Conceit deceitful, so compact, so kind,
> That for Achilles' image stood his spear
> Grasped in an armed hand; himself behind
> Was left unseen, save to the eye of mind.

[We have hitherto spoken chiefly of Mr. Poe's *collected* tales, as by them he is more widely known than by those published since in various magazines, and which we hope soon to see collected. In these he has more strikingly displayed his analytic propensity.] [6]

Beside the merit of conception, Mr. Poe's writings have also that of form. His style is highly finished, graceful, and truly classical. It would be hard to find a living author who had displayed such varied powers. As an example of his style we would refer to one of his tales, *The House of Usher*, in the first volume of his *Tales of the Grotesque and Arabesque*. It has a singular charm for us, and we think that no one could read it without being strongly moved by its serene and somber beauty.

[6] Since the publication of the *Tales of the Grotesque and Arabesque*, Mr. P. has written, for this and other journals, the following *tales,* independently of essays, criticisms, etc.: *The Mystery of Marie Rogêt, Never Bet Your Head, A Tale of the Ragged Mountains, The Masque of the Red Death, The Colloquy of Monos and Una, The Landscape Garden, The Pit and the Pendulum, The Tell-Tale Heart, The Black Cat, The Man of the Crowd, The System of Doctors Tarr and Fether, The Spectacles, The Elk, The Business Man, The Premature Burial, The Oblong-Box, Thou Art the Man, Eleonora, Three Sundays in a Week, The Island of the Fay, Life in Death, The Angel of the Odd, The Literary Life of Thingum-Bob, The Descent into the Maelstrom, The 1002d Tale of Scheherazade, Mesmeric Revelation, The Murders in the Rue Morgue, The Purloined Letter,* and *The Gold-Bug.* He is also the author of the late *Balloon-Hoax.* The *Grotesque and Arabesque* included twenty-five tales.]

Had its author written nothing else it would alone have been enough to stamp him as a man of genius, and the master of a classic style. In this tale occurs one of the most beautiful of his poems. It loses greatly by being taken out of its rich and appropriate setting, but we cannot deny ourselves the pleasure of copying it here. We know no modern poet who might not have been justly proud of it.

/ "The Haunted Palace" was quoted here. /

Was ever the wreck and desolation of a noble mind so musically sung?

A writer in the *London Foreign Quarterly Review,* who did some faint justice to Mr. Poe's poetical abilities, speaks of his resemblance to Tennyson. The resemblance, if there be any, is only in so sensitive an ear to melody as leads him sometimes into quaintness, and the germ of which may be traced in his earliest poems, published several years before the first of Tennyson's appeared.

We copy one more of Mr. Poe's poems, whose effect cannot fail of being universally appreciated.

/ "Lenore" was quoted here. /

How exquisite, too, is the rhythm!

Beside his *Tales of the Grotesque and Arabesque,* and some works unacknowledged, Mr. Poe is the author of *Arthur Gordon Pym,* a romance, in two volumes, which has run through many editions in London; of a system of Conchology, of a digest and translation of Lemonnier's *Natural History,* and has contributed to several reviews in France, in England, and in this country. He edited the *Southern Literary Messenger* during its novitiate, and by his own contributions gained it most of its success and reputation. He was also, for some time, the editor of this magazine, and our readers will bear testimony to his ability in that capacity.

Mr. Poe is still in the prime of life, being about thirty-two years of age, and has probably as yet given but an earnest of his powers. As a critic, he has shown so superior an ability that we cannot but hope that he will collect his essays of this kind and give them a more durable form. They would be a very valuable contribution to our literature, and would fully justify all we have said in his praise. We could refer to many others of his poems than those we have quoted, to prove that he is the possessor of a pure and original vein. His tales and essays have equally shown him a master in prose. It is not for us to assign him his definite rank among contemporary authors, but we may be allowed to say that we know of *none* who has displayed more varied and striking abilities.

In the 1850 version by Griswold the ending of Lowell's essay is radically changed from the sentence introducing "The Haunted Palace." That sentence reads: "In this tale occurs one of the most beautiful of his poems." Omitting the poem and the remaining paragraphs, Griswold substituted the following ending:

The great masters of imagination have seldom resorted to the vague and the unreal as sources of effect. They have not used dread and horror alone, but only in combination with other qualities, as means of subjugating the fancies of their readers. The loftiest muse has ever a household and fireside charm about her. Mr. Poe's secret lies mainly in the skill with which he has employed the strange fascination of mystery and terror. In this his success is so great and striking as to deserve the name of art, not artifice. We cannot call his materials the noblest or purest, but we must concede to him the highest merit of construction.

As a critic, Mr. Poe was aesthetically deficient. Unerring in his analysis of dictions, meters, and plots, he seemed wanting in the faculty of perceiving the profounder ethics of art. His criticisms are, however, distinguished for scientific precision and coherence of logic. They have the exactness, and, at the same time, the coldness of mathematical demonstrations. Yet they stand in strikingly refreshing contrast with the vague generalisms and sharp personalities of the day. If deficient in warmth, they are also without the heat of partisanship. They are especially valuable as illustrating the great truth, too generally overlooked, that analytic power is a subordinate quality of the critic.

On the whole, it may be considered certain that Mr. Poe has attained an individual eminence in our literature, which he will keep. He has given proof of power and originality. He has done that which could only be done once with success or safety, and the imitation or repetition of which would produce weariness.

Although admiring MARGARET FULLER [1810–50] as a critic, Poe satirized her in "How to Write a Blackwood Article" [1838], and elsewhere described her as "an ill-tempered and very inconsistent *Old Maid*." However, she was able to perceive in the tales of Poe "the fruit of genuine observations and experience, combined with an invention which is . . . a penetration into the causes of things." Despite its brevity, this is one of the better early reviews.

Poe's Tales

MARGARET FULLER

Mr. Poe's tales need no aid of newspaper comment to give them popularity; they have secured it. We are glad to see them given to the public in this neat form, so that thousands more may be entertained by them without injury to their eyesight.

No form of literary activity has so terribly degenerated among us as the tale. Now that everybody who wants a new hat or bonnet takes this way to earn one from the magazines or annuals, we are inundated with the very flimsiest fabrics ever spun by mortal brain. Almost every person of feeling or fancy could supply a few agreeable and natural narratives, but when instead of using their materials spontaneously they set to work with geography in hand to find unexplored nooks of wild scenery in which to locate their Indians or interesting farmers' daughters, or with some abridgment of history to hunt monarchs or heroes yet unused to become the subjects of their crude coloring, the sale-work produced is a sad affair indeed and "gluts the market" to the sorrow both of buyers and lookers-on.

In such a state of things the writings of Mr. Poe are a refreshment, for they are the fruit of genuine observations and experience, combined with an invention which is not "making up," as children call their way of contriving stories, but a penetration into the causes of things which leads to original but credible results. His narrative proceeds with vigor, his colors are applied with discrimination, and where the effects are fantastic they are not unmeaningly so.

The "Murders in the Rue Morgue" especially made a great impression upon those who did not know its author and were not

From the New York *Daily Tribune*, July 11, 1845.

familiar with his mode of treatment. Several of his stories make us wish he would enter the higher walk of the metaphysical novel and, taking a mind of the self-possessed and deeply marked sort that suits him, give us a deeper and longer acquaintance with its life and the springs of its life than is possible in the compass of these tales.

As Mr. Poe is a professed critic and of all the band the most unsparing to others, we are surprised to find some inaccuracies in the use of words, such as these: "he had with him many books, but rarely *employed* them."—"His results have, in truth, the *whole air* of intuition."

The degree of skill shown in the management of revolting or terrible circumstances makes the pieces that have such subjects more interesting than the others. Even the failures are those of an intellect of strong fiber and well-chosen aim.

MARTIN FARQUHAR TUPPER [1810–89], English author and reviewer, is remembered chiefly for his moralistic, blank-verse *Proverbial Philosophy*. The review reprinted here is an example of the manner in which Poe's tales of terror and horror were often censured in England as well as in the United States on grounds of their alleged immorality or incredibility. Tupper devotes most of his space to praising "The Gold Bug" and "Descent into the Maelström," with long excerpts (here omitted) as a way of introducing his readers to these tales.

American Romance

MARTIN FARQUHAR TUPPER

Tales. By Edgar Allan Poe. Pp. 228. Wiley and Putnam.

[In the *Literary Gazette*, No. 1490, p. 528, we briefly noticed the following work,—so briefly that a valued correspondent had not observed it, and thought we had altogether neglected a volume of very considerable talent and imagination. To repair this wrong, he favoured us with his opinion of it; and agreeing

From the London *Literary Gazette*, January 31, 1846.

with him in his estimate, we have pleasure in adopting it as our own, and thus doing more justice to a Transatlantic writer of original powers.—Ed. *L. G.*]

"Fresh fields and pastures new" are obviously the likeliest places wherein to look for inventive genius and original power; accordingly, we are not surprised to hear that the author of this remarkable volume is an American. His work has come to our shores recommended by success upon its own; and that such success is no more than it deserves we will undertake to demonstrate to our readers, before we put the finishing point to our note of admiration.

First, however, and by way of getting a troublesome duty out of the way at once, we must qualify our coming praises, by a light and wholesome touch of censure. This, in a general way, and without descending into a specification of instances, must be held to apply to such a tale as the "Black Cat," which is impossible and revolting; to such an argument as "Mesmeric Revelation," which far too daringly attempts a solution of that deepest of riddles, the nature of the Deity; to such a dialogue as "Lionising," simply foolish; and to such a juvenile production as the "Fall of the House of Usher." These, though not without their own flashes of genius, might have been omitted to great advantage: and the remainder of the volume, acute, interesting, and graphic, would then have stood consistent with itself—*totus, teres, atque rotundus.*

Induction, and a microscopic power of analysis, seem to be the pervading characteristics of the mind of Edgar Poe. Put him on any trail, and he traces it as keenly as a Blackfoot or Ojibway; give him any clue, and he unravels the whole web of mystery: never was bloodhound more sagacious in scenting out a murderer; nor Œdipus himself more shrewd in solving an enigma. He would make a famous Transatlantic Vidocq, and is capable of more address and exploit than a Fouché; he has all his wits about him ready for use, and could calmly investigate the bursting of a bombshell; he is a hound never at fault, a moral tightrope dancer never thrown from his equilibrium; a close keen reasoner, whom no sophistry distracts—nothing foreign or extraneous diverts him from his inquiry.

But it is time to present the reader with specimens of some of our author's peculiarities. "The Gold-Bug," a strange tale of

treasure-seeking, forcibly demonstrates how able an ally Dr.
Young and M. Champollion would have found in Edgar Poe,
whilst engaged in deciphering Egyptian hieroglyphics.

. . . .

Take, again, the marvellous train of analytical reasoning whereby
he arrives at truth in the "Rue Morgue Murders"; a tale wherein
the horror of the incidents is overborne by the acuteness of the
arguments; and is introduced by a specimen of mind-reading
which Dr. Elliotson's Adolphe or Okey might vainly attempt to
equal. "The Mystery of Marie Rogêt" is similar in keenness;
and to us at least the only mystery in the matter now is,—why
was not the "dark sailor" apprehended? Additional interest is
given to these twin tales of terror from their historic truth; and
from the strange fact that the guesser's sagacity has anticipated
in the last case the murderer's confession.

Let us now turn to other pages equally brightened by
genius, while they are untarnished with the dread details of
crime. "A Descent into the Maelström" has but one fault; it is
too deliberate; there is too little in it of the rushing havoc, the
awful eddying of that northern sea's black throat. Still there is
magnificent writing in the tale; and a touch is given below of
our author's peculiar presence of mind which would stand him
in good stead on a barrel of ignited gunpowder.

/ Here was quoted a passage from "A Descent into the Maelström." /

The "Conversation Between Eiros and Charmion" is full of
terror and instruction; true to philosophy and to holy writ, it
details the probable mode of the final conflagration:

/ Here was quoted a passage from "Conversation Between Eiros
and Charmion." /

If the *Vestiges of Creation* have obtained so much celebrity
from attempting to shew and explain to mankind the *Beginning*
of things, we may surely anticipate fame for the author who
has thus, in a like philosophizing excursus, depicted to us their
Ending.

Let us, in conclusion, draw the reader's attention to the
only piece of Poe-try—(the pun is quite irresistible)—wherewith
Mr. Poe has favoured us in this book. It occurs in the otherwise
condemned tale of "Usher"; and not only half redeems that ill-

considered production, but makes us wish for many more such staves. Its title is the "Haunted Palace," and it purports to be a madman's rhapsody on his own mind:

/ Here was quoted a passage from "The Haunted Palace." /

After perusing these extracts, and our own honest verdict of the book, we are sure that our readers will not long be strangers to the Tales of Edgar Poe.

———————

In this "postscript" to Lowell's article, P. PENDLETON COOKE [1816–50] heaps unqualified praise on Poe's poetry for its "perhaps perfect" rhythm and vocabulary—especially "The Raven," which he calls "a singularly beautiful poem." He identifies Poe's genius with a "daring and wild" imagination and a Defoe-like verisimilitude in the tales, although for himself Cooke would prefer to have Poe compose "one cheerful book . . . a book full of homely doings, of successful toils, of ingenious shifts and contrivances, of ruddy firesides . . . a book for the million," rather than for the few.

Edgar A. Poe

P. PENDLETON COOKE

[The following paper is a sequel to Mr. Lowell's memoir (socalled,) of Mr. Poe, published two or three years since in Graham's Magazine. Mr. P. edited the Messenger for several years, and the pages of that magazine would seem, therefore, a proper place for the few hurried observations which I have here made upon his writings and genius.—P. P. C.]

Since the memoir of Mr. Poe, written by James Russell Lowell, appeared, Mr. P. has written some of his best things; amongst them The Raven, and Dreamland—poems—and M. Valdemar's case—a prose narrative.

"The Raven" is a singularly beautiful poem. Many readers who prefer sunshine to the weird lights with which Mr. Poe fills his sky, may be dull to its beauty, but it is none the less a great

From the *Southern Literary Messenger*, January 1848, reprinted in the Harrison edition of Poe's *Works*, I, 383–92.

triumph of imagination and art. Notwithstanding the extended
publication of this remarkable poem, I will quote it almost entire
—as the last means of justifying the praise I have bestowed
upon it.

The opening stanza rapidly and clearly arranges time, place,
etc., for the mysteries that follow.

Once upon a midnight dreary, while I pondered, weak and weary,
Over many a quaint and curious volume of forgotten lore,
While I nodded, nearly napping, suddenly there came a tapping
As of some one gently rapping, rapping at my chamber door,
' 'T is some visiter,' I muttered, tapping at my chamber door—
                    Only this, and nothing more.'

Observe how artistically the poet has arranged the circumstances of this opening—how congruous all are. This congruity
extends to the phraseology; every word is admirably selected
and placed with reference to the whole. Even the word "napping" is well chosen, as bestowing a touch of the fantastic, which
is subsequently introduced as an important component of the
poem. Stanza 2d increases the distinctness and effect of the
picture as already presented to us. The "Midnight Dreary" is
a midnight "in the bleak December," and the "dying embers"
are assuming strange and fantastic shapes upon the student's
hearth. We now pass these externals and some words of exquisite melody let us into the secret of the rooted sorrow which
has led to the lonely night-watching and fruitless study.

                    Vainly I had sought to borrow
From my books surcease of sorrow—sorrow for the lost Lenore—
For the rare and radiant maiden, *whom the angels named Lenore,*
                    Nameless here forever more.

A death was never more poetically told than in the italicised
words:
The "tapping" is renewed—

And the silken, sad, uncertain, rustling of each purple curtain
Thrilled me, filled me, with fantastic terrors never felt before,
So that now, to still the beating of my heart, I stood repeating
' 'T is some visiter entreating entrance at my chamber door,
Some late visiter entreating entrance at my chamber door,
                    Only this and nothing more.'

After some stanzas, quaint and highly artistical, the raven is found at the window; I quote now continuously to the end.

/ Here was quoted "The Raven." /

The rhythm of this poem is exquisite, its phraseology is in the highest degree musical and apt, the tone of the whole is wonderfully sustained and appropriate to the subject, which, full as it is of a wild and tender melancholy, is admirably well chosen. This is my honest judgment; I am fortified in it by high authority. Mr. Willis says:—"It is the most effective single example of fugitive poetry ever published in this country, and unsurpassed in English poetry for subtle conception, masterly ingenuity of versification, and consistent sustaining of imaginative lift. It is one of those dainties which we *feed on.* It will stick to the memory of every one who reads it."

Miss Barrett says:—"This vivid writing!—this power *which is felt!* 'The Raven' has produced a sensation—a 'fit horror' here in England. Some of my friends are taken by the fear of it, and some by the music. I hear of persons *haunted* by the Nevermore, and one acquaintance of mine, who has the misfortune of possessing a bust of Pallas, never can bear to look at it in the twilight. Our great poet, Mr. Browning, author of Paracelsus, etc., is enthusiastic in his admiration of the rhythm. . . . Then there is a tale of his which I do not find in this volume, but which is going the rounds of the newspapers, about mesmerism, throwing us all into most 'admired disorder,' or dreadful doubts as to whether it can be true, as the children say of ghost stories. The certain thing in the tale in question is the power of the writer, and the faculty he has of making horrible improbabilities seem near and familiar."

The prose narrative, "M. Valdemar's Case"—the story of which Miss Barrett speaks—is the most truth-like representation of the impossible ever written. M. Valdemar is mesmerized *in articulo mortis.* Months pass away, during which he appears to be in mesmeric sleep; the mesmeric influence is withdrawn, and instantly his body becomes putrid and loathsome—*he has been many months dead.* Will the reader believe that men were found to credit this wild story? And yet some very respectable people believed in its truth firmly. The editor of the Baltimore Visiter republished it as a statement of facts, and was at the pains to vouch for Mr. Poe's veracity. If the letter of a Mr. Collier, published just after the original appearance of the story, was not a quiz, he also fell into the same trap. I understand that some foreign mesmeric journals, German and French, reprinted it as being what it purported to be—a true account of mesmeric phenomena. That many others were deceived in like manner by this strange tale, in which, as Miss Barrett says, "the wonder and question are, can it be true?" is very probable.

With Mr. Poe's more recent productions I am not at all acquainted—excepting a review of Miss Barrett's works, and an essay on the philosophy of composition. The first of these contains a great deal of noble writing and excellent criticism; the last is an admirable specimen of analysis. I believe Mr. P. has been for some time ill—has recently sustained a heavy domestic bereavement—and is only now returning to his literary labors. The public will doubtless welcome the return of so favorite an author to pursuits in which heretofore he has done so much and so well.

Unnecessary as the labor may be, I will not conclude this postscript to Mr. Lowell's memoir, without making some remarks upon Mr. Poe's genius and writings generally.

Mr. P.'s most distinguishing power is that which made the extravagant fiction of M. Valdemar's Case sound like truth. He has De Foe's peculiar talent for filling up his pictures with minute life-like touches—for giving an air of remarkable naturalness and truth to whatever he paints. Some of his stories, written many years ago, are wonderful in this fidelity and distinctness of portraiture; "Hans Phaal," "A Descent into the Maelström," and "MS. Found in a Bottle," show it in an eminent degree. In the first of these a journey to the moon is described with the fullness and particularity of an ordinary traveller's journal; entries, astronomical and thermical, and, on reaching the moon, botanical, and zoölogical, are made with an inimitable matter-of-fact air. In A Descent into the Maelström you are made fairly to feel yourself on the descending round of the vortex, convoying fleets of drift timber, and fragments of wrecks; the terrible whirl makes you giddy as you read. In the "MS. Found in a Bottle" we have a story as wild as the mind of man ever conceived, and yet made to sound like the most matter-of-fact veracious narrative of a seaman.

But in Mr. Poe, the peculiar talent to which we are indebted for Robinson Crusoe, and the memoirs of Captain Monroe, has an addition. Truthlike as nature itself, his strange fiction shows constantly the presence of a singularly adventurous, very wild, and thoroughly poetic imagination. Some sentences from them, which always impressed me deeply, will give full evidence of the success with which this rare imaginative power is made to adorn and ennoble his truthlike pictures. Take this passage from Ligeia, a wonderful story, written to show the triumph of the human will even over *death.* Ligeia, in whom the struggle between the will to live, and the power of death, has seemed to terminate in the defeat of the passionate will, is consigned to the tomb. Her husband married a second wife, "the fair-haired and blue-eyed Lady Rowena." By the sick bed of this second wife, who is dying from some mysterious cause, he sits.

. . . .

Again take this passage from the Fall of the House of Usher.

. . . .

These quoted passages—the "white and ghastly spectrum of the teeth" in "Berenice"—the visible vulture eye, and audible heart-beat in the "Tell-tale Heart"—the resemblance in "Morella" of the living child to the dead mother, becoming gradually fearful, until the haunting eyes gleam out a terrible *identity,* and prove as in Ligeia the final conquest of the will over death—these and a thousand such clinging ideas, which Mr. P.'s writings abound in, prove indisputably that the fires of a great poet are seething under those analytic and narrative powers *in which no living writer equals him.*

This added gift of a daring and wild imagination is the source of much of the difference between our author and De Foe. De Foe loves and deals always with the homely. Mr. Poe is nervously afraid of the homely—has a creed that Beauty is the goddess of the Poet:—not Beauty with swelling bust, and lascivious carriage, exciting passions of the blood, but Beauty sublimated and cherished by the soul—the beauty of the Uranian, not Dionean Venus. De Foe gives us in the cheerful and delightful story of his colonist of the desert isles, (which has as sure a locality in a million minds as any genuine island has upon the maps,) a clear, plain, true-sounding narrative of matters that might occur any day. His love for the real

makes him do so. The "real" of such a picture has not strangeness enough in its proportions for Mr. Poe's imagination; and,
with the same talent for truthlike narrative, to what different
results of creation does not this imagination, scornful of the
soberly real, lead him! Led by it he loves to adventure into
what in one of his poems he calls—

> a wild weird clime
> Out of space, out of time;—

deals in mysteries of "life in death," dissects monomanias, exhibits convulsions of soul—in a word, wholly leaves beneath and
behind him the wide and happy realm of the common cheerful
life of man.

That he would be a greater favorite with the majority of
readers if he brought his singular capacity for vivid and truthlike narrative to bear on subjects nearer ordinary life, and of a
more cheerful and happy character, does not, I think, admit of
a doubt. But whether with the few he is not all the more appreciable from the difficult nature of the fields which he has principally chosen, is questionable. For what he has done, many of
the best minds of America, England and France, have awarded
him praise; labors of a tamer nature might not have won it from
such sources. For my individual part, having the seventy or
more tales, analytic, mystic, grotesque, arabesque, always wonderful, often great, which his industry and fertility have already
given us, I would like to read one cheerful book made by his
invention, with little or no aid from its twin brother *imagination*
—a book in his admirable style of full, minute, never tedious
narrative—a book full of homely doings, of successful toils, of
ingenious shifts and contrivances, of ruddy firesides—a book
healthy and happy throughout, and with no poetry in it at all
anywhere, except a good old English "poetic justice" in the end.
Such a book, such as Mr. Poe could make it, would be a book
for the million, and if it did nothing to exalt him with the few,
would yet certainly *endear* him to them.

Mr. Lowell has gone deeply and discriminatingly into Mr.
Poe's merits as a poet. Any elaborate remarks of mine on the
same subject, would be out of place here. I will not, however,
lose this opportunity of expressing an admiration which I have
long entertained of the singular mastery of certain externals of

his art which he everywhere exhibits in his verse. His rhythm, and his vocabulary, or phraseology, are perhaps perfect. The reader has perceived the beauty of the rhythm in The Raven. Some other verses from poems to which Mr. Lowell has referred, are quite as remarkable for this beauty. Read these verses from Lenore:—

. . . .

And take these, in the most graceful of all measures—they are from "To One in Paradise."

> And all my days are trances
>   And all my nightly dreams
> Are where thy dark eye glances,
>   And where thy footstep gleams—
> In what ethereal dances,
>   By what eternal streams.

Along with wonderful beauty of rhythm, these verses show the exquisite taste in phraseology, the nice sense of melody and aptness in words, of which I spoke. We have direct evidence of this nice sense of verbal melody in some quotations which are introduced into the dramatic fragment "Politian." Lalage reads from a volume of our elder English Dramatists:

. . . .

I must conclude these insufficient remarks upon a writer worthy of high and honorable place amongst the leading creative minds of the age.

As regards the Wiley & Putnam publication of Mr. Poe's tales—a volume by which his rare literary claims have been most recently presented to the public—I think the book in some respects does him injustice. It contains twelve tales out of more than seventy; and it is made up almost wholly of what may be called his analytic tales. This is not *representing* the author's mind in its various phases. A reader gathering his knowledge of Mr. Poe from this Wiley & Putnam issue would perceive nothing of the diversity and variety for which his writings are in fact remarkable. Only the publication of all his stories, at one issue, in one book, would show this diversity and variety in their *full* force; but much more might have been done to represent his mind by a judicious and not wholly one-toned selection.

THE REVEREND RUFUS WILMOT GRISWOLD [1815–57], Vermont-born author, Baptist minister, protégé of Horace Greeley, and editor of *Graham's Magazine*, became by the poet's own request Poe's literary executor. The irony of this misplaced trust became evident on the very day of Poe's funeral, October 9, 1849, when Griswold published his slanderous letter signed "Ludwig," which, because it was considered authoritative and was widely reprinted, did irreparable damage to Poe. While it is true that some of the errors in biographical fact are traceable to Poe's autobiographical sketch sent to Griswold in 1841, it was the effect of Griswold's own deliberate distortions, further magnified in his 1850 "Memoir," which, in spite of the efforts of Poe's friends to come to his defense, blackened Poe's reputation as a man and a writer here and abroad for decades to come.

The "Ludwig" Article

RUFUS WILMOT GRISWOLD

Edgar Allan Poe is dead. He died in Baltimore the day before yesterday. This announcement will startle many, *but few will be grieved by it.* The poet was well known personally or by reputation, in all this country; he had readers in England, and in several of the states of Continental Europe; *but he had few or no friends;* and the regrets for his death will be suggested principally by the consideration that in him literary art lost one of its most brilliant, but erratic, stars.

The family of Mr. Poe, we learn from Griswold's "Poets and Poetry of America," from which a considerable portion of the facts in this notice are derived, was one of the oldest and most respectable in Baltimore. David Poe, his paternal grandfather, was a Quartermaster-General in the Maryland line during the Revolution, and the intimate friend of Lafayette, who during his last visit to the United States, called personally upon the General's widow, and tendered her acknowledgments for the services rendered to him by her husband. His great-grandfather, John Poe, married in England, Jane, a daughter of Admiral James McBride, noted in British naval history, and claiming kindred with some of the most illustrious English families. His father and mother,—both of whom were in some way connected with the theatre, and lived as precariously as their

New York *Daily Tribune* of October 9, 1849.

more gifted, and more eminent son,—died within a few weeks
of each other, of consumption, leaving him an orphan at two
years of age. Mr. John Allan, a wealthy gentleman of Richmond, took a fancy to him, and persuaded his grandfather to
suffer him to adopt him. He was brought up in Mr. Allan's family; and as that gentleman had no other children, he was regarded
as his son and heir. In 1816 he accompanied Mr. and Mrs.
Allan to Great Britain, visited every portion of it, and afterward
passed four or five years in a school kept at [Stoke] Newington,
near London, by Rev. Dr. Bransby. He returned to America
in 1822, and in 1825 went to the Jefferson University, at Charlottesville, in Virginia, where he led a very dissipated life, the
manners of the College at that time being extremely dissolute.
He took the first honors, however, and went home greatly in
debt. Mr. Allan refused to pay some of his debts of *honor,* and
he hastily quitted the country on a quixotic expedition to join
the Greeks, then struggling for liberty. He did not reach his
original destination, however, but made his way to St. Petersburg, in Russia, when he became involved in difficulties, from
which he was extricated by the late Henry Middleton, the American Minister at that Capital. He returned home in 1829, and
immediately afterwards entered the Military Academy at West-
Point. In about eighteen months from that time, Mr. Allan, who
had lost his first wife while Mr. Poe was in Russia, married again.
He was sixty-five years of age, and the lady was young; Poe
quarreled with her, and the veteran husband, taking the part
of his wife, addressed him an angry letter, which was answered
in the same spirit. He died soon after, leaving an infant son
heir to his property, and bequeathing Poe nothing.

The army, in the opinion of the young poet, was not a place
for a poor man; so he left West Point abruptly, and determined
to maintain himself by authorship. He printed, in 1827, a small
volume of poems, most of which were written in early youth.
Some of these poems are quoted in a review by Margaret
Fuller, in *The Tribune* in 1846, and are justly regarded as among
the most wonderful exhibitions of the precocious developments
of genius. They illustrated the character of his abilities, and
justified his anticipations of success. For a considerable time,
however, though he wrote readily and brilliantly, his contributions to the journals attracted little attention, and his hopes of

gaining a livelihood by the profession of literature was nearly ended at length in sickness, poverty and despair.

But in 1831 [1833], the proprietor of a weekly gazette, in Baltimore, offered two premiums, one for the best story in prose, and the other for the best poem.

In due time Poe sent in two articles, and he waited anxiously for the decision. One of the Committee was the accomplished author of "Horseshoe Robinson," John P. Kennedy, and his associates were scarcely less eminent than he for wit and critical sagacity. Such matters were usually disposed of in a very off-hand way; committees to award literary prizes drink to the payer's health, in good wines, over the unexamined MSS., which they submit to the discretion of the publisher, with permission to use their names in such a way as to promote the publisher's advantage. So it would have been in this case, but that one of the Committee, taking up a small book, in such exquisite calligraphy as to seem like one of the finest issues of the press of Putnam, was tempted to read several pages, and being interested, he summonsed the attention of the company to the half-dozen compositions in the volume. It was unanimously decided that the prizes should be paid to the first of geniuses who had written legibly. Not another MS. was unfolded. Immediately the confidential envelope was opened, and the successful competitor was found to bear the scarcely known name of Poe.

The next day the publisher called to see Mr. Kennedy, and gave him an account of the author that excited his curiosity and sympathy, and caused him to request that he should be brought to his office. Accordingly he was introduced; the prize money had not yet been paid, and he was in the costume in which he had answered the advertisement of his good fortune. Thin, and pale even to ghastliness, his whole appearance indicated sickness and the utmost destitution. A tattered frock-coat concealed the absence of a shirt, and the ruins of boots disclosed more than the want of stockings. But the eyes of the young man were luminous with intelligence and feeling, and his voice and conversation, and manners, all won upon the lawyer's regard. Poe told his history, and his ambitions, and it was determined that he should not want means for a suitable appearance in society, nor opportunity for a just display of his abilities in literature. Mr. Kennedy accompanied him to a clothing store, and purchased for him a respectable suit, with changes of linen, and sent him to a bath, from which he returned with the suddenly regained bearing of a gentleman.

The late Mr. Thomas W. White had then recently established *The Southern Literary Messenger,* at Richmond, and upon the warm recommendation of Mr. Kennedy, Poe was engaged at a small salary—we believe of $500 a year—to be its editor. He entered upon his duties with letters full of expression of the warmest gratitude to his friends in Baltimore, who in five or six weeks were astonished to learn that with characteristic recklessness of consequence, he was hurriedly married to a girl as *poor as himself.* Poe continued in this situation for about a year and a half, in which he wrote many brilliant articles, and raised the *Messenger* to the first rank of literary periodicals.

He next removed to Philadelphia, to assist William E. Burton in the editorship of the *Gentleman's Magazine,* a miscellany that in 1840 was merged in *Graham's Magazine,* of which Poe became one of the principal writers, particularly in criticism, in which his papers attracted much attention by their careful and skilful analysis, and general caustic severity. At this period, however, he appeared to have been more ambitious of securing distinction in romantic fiction, and a collection of his compositions in this department, published in 1841, under the title of Tales of the Grotesque and the Arabesque, established his reputation for ingenuity, imagination, and extraordinary power in tragical narration.

Near the end of 1844 Poe removed to New York, where he conducted for several months a literary miscellany called the *Broadway Journal.* In 1845 he published a volume of "Tales" in Wiley and Putnam's "Library of American Books"; and in the same series a collection of his poems. Besides these poems he was the author of "Arthur Gordon Pym," a romance; "Eureka," an essay on the spiritual and material universe; a work which he wishes to have "judged as a poem"; and several extended series of papers in the periodicals, the most noteworthy of which are "Marginalia," embracing opinions of books and authors; "Secret Writing," "Autography"; and "Sketches of the Literati of New York."

His wife died in 1847, at Fordham, near this city, and some of our readers will remember the paragraphs in the papers of the time, upon his destitute condition. We remember that Col. Webb collected in a few moments fifty or sixty dollars for him at the Metropolitan Club; Mr. Lewis, of Brooklyn, sent a similar sum from one of the courts, in which he was engaged when he saw the statement of the poet's poverty; and others illustrated in the same manner the effect of such an appeal to the popular heart.

Since that time Mr. Poe had lived quietly, and with an income from his literary labors sufficient for his support. A few weeks ago he proceeded to Richmond, in Virginia, where he lectured upon the poetical character, etc.; and it was understood by some of his correspondents here that he was this week to be married, most advantageously, to a lady of that city, a widow, to whom he had been previously engaged while a student in the University.

The character of Mr. Poe we cannot attempt to describe in this very hastily written article. We can but allude to some of the more striking phases.

His conversation was at times almost supramortal in its eloquence. His voice was modulated with astonishing skill, and his large and variably expressive eyes looked reposed or shot fiery tumult into theirs who listened, while his own face glowed or was changeless in pallor, as his imagination quickened his blood, or drew it back frozen to his heart. His imagery was from the worlds which no mortal can see but with the vision of genius. Suddenly starting from a proposition exactly and sharply defined in terms of utmost simplicity and clearness, he rejected the forms of customary logic, and in a crystalline process of accretion, built up his ocular demonstrations in forms of gloomiest and ghostliest grandeur, or in those of the most airy and delicious beauty, so minutely, and so distinctly, yet so rapidly, that the attention which was yielded to him was chained till it stood among his wonderful creations—till he himself dissolved the spell, and brought his hearers back to common and base existence, by vulgar fancies or by exhibitions of the ignoble passions.

He was at times a dreamer—dwelling in ideal realms—in heaven or hell, peopled with creations and the accidents of his brain. He walked the streets, in madness or melancholy, with lips moving in indistinct curses, or with eyes upturned in pas-

sionate prayers (never for himself, for he felt, or professed to
feel, that he was already damned), but for their happiness who
at that moment were objects of his idolatry; or with his glance
introverted to a heart gnawed with anguish, and with a face
shrouded in gloom, he would brave the wildest storms; and all
night, with drenched garments and arms wildly beating the
wind and rain, he would speak as if to spirits that at such times
o ily could be evoked by him from that Aidenn close by whose
portals his disturbed soul sought to forget the ills to which his
constitution subjected him—close by that Aidenn where were
those he loved—the Aidenn which he might never see but in fitful glimpses, as its gates opened to receive the less fiery and
more happy natures whose listing to sin did not involve the
doom of death. He seemed, except when some fitful pursuit
subjected his will and engrossed his faculties, always to bear
the memory of some controlling sorrow. The remarkable poem
of *The Raven* was probably much more nearly than has been
supposed, even by those who were very intimate with him, a
reflection and an echo of his own history. He was the bird's

> —unhappy master,
> Whom unmerciful disaster
> Followed fast and followed faster
> Till his song the burden bore—
> Melancholy burden bore
> Of "Nevermore," of "Nevermore."

Every genuine author in a greater or less degree leaves in
his works, whatever their design, traces of his personal character; elements of his immortal being, in which the individual
survives the person. While we read the pages of the *Fall of the
House of Usher,* or of *Mesmeric Revelation,* we see in the solemn
and stately gloom which invests one, and in the subtle metaphysical analysis of both, indications of the idiosyncrasies,—of
what was most peculiar—in the author's intellectual nature. But
we see here only the better phases of this nature, only the symbols of his juster action, for his harsh experience had deprived
him of all faith in man or woman.

He had made up his mind upon the numberless complexi-
ties of the social world, and the whole system was with him an
imposture. This conviction gave a direction to his shrewd and

naturally unamiable character. Still though he regarded society as composed of villains, the sharpness of his intellect was not of that kind which enabled him to cope with villainy, while it continually caused him overshots, to fail of the success of honesty. He was in many respects like Francis Vivian in Bulwer's novel of the "Caxtons." "Passion, in him, comprehended many of the worst emotions which militate against human happiness. You could not contradict him, but you raised quick choler; you could not speak of wealth, but his cheek paled with gnawing envy. The astonishing natural advantage of this poor boy—his beauty, his readiness, the daring spirit that breathed around him like a fiery atmosphere—had raised his constitutional self-confidence into an arrogance that turned his very claims to admiration into prejudice against him. Irascible, envious—bad enough, but not the worst, for these salient angles were all varnished over with a cold repellant cynicism while his passions vented themselves in sneers. There seemed to him no moral susceptibility; and what was more remarkable in a proud nature, little or nothing of the true point of honor. He had, to a morbid excess, that desire to rise which is vulgarly called ambition, but no wish for the esteem or the love of his species; only the hard wish to succeed—not shine, not serve—succeed, that he might have the right to despise a world which galled his self-conceit."[1]

We have suggested the influence of his aims and vicissitudes upon his literature. It was more conspicuous in his later than his earlier writing. Nearly all that he wrote in the last two or three years—including much of his best poetry—was in some sense biographical; in draperies of his imagination, those who had taken the trouble to trace his steps, could perceive, but slightly covered, the figure of himself.

There are perhaps some of our readers who will understand the allusions of the following beautiful poem. Mr. Poe presented it in MS. to the writer of these paragraphs, just before he left New York recently, remarking it was the last thing he had written.

/ Here was quoted "Annabel Lee." /

We must omit any particular criticism of Mr. Poe's works. As a writer of tales it will be admitted generally, that he was

---

[1] When reprinted without quotation marks in Griswold's "Memoir" of Poe, this verbatim description of Bulwer's Vivian seemed to describe Poe's character.— Editor's note.

scarcely surpassed in ingenuity of construction or effective painting; as a critic, he was more remarkable as a dissector of sentences than as a commenter upon ideas. *He was little better than a carping grammarian.* As a poet, he will retain a most honorable rank. Of his "Raven," Mr. Willis observes, that in his opinion, "it is the most effective single example of fugitive poetry ever published in this country, and is unsurpassed in English poetry for subtle conceptions, masterly ingenuity of versification, and consistent sustaining of imaginative lift." In poetry, as in prose, he was most successful in the metaphysical treatment of the passions. His poems are constructed with wonderful ingenuity, and finished with consummate art. They illustrate a morbid sensitiveness of feeling, a shadowy and gloomy imagination, and a taste almost faultless in the apprehension of that sort of beauty most agreeable to his temper.

We have not learned the circumstance of his death. It was sudden, and from the fact that it occurred in Baltimore, it is presumed that he was on his return to New York.

"After life's fitful fever he sleeps well."

—Ludwig

NATHANIEL PARKER WILLIS [1806–67], Maine author, and editor of several journals, inserted this note in the *Home Journal* for October 13, 1849: "Edgar Poe is no more. He died at Baltimore on Sunday last, in the fortieth year of his age. He was a man of genius and a poet of remarkable power. Peace to his manes." Then, on October 20, came his "Death of Edgar A. Poe," a sincere defense of Poe's character. Near the beginning Willis quoted six paragraphs, not reprinted here, from the "Ludwig" article: in addition to paragraph one, they consisted of the section from "His conversation . . ." (p. 32) through "the figure of himself" (p. 34). The most damaging passage was probably the description of Bulwer's Vivian, which later appeared without the quotation marks in the memoirs by Willis and Griswold as reprinted in the latter's several editions of Poe's works. Willis himself emphasized that the Poe *he* had known as associate editor of the *Mirror* from 1844 had been "a quiet, patient, industrious, and most gentlemanly person." Poe's reported bad traits he attributed to the effects of occasional drinking, about which he had heard but which he had never witnessed. Poe's good traits Willis conveyed by reprinting several of Poe's letters, and by describing Mrs. Clemm's loyalty to him and willing sacrifices for him.

Death of Edgar Allan Poe

NATHANIEL PARKER WILLIS

The ancient fable of two antagonistic spirits imprisoned in one body, equally powerful and having the complete mastery by turns—of one man, that is to say, inhabited by both a devil and an angel—seems to have been realized, if all we hear is true, in the character of the extraordinary man whose name we have written above. Our own impression of the nature of Edgar A. Poe, differs in some important degree, however, from that which has been generally conveyed in the notices of his death. Let us, before telling what we personally know of him, copy a graphic and highly finished portraiture, from the pen of Dr. Rufus W. Griswold, which appeared in a recent number of the *Tribune:*—

/ Here were quoted passages from Griswold's "Ludwig" article. /

Apropos of the disparaging portion of the above well-written sketch, let us truthfully say:—

Some four or five years since, when editing a daily paper in this city, Mr. Poe was employed by us, for several months, as critic and subeditor. This was our first personal acquaintance with him. He resided with his wife and mother at Fordham, a few miles out of town, but was at his desk in the office, from nine in the morning till the evening paper went to press. With the highest admiration for his genius, and a willingness to let it atone for more than ordinary irregularity, we were led by common report to expect a very capricious attention to his duties, and occasionally a scene of violence and difficulty. Time went on, however, and he was invariably punctual and industrious. With his pale, beautiful and intellectual face, as a reminder of what genius was in him, it was impossible, of course, not to treat him always with deferential courtesy, and, to our occasional request that he would not probe too deep in a criticism, or that he would erase a passage colored too highly with his resentments against society and mankind, he readily and courteously assented—far more yielding than most men, we thought, on points so excusably sensitive. With a prospect of taking the lead in another periodical, he, at last, voluntarily gave up his employ-

From *Home Journal,* October 20, 1849.

ment with us, and, through all this considerable period, we had
seen but one presentment of the man—a quiet, patient, industrious, and most gentlemanly person, commanding the utmost respect and good feeling by his unvarying deportment and ability.

Residing as he did in the country, we never met Mr. Poe
in hours of leisure; but he frequently called on us afterwards at
our place of business, and we met him often in the street—invariably the same sad-mannered, winning, and refined gentleman,
such as we had always known him. It was by rumor only, up
to the day of his death, that we knew of any other development
of manner or character. We heard, from one who knew him well,
(what should be stated in all mention of his lamentable irreg-
ularities), that, with a *single glass* of wine, his whole nature
was reversed, the demon became uppermost, and, though none
of the usual signs of intoxication were visible, his *will* was palpably insane. Possessing his reasoning faculties in excited activity,
at such times, and seeking his acquaintances with his wonted
look and memory, he easily seemed personating only another
phase of his natural character, and was accused, accordingly, of
insulting arrogance and bad-heartedness. In this reversed character, we repeat, it was never our chance to see him. We know
it from hearsay, and we mention it in connection with this sad
infirmity of physical constitution, which puts it upon very nearly
the ground of a temporary and almost irresponsible insanity.

The arrogance, vanity and depravity of heart, of which
Mr. Poe was generally accused, seem, to us, referable altogether
to this reversed phase of his character. Under that degree of
intoxication which only acted upon him by demonizing his sense
of truth and right, he doubtless said and did much that was
wholly irreconcilable with his better nature; but, when himself,
and as we knew him only, his modesty and unaffected humility,
as to his own deservings, were a constant charm to his character. His letters (of which the constant application for auto-
graphs has taken from us, we are sorry to confess, the greater
portion) exhibited this quality very strongly. In one of the carelessly written notes of which we chance still to retain possession,
for instance, he speaks of "The Raven"—that extraordinary poem
which electrified the world of imaginative readers, and has become the type of a school of poetry of its own—and, in evident
earnest, attributes its success to the few words of commendation

with which we had prefaced it in this paper. It will throw light on his sane character to give a literal copy of the note:—

Fordham, April 20, 1849.

My Dear Willis:—The poem which I enclose, and which I am so vain as to hope you will like, in some respects, has been just published in a paper for which sheer necessity compels me to write, now and then. It pays well as times go—but unquestionably it ought to pay ten prices; for whatever I send it I feel I am consigning to the tomb of the Capulets. The verses accompanying this, may I beg you to take out of the tomb, and bring them to light in the *Home Journal?* If you can oblige me so far as to copy them, I do not think it will be necessary to say 'From the ——,' —— that would be too bad; —— and, perhaps, 'from a late —— paper,' would do.

I have not forgotten how a 'good word in season' from you made 'The Raven,' and made 'Ulalume,' (which, by-the-way, people have done me the honor of attributing to you)—therefore I *would* ask you, (if I dared), to say something of these lines—if they please you.

Truly yours ever,
Edgar A. Poe.

In double proof—of his earnest disposition to do the best for himself, and of the trustful and grateful nature which has been denied him—we give another of the only three of his notes which we chance to retain:—

Fordham, January 22, 1848.

My dear Mr. Willis:—I am about to make an effort at re-establishing myself in the literary world, and *feel* that I may depend upon your aid.

My general aim is to start a Magazine, to be called *'The Stylus';* but it would be useless to me, even when established, if not entirely out of the control of a publisher. I mean, therefore, to get up a Journal which shall be *my own,* at all points. With this end in view, I must get a list of, at least, five hundred subscribers to begin with:—nearly two hundred I have already. I propose, however, to go South and West, among my personal and literary friends— old college and West Point acquaintances—and see what I can do. In order to get the means of taking the first step, I propose to lecture at the Society Library, on Thursday, the 3d of February—and, that there may be no cause of *squabbling,* my subject shall *not be literary* at all. I have chosen a broad text—'The Universe.'

Having thus given you *the facts* of the case, I leave all the rest to the suggestions of your own tact and generosity. Gratefully—*most* gratefully—

Your friend always,
Edgar A. Poe.

Brief and chance-taken, as these letters are, we think they sufficiently prove the existence of the very qualities denied to Mr. Poe—humility, willingness to persevere, belief in another's kindness, and capability of cordial and grateful friendship! Such he assuredly was *when sane.* Such only he has invariably seemed to us, in all we have happened personally to know of him, through a friendship of five or six years. And so much easier is it to believe what we have seen and known, than what we *hear of* only, that we remember him but with admiration and respect —these descriptions of him, when morally insane, seeming to us like portraits, painted in sickness, of a man we have only known in health.

But there is another, more touching, and far more forcible evidence that there *was goodness* in Edgar A. Poe. To reveal it, we are obliged to venture upon the lifting of the veil which sacredly covers grief and refinement in poverty—but we think it may be excused, if so we can brighten the memory of the poet, even were there not a more needed and immediate service which it may render to the nearest link broken by his death.

Our first knowledge of Mr. Poe's removal to this city was by a call which we received from a lady who introduced herself to us as the mother of his wife. She was in search of employment for him, and she excused her errand by mentioning that he was ill, that her daughter was a confirmed invalid, and that their circumstances were such as compelled her taking it upon herself. The countenance of this lady, made beautiful and saintly with an evidently complete giving up of her life to privation and sorrowful tenderness, her gentle and mournful voice urging its plea, her long-forgotten but habitually and unconsciously refined manners, and her appealing and yet appreciative

mention of the claims and abilities of her son, disclosed at once
the presence of one of those angels upon earth that women in
adversity can be. It was a hard fate that she was watching over.
Mr. Poe wrote with fastidious difficulty, and in a style too much
above the popular level to be well paid. He was always in
pecuniary difficulty, and, with his sick wife, frequently in want
of the merest necessaries of life. Winter after winter, for years,
the most touching sight to us, in this whole city, has been that
tireless minister to genius, thinly and insufficiently clad, going
from office to office with a poem, or an article on some literary
subject, to sell—sometimes simply pleading in a broken voice that
he was ill, and begging for him—mentioning nothing but that "he
was ill," whatever might be the reason for his writing nothing—
and never, amid all her tears and recitals of distress, suffering one
syllable to escape her lips that could convey a doubt of him, or
a complaint, or a lessening of pride in his genius and good intentions. Her daughter died, a year and a half since, but she did
not desert him. She continued his ministering angel—living with
him—caring for him—guarding him against exposure, and, when
he was carried away by temptation, amid grief and the loneli-
ness of feelings unreplied to, and awoke from his self-abandon-
ment prostrated in destitution and suffering, *begging* for him
still. If woman's devotion, born with a first love, and fed with
human passion, hallow its object, as it is allowed to do, what
does not a devotion like this—pure, disinterested and holy as the
watch of an invisible spirit—say for him who inspired it?

We have a letter before us, written by this lady, Mrs.
Clemm, on the morning in which she heard of the death of this
object of her untiring care. It is merely a request that we would
call upon her, but we will copy a few of its words—sacred as its
privacy is—to warrant the truth of the picture we have drawn
above, and add force to the appeal we wish to make for her:—

> I have this morning heard of the death of my darling
> Eddie. . . . Can you give me any circumstances or partic-
> ulars. . . . Oh! do not desert your poor friend in this bit-
> ter affliction. . . . Ask Mr. —— to come, as I must deliver a
> message to him from my poor Eddie. . . . I need not ask
> you to notice his death and to speak well of him. I know
> you will. But say what an affectionate son he was to me,
> his poor desolate mother. . . .

To hedge round a grave with respect, what choice is there, between the relinquished wealth and honors of the world, and the story of such a woman's unrewarded devotion! Risking what we do, in delicacy, by making it public, we feel—other reasons aside—that it betters the world to make known that there are such ministrations to its erring and gifted. What we have said will speak to some hearts. There are those who will be glad to know how the lamp, whose light of poetry has beamed on their far-away recognition, was watched over with care and pain— that they may send to her, who is more darkened than they by its extinction, some token of their sympathy. She is destitute, and alone. If any, far or near, will send to us what may aid and cheer her through the remainder of her life, we will joyfully place it in her hands.

EVERT AUGUSTUS DUYCKINCK [1816–78], American author and editor, owned and edited, with his brother George Long Duyckinck, the foremost literary weekly of that period, the *Literary World.* He was a friend and adviser to Poe during the last four years of Poe's life, when such support was desperately needed. However, this review by Duyckinck of Griswold's 1850 edition of Poe finds fault with Poe as a writer, as well as praising certain of his qualities. A later view of Poe as a symbolist was anticipated by Duyckinck's impression of Poe as an "ideologist—a man of ideas . . . and dealt solely in abstractions." In the September 26, 1850, issue Duyckinck questioned Griswold's "Memoir": "the opinions we find expressed are about as dishonest as they well could be."

Poe's Works

EVERT AUGUSTUS DUYCKINCK

The Works of the Late Edgar Allan Poe: with Notices of his Life and Genius. By N. P. Willis, J. R. Lowell, and R. W. Griswold. In two vols. J. S. Redfield.

From the announcement we expected a somewhat fuller account of the life of Mr. Poe than is furnished in the few pages prefixed to this collection of his writings. If we had considered carefully

From the *Literary World,* January 26, 1850.

the character of the man's talent this expectation would have been found to be ill-founded. Poe was strictly impersonal; as greatly so as any man whose acquaintance we have enjoyed. In a knowledge of him extending through several years, and frequent opportunities, we can scarcely remember to have had from him any single disclosure or trait of personal character; anything which marked him as a mover or observer among men. Although he had traveled in distant countries, sojourned in cities of our own country, and had, at different times, under favorable opportunities, been brought into contact with life and character of many phases, he had no anecdote to tell, no description of objects, dress, or appearance. Nothing, in a word, to say of things. Briefly, he was what Napoleon named an ideologist—a man of ideas. He lived entirely apart from the solidities and realities of life: was an abstraction; thought, wrote, and dealt solely in abstractions. It is this which gives their peculiar feature to his writings. They have no color, but are in pure outline, delicately and accurately drawn, but altogether without the glow and pulse of humanity. His genius was mathematical, rather than pictorial or poetical. He demonstrates instead of painting. Selecting some quaint and abstruse theme, he proceeded to unfold it with the closeness, care, and demonstrative method of Euclid; and you have, to change the illustration, fireworks for fire; the appearance of water for water; and a great shadow in the place of an actual, moist, and thunderbearing sky. His indifference to living, flesh and blood subjects, explains his fondness for the mechanism and music of verse, without reference to the thought or feeling. He is therefore a greater favorite with scholars than with the people; and would be (as a matter of course) eagerly followed by a train of poetastering imitators, who, to do them justice in a familiar image, "hear the bell ring and don't know where the clapper hangs." Poe is an object of considerable, or more than considerable size; but the imitation of Poe is a shadow indescribably small and attenuated. We can get along, for a while, on a diet of common air—but the exhausted receiver of the air-pump is another thing! The method and management of many of Mr. Poe's tales and poems are admirable, exhibiting a wonderful ingenuity, and completely proving him master of the weapon he had chosen for his use. He lacks reality, imagination, everyday power, but he is remarkably subtle, acute, and earnest in his own way. His instrument is neither an organ nor a harp; he is neither a King David nor a Beethoven, but rather a Campanologian, a Swiss bell-ringer, who from little contrivances of his own, with an ingeniously devised hammer, strikes a sharp melody, which has all that is delightful and affecting, that is attainable without a soul. We feel greatly obliged to Messrs. Willis, Lowell, and Griswold, for helping to wheel forward into public view this excellent machine; to which Mr. Redfield has furnished an appropriate cloth and cover, with the performer's head, as large and as true as life, stamped on its front, in an excellent daguerreotype portrait.

In addition to his 1852 and 1856 essays on Poe, CHARLES BAUDELAIRE [1821–67] wrote this one, the preface to his second volume of translations [1857]. To Baudelaire Poe is the *poète maudit*, symbol of the alienated artist in frustrated rebellion against materialism. He exalts Poe's insight into the "democratic illusions" of his time—democracy as a social philosophy, the idea of inevitable progress, the Rousseauistic worship of the primitive. In Poe's aesthetic theory and practice, Baudelaire found confirmation of his own doctrine of poetry and of the "Literature of Decadence" generally.

New Notes on Edgar Poe

CHARLES BAUDELAIRE

I

Decadent literature!—Empty words which we often hear fall, with the sonority of a deep yawn, from the mouths of those unenigmatic sphinxes who keep watch before the sacred doors of classical Aesthetics. Each time that the irrefutable oracle resounds, one can be sure that it is about a work more amusing than the *Iliad*. It is evidently a question of a poem or of a novel, all of whose parts are skillfully designed for surprise, whose

"Notes nouvelles sur Edgar Poe," translated by Lois and Francis Hyslop. Preface to *Nouvelles histoires extraordinaires par Edgar Poe*, 1857.

style is magnificently embellished, where all the resources of language and prosody are utilized by an impeccable hand. When I hear the anathema boom out—which, I might say in passing, usually falls on some favorite poet—I am always seized with the desire to reply: Do you take me for a barbarian like you and do you believe me capable of amusing myself as dismally as you do? Then grotesque comparisons stir in my brain; it seems to me that two women appear before me: one, a rustic matron, repugnant in her health and virtue, plain and expressionless, in short, *owing everything to simple nature;* the other, one of those beauties who dominate and oppress one's memory, adding all the eloquence of dress to her profound and original charm, well poised, conscious and queen of herself—with a speaking voice like a well-tuned instrument, and eyes laden with thoughts but revealing only what they wish. I would not hesitate in my choice, and yet there are pedagogical sphinxes who would reproach me for my failure to respect classical honor.— But, putting aside parables, I think it is permissible to ask these wise men if they really understand all the vanity, all the futility of their wisdom. The phrase *decadent literature* implies that there is a scale of literatures, an infantile, a childish, an adolescent, etc. This term, in other words, supposes something fatal and providential, like an ineluctable decree; and it is altogether unfair to reproach us for fulfilling the mysterious law. All that I can understand in this academic phrase is that it is shameful to obey this law with pleasure and that we are guilty to rejoice in our destiny.—The sun, which a few hours ago overwhelmed everything with its direct white light, is soon going to flood the western horizon with variegated colors. In the play of light of the dying sun certain poetic spirits will find new delights; they will discover there dazzling colonnades, cascades of molten metal, paradises of fire, a sad splendor, the pleasure of regret, all the magic of dreams, all the memories of opium. And indeed the sunset will appear to them like the marvelous allegory of a soul filled with life which descends behind the horizon with a magnificent store of thoughts and dreams.

But what the narrow-minded professors have not realized is that, in the movement of life, there may occur some complication, some combination quite unforeseen by their schoolboy wisdom. And then their inadequate language fails, as in the case

—a phenomenon which perhaps will increase with variants—of a nation which begins with decadence and thus starts where others end.

Let new literatures develop among the immense colonies of the present century and there will result most certainly spiritual accidents of a nature disturbing to the academic mind. Young and old at the same time, America babbles and rambles with an astonishing volubility. Who could count its poets? They are innumerable. Its *blue stockings?* They clutter the magazines. Its critics? You may be sure that they have pedants who are as good as ours at constantly recalling the artist to ancient beauty, at questioning a poet or a novelist on the morality of his purpose and the merit of his intentions. There can be found there as here, but even more than here, men of letters who do not know how to spell; a childish, useless activity; compilers in abundance, hack writers, plagiarists of plagiaries, and critics of critics. In this maelstrom of mediocrity, in this society enamored of material perfections—a new kind of scandal which makes intelligible the grandeur of inactive peoples—in this society eager for surprises, in love with life, but especially with a life full of excitements, a man has appeared who was great not only in his metaphysical subtlety, in the sinister or bewitching beauty of his conceptions, in the rigor of his analysis, but also great and not less great as a *caricature.*—I must explain myself with some care; for recently a rash critic, in order to disparage Edgar Poe and to invalidate the sincerity of my admiration, used the word jongleur which I myself had applied to the noble poet as a sort of praise.

From the midst of a greedy world, hungry for material things, Poe took flight in dreams. Stifled as he was by the American atmosphere, he wrote at the beginning of *Eureka:* "I offer this book to those who have put faith in dreams as in the only realities!" He was in himself an admirable protest, and he made his protest in his own particular way. The author who, in "The Colloquy of Monos and Una," pours out his scorn and disgust for democracy, progress and *civilization,* this author is the same one who, in order to encourage credulity, to delight the stupidity of his contemporaries, has stressed human sovereignty most emphatically and has very ingeniously fabricated hoaxes flattering to the pride of *modern man.* Considered in this light, Poe seems like a helot who wishes to make his master blush. Finally, to state my thought even more clearly, Poe was always great not only in his noble conceptions but also as a prankster.

II

For he was never a dupe! I do not think that the Virginian who calmly wrote in the midst of a rising tide of democracy: "People have nothing to do with laws except to obey them," has ever been a victim of modern wisdom; and: "The nose of a mob is its imagination. By this, at any time, it can be quietly led"—and a hundred other passages in which mockery falls thick and fast like a hail of bullets but still remains proud and indifferent. —The Swedenborgians congratulate him on his "Mesmeric Revelation," like those naïve Illuminati who formerly hailed in the author of the *Diable amoureux* a discoverer of their mysteries; they thank him for the great truths which he has just proclaimed —for they have discovered (O verifiers of the unverifiable!) that all that which he has set forth is absolutely true;—although, at first, these good people confess, they had suspected that it might well have been merely fictitious. Poe answers that, so far as he is concerned, he has never doubted it.—Must I cite in addition this short passage which catches my eye while scanning for the hundredth time his amusing "Marginalia," which are the secret chambers, as it were, of his mind: "The enormous multiplication of books in all branches of knowledge is one of the greatest scourges of this age, for it is one of the most serious obstacles to the acquisition of all positive knowledge." Aristocrat by nature even more than by birth, the Virginian, the Southerner, the Byron gone astray in a bad world, has always kept his philosophic impassability and, whether he defines the nose of the mob, whether he mocks the fabricators of religions, whether he scoffs at libraries, he remains what the true poet was and always will be—a truth clothed in a strange manner, an apparent paradox, who does not wish to be elbowed by the crowd and who runs to the far east when the fireworks go off in the west.

But more important than anything else: we shall see that this author, product of a century infatuated with itself, child of a nation more infatuated with itself than any other, has clearly seen, has imperturbably affirmed the natural wickedness of man. There is in man, he says, a mysterious force which modern philosophy does not wish to take into consideration; nevertheless, without this nameless force, without this primordial bent, a host of human actions will remain unexplained, inexplicable. These actions are attractive only *because* they are bad or dangerous; they possess the fascination of the abyss. This primitive, irresistible force is natural Perversity, which makes man constantly and simultaneously a murderer and a suicide, an assassin and a hangman;—for he adds, with a remarkably satanic subtlety, the impossibility of finding an adequate rational motive for certain wicked and perilous actions could lead us to consider them as the result of the suggestions of the Devil, if experience and history did not teach us that God often draws from them the establishment of order and the punishment of scoundrels;—*after having used the same scoundrels as accomplices!* such is the thought which, I confess, slips into my mind, an implication as inevitable as it is perfidious. But for the present I wish to consider only the great forgotten truth—the primordial perversity of man—and it is not without a certain satisfaction that I see some vestiges of ancient wisdom return to us from a country from which we did not expect them. It is pleasant to know that some fragments of an old truth are exploded in the faces of all these obsequious flatterers of humanity, of all these humbugs and quacks who repeat in every possible tone of voice: "I am born good, and you too, and all of us are born good!" forgetting, no! pretending to forget, like misguided equalitarians, that we are all born marked for evil!

Of what lies could he be a dupe, he who sometimes—sad necessity of his environment—dealt with them so well? What scorn for pseudophilosophy on his good days, on the days when he was, so to speak, inspired! This poet, several of whose compositions seem deliberately made to confirm the alleged omnipotence of man, has sometimes wished to purge himself. The day that he wrote: "All certainty is in dreams," he thrust back his own Americanism into the region of inferior things; at other times, becoming again the true poet, doubtless obeying the ineluctable truth which haunts us like a demon, he uttered the ardent sighs of *the fallen angel who remembers heaven;* he lamented the olden age and the lost Eden; he wept over all the magnificence of nature *shrivelling up before the hot breath of fiery furnaces;* finally, he produced those admirable pages: "The Colloquy of Monos and Una" which would have charmed and troubled the impeccable de Maistre.

It is he who said about socialism at a time when the latter did not yet have a name, or when, at least, this name was not completely popularized: "The world is infested, just now, by a new sect of philosophers, who have not yet suspected themselves of forming a sect, and who, consequently, have adopted no name. They are the *Believers in everything Old.* Their High Priest in the East, is Charles Fourier—in the West, Horace Greeley; and they are well aware that they are high priests. The only common bond among the members is Credulity:—let us call it Insanity at once, and be done with it. Ask any one of them *why* he believes this or that, and, if he be conscientious (ignorant people usually are), he will make you very much such a reply as Talleyrand made when asked why he believed in the Bible. 'I believe in it first,' said he, 'because I am Bishop of Autun; and, secondly, because I don't know the least thing about it.' What these philosophers call 'argument' is a way they have 'de nier ce qui est et d'expliquer ce qui n'est pas.' "

Progress, that great heresy of decay, likewise could not escape Poe. The reader will see in different passages what terms he used to characterize it. One could truly say, considering the fervor that he expends, that he had to vent his spleen on it, as on a public nuisance or as on a pest in the street. How he would have laughed, with the poet's scornful laugh, which alienates simpletons, had he happened, as I did, upon this wonderful statement which reminds one of the ridiculous and deliberate absurdities of clowns. I discovered it treacherously blazoned in an eminently serious magazine:—*The unceasing progress of science has very recently made possible the rediscovery of the lost and long sought secret of* . . . (Greek fire, the tempering of copper, something or other which has vanished), *of which the most successful applications date back to a* barbarous *and very old period!!!* That is a sentence which can be called a real find, a brilliant discovery, even in a century of *unceasing progress;* but I believe that the mummy Allamistakeo would not have failed to ask with a gentle and discreet tone of superiority, if it were also thanks to *unceasing progress*—to the fatal, irresistible law of progress—that this famous secret had been lost.—Moreover, to become serious about a subject which is as sad as it is laughable, is it not a really stupefying thing to see a nation, several nations, and presently all humanity, say to its wise men, its magicians: I shall love you and I shall make you great if you convince me that we are progressing unconsciously, inevitably— while sleeping; rid us of responsibility, veil for us the humiliation of comparisons, turn history into sophistries and you will be able to call yourselves the wisest of the wise? Is it not a cause for astonishment that this simple idea does not flash into everyone's mind: that progress (in so far as there is progress) perfects sorrow to the same extent that it refines pleasure and that, if the epidermis of peoples is becoming delicate, they are evidently pursuing only an *Italiam fugientem,* a conquest lost every minute, a progress always negating itself?

But these illusions which, it must be added, are selfish, originate in a foundation of perversity and falsehood—meteors rising from swamps—which fill with disdain souls in love with the eternal fire, like Edgar Poe, and exasperate foggy minds like Jean-Jacques [Rousseau], in whom a wounded and rebellious sensibility takes the place of philosophy. That he was justified in his attack on the *depraved animal* is undeniable; but the depraved animal has the right to reproach him for invoking simple nature. Nature produces only monsters, and the whole question is to understand the word *savages.* No philosopher will dare to propose as models those wretched, rotten hordes, victims of the elements, prey of the animals, as incapable of manufacturing arms as of conceiving the idea of a spiritual and supreme power. But, if one wishes to compare modern man, civilized man, with the savage, or rather a so-called civilized nation with a so-called savage nation, that is to say one deprived of all the ingenious inventions which make heroism unnecessary, who does not see that all honor goes to the savage? By his nature, by very necessity itself, he is encyclopedic, while civilized man finds himself confined to the infinitely small regions of specialization. Civilized man invents the philosophy of progress to console himself for his abdication and for his downfall; whereas the savage man, redoubtable and respected husband, warrior forced to personal bravery, poet in the melancholy hours when the setting sun inspires songs of the past and of his forefathers, skirts more closely the edge of the ideal. Of what lack shall we dare accuse him? He has the priest, he has the magician and the doctor. What am I saying? He has the dandy, supreme incarnation of the idea of the beautiful given expression in material life, he who dictates form and governs manners. His clothing, his adornments, his weapons, his pipe give proof of an inventive faculty which for a long time has deserted us. Shall we compare our sluggish eyes and our deafened ears to those eyes which pierce the mist, to those ears *which would hear the grass growing?* And the savage woman with a simple and childlike soul, an obedient and winning animal, giving herself entirely and knowing that she is only half of a destiny, shall we declare her inferior to the American woman whom M. Bellegarigue (editor of the *Grocer's Bulletin!*) thought he was praising by saying that she was the ideal of the kept woman? This same woman, whose overpractical manners inspired Edgar Poe, he who was so gallant, so respectful of beauty, to write the following sad lines: "The frightfully long money-pouches—'like the Cucumber called the Gigantic'—which have come in vogue among our belles—are *not* of Parisian origin, as many suppose, but are strictly indigenous here. The fact is, such a fashion would be quite out of place in Paris, where it is money *only* that women keep in a purse. The purse of an American lady, however, must be large enough to carry both her money and the soul of its owner." As for religion, I shall not speak of Vitzilipoutzli as lightly as Alfred de Musset has done; I confess without shame that I much prefer the cult of Teutatès to that of Mammon; and the priest who offers to the cruel extorter of human sacrifices victims who die *honorably,* victims who *wish* to die, seems to me a quite sweet and human being compared to the financier who immolates whole populations solely in his own interest. Now and then, these matters are still understood, and I once found in an article by M. Barbey d'Aurevilly an exclamation of philosophic sadness which sums up everything that I should like to say about the subject: "Civilized peoples, who keep casting stones at savages, soon you will not deserve to be even idolaters!"

Such an environment—although I have already said so, I cannot resist the desire to repeat it—is hardly made for poets. What a French mind, even the most democratic, understands by a State, would find no place in an American mind. For every intellect of the old world, a political State has a center of movement which is its brain and its sun, old and glorious memories, long poetic and military annals, an aristocracy to which poverty, daughter of revolutions, can add only a paradoxical luster; but That! that mob of buyers and sellers, that nameless creature, that headless monster, that outcast on the other side of the ocean, you call that a State!—I agree, if a vast tavern where the customer crowds in and conducts his business on dirty tables, amid the din of coarse speech, can be compared to a *salon*, to what we formerly called a salon, a republic of the mind presided over by beauty!

It will always be difficult to exercise, both nobly and fruitfully, the profession of a man of letters, without being exposed to defamation, to the slander of the impotent, to the envy of the rich—that envy which is their punishment!—to the vengeance of bourgeois mediocrity. But what is difficult in a limited monarchy or in an ordinary republic becomes almost impossible in a sort of Capernaum where each policeman of public opinion keeps order in the interest of his vices—or of his virtues, for it is all one and the same thing;—where a poet, a novelist of a country in which slavery exists, is a detestable writer in the eyes of an abolitionist critic; where one does not know which is more scandalous—the disorder of cynicism or the imperturbability of Biblical hypocrisy. To burn chained Negroes guilty of having felt their black cheeks sting with the blush of honor, to play with guns in the pit of a theater, to establish polygamy in the paradises of the West, which the savages (this term seems unjust) had not yet soiled with these shameful Utopias, to post on walls, doubtless to sanctify the principle of unlimited liberty, *the cure for nine months' illnesses,* such are some of the salient characteristics, some of the moral examples of the noble country of Franklin, the inventor of a counting-house morality, the hero of a century devoted to materialism. It is good to consider constantly these extraordinary examples of gross behavior in a time when americanomania has become almost a fashionable passion, to the extent that an archbishop has been able to promise us quite seriously that Providence would soon call us to enjoy this transatlantic ideal.

Such a social environment necessarily engenders corresponding literary errors. Poe reacted against these errors as often as he could, and with all his might. We must not be surprised then that American writers, though recognizing his singular power as a poet and as a storyteller, have always tended to question his ability as a critic. In a country where the idea of utility, the most hostile in the world to the idea of beauty, dominates and takes precedence over everything, the perfect critic will be the most *respectable,* that is to say the one whose tendencies and desires will best approximate the tendencies and desires of his public—the one who, confusing the intellectual faculties of the writer and the categories of writing, will assign to all a single goal—the one who will seek in a book of poetry the means of perfecting conscience. Naturally he will become all the less concerned with the real, the positive beauties of poetry; he will be all the less shocked by imperfections and even by faults in execution. Edgar Poe, on the contrary, dividing the world of the mind into pure *Intellect, Taste,* and *Moral Sense,* applied criticism in accordance with the category to which the object of his analysis belonged. He was above all sensitive to perfection of plan and to correctness of execution; taking apart literary works like defective pieces of machinery (considering the goal that they wished to attain), noting carefully the flaws of workmanship; and when he passed to the details of the work, to its plastic expression, in a word, to style, examining meticulously and without omissions the faults of prosody, the grammatical errors and all the mass of dross which, among writers who are not artists, besmirch the best intentions and deform the most noble conceptions.

For him, Imagination is the queen of faculties; but by this word he understands something greater than that which is understood by the average reader. Imagination is not fantasy; nor is it sensibility, although it may be difficult to conceive of an imaginative man who would be lacking in sensibility. Imagination is an almost divine faculty which perceives immediately and without philosophical methods the inner and secret relations of things, the correspondences and the analogies. The honors and functions which he grants to this faculty give it such value (at least when the thought of the author has been well understood) that a scholar without imagination appears only as a pseudoscholar, or at least as an incomplete scholar.

Among the literary domains where imagination can obtain the most curious results, can harvest treasures, not the richest, the most precious (those belong to poetry), but the most numerous and the most varied, there is one of which Poe is especially fond; it is the *Short Story*. It has the immense advantage over the novel of vast proportions that its brevity adds to the intensity of effect. This type of reading, which can be accomplished in one sitting, leaves in the mind a more powerful impression than a broken reading, often interrupted by the worries of business and the cares of social life. The unity of impression, the *totality* of effect is an immense advantage which can give to this type of composition a very special superiority, to such an extent that an extremely short story (which is doubtless a fault) is even better than an extremely long story. The artist, if he is skillful, will not adapt his thoughts to the incidents but, having conceived deliberately and at leisure an effect to be produced, will invent the incidents, will combine the events most suitable to bring about the desired effect. If the first sentence is not written with the idea of preparing this final impression, the work has failed from the start. There must not creep into the entire composition a single word which is not intentional, which does not tend, directly or indirectly, to complete the premeditated design.

There is one point in which the short story is superior even to the poem. Rhythm is necessary to the development of the idea of beauty, which is the greatest and the most noble aim of poetry. Now, the artifices of rhythm are an insurmountable obstacle to the detailed development of thought and expression which has *truth* as its object. For truth can often be the goal of the short story, and reasoning the best tool for the construction of a perfect short story. That is why this type of composition, which is not as high on the scale as pure poetry, can provide more varied results, more easily appreciated by the average reader. Moreover, the author of a short story has at his disposal a multitude of tones, of nuances of language, the rational tone, the sarcastic, the humorous, which are repudiated by poetry and which are, as it were, dissonances, outrages to the idea of pure beauty. And that is also why the author who seeks in the short story the single goal of beauty works only at a great disadvantage, deprived as he is of the most useful instrument, rhythm. I know that in all literatures efforts have been made, often successful, to create purely poetic short stories; Edgar Poe himself has written some very beautiful ones. But they are struggles and efforts which serve only to prove the strength of the true means adapted to the corresponding goals, and I am inclined to believe that in the case of some authors, the greatest that can be chosen, these heroic attempts spring from despair.

IV

"*Genus irritabile vatum!* That poets (using the word comprehensively, as including artists in general) are a *genus irritabile*, is well understood; but the *why,* seems not to be commonly seen. An artist *is* an artist only by dint of his exquisite sense of Beauty—a sense affording him rapturous enjoyment but at the same time implying, or involving, an equally exquisite sense of Deformity or disproportion. Thus a wrong—an injustice—done a poet who is really a poet, excites him to a degree which, to ordinary apprehension, appears disproportionate with the wrong. Poets *see* injustice—*never* where it does not exist—but very often where the unpoetical see no injustice whatever. Thus the poetical irritability has no reference to 'temper' in the vulgar sense but merely to a more than usual clear-sightedness in respect to Wrong:—this clear-sightedness being nothing more than a corollary from the vivid perception of Right—of justice—of proportion —in a word, of the beautiful. But one thing is clear—that the man who is *not* 'irritable' (to the ordinary apprehension) is *no poet.*"

Thus the poet himself speaks, preparing an excellent and irrefutable apologia for all those of his race. Poe carried this sensibility into his literary affairs, and the extreme importance which he attached to things poetic often led him to use a tone in which, according to the judgment of the weak, a feeling of superiority became too evident. I have already mentioned, I believe, that several prejudices which he had to combat, false ideas, commonplace opinions which circulated around him, have for a long time infected the French press. It will not be useless then to give a brief account of some of his most important opinions relative to poetic composition. The parallelism of error will make their application quite easy.

But above all, I must point out that in addition to the share which Poe granted to a natural, innate poetic gift, he gave an importance to knowledge, work, and analysis that will seem excessive to arrogant and unlettered persons. Not only has he expended considerable efforts to subject to his will the fleeting spirit of happy moments, in order to recall at will those exquisite sensations, those spiritual longings, those states of poetic health, so rare and so precious that they could truly be considered as graces exterior to man and as visitations; but also he has subjected inspiration to method, to the most severe analysis. The choice of means! he returns to that constantly, he insists with a learned eloquence upon the adjustment of means to effect, on the use of rhyme, on the perfecting of the refrain, on the adaptation of rhythm to feeling. He maintained that he who cannot seize the intangible is not a poet; that he alone is a poet who is master of his memory, the sovereign of words, the record book of his own feelings always open for examination. Everything for the conclusion! he often repeats. Even a sonnet needs a plan, and the construction, the armature, so to speak, is the most important guarantee of the mysterious life of works of the mind.

I turn naturally to the article entitled "The Poetic Principle," and I find from the very beginning a vigorous protest against what could be called, in the field of poetry, the heresy of length or of dimension—the absurd importance attributed to bulky poems. "I hold that a long poem does not exist. I maintain that the phrase, 'a long poem,' is simply a flat contradiction in terms." In fact, a poem deserves its title only insomuch as it excites and uplifts the soul, and the real merit of a poem is due to this excitation, to this *uplifting* of the soul. But, from psychological necessity, all these excitations are fugitive and transitory. This strange mood into which the soul of the reader has been drawn by force, as it were, will certainly not last as long as the reading of a poem which exceeds human capacity for enthusiasm.

It is obvious then that the epic poem stands condemned. For a work of that length can be considered poetic only insofar as one sacrifices the vital condition of every work of art, Unity; —I do not mean unity in the conception but unity in the impression, the *totality* of effect, as I said when I had occasion to compare the novel with the short story. The epic poem then appears to us, aesthetically speaking, as a paradox. Bygone ages may have produced a series of lyric poems, later compiled into epic poems; but every *epic intention* obviously is the result of an imperfect sense of art. The time for these artistic anomalies has passed, and it is even very doubtful that a long poem has ever been truly popular in the full meaning of the word.

It must be added that a too short poem, one which does not furnish a *pabulum* that will sustain the excitation created, one which is not equal to the natural appetite of the reader, is also very defective. However brilliant and intense the effect may be, it is not lasting; memory does not retain it; it is like a seal which, placed too lightly and too hastily, has not had time to imprint its image on the wax.

But there is another heresy which, thanks to the hypocrisy, to the dullness, and to the baseness of human minds, is even more formidable and has a greater chance of survival—an error which has a hardier life—I wish to speak of the heresy of *teaching a lesson* which includes as inevitable corollaries the heresy of *passion,* of *truth,* and of *morality.* A great many people imagine that the aim of poetry is a lesson of some sort, that it must now fortify the conscience, now perfect morals, now in short *prove* something or other which is useful. Edgar Poe claims that Americans especially have supported this heterodox idea; alas! there is no need to go as far as Boston to encounter the heresy in question. Even here it attacks and breaches true poetry every day. Poetry, if only one is willing to seek within himself, to question his heart, to recall his memories of enthusiasm, has no other goal than itself; it cannot have any other, and no poem will be so great, so noble, so truly worthy of the name of poetry as that which will have been written solely for the pleasure of writing a poem.

I do not mean that poetry does not ennoble manners—let there be no mistake about it—that its final result is not to raise man above the level of vulgar interests; that would obviously be an absurdity. I say that, if the poet has pursued a moral aim, he has diminished his poetic force; and it is not rash to wager that his work will be bad. Poetry cannot, under penalty of death or failure, be assimilated to science or morality; it does not have Truth as its object, it has only Itself. The means for demonstrating truth are other and are elsewhere. Truth has nothing to do with songs. All that constitutes the grace, the charm, the irresistible attraction of a song, would take from Truth its authority and its power. Cold, calm, impassive, the demonstrative mood rejects the diamonds and the flowers of the Muse; it is then absolutely the inverse of the poetic mood.

Pure Intellect aims at Truth, Taste reveals Beauty, and Moral Sense teaches us what is Right. It is true that taste is intimately connected with the other two, and is separated from Moral Sense only by so slight a difference that Aristotle has not hesitated to include among the virtues some of its delicate operations. Thus, what especially exasperates the man of taste in the spectacle of vice is its deformity, its disproportion. Vice injures the just and the true, revolts the intellect and the conscience; but, as an outrage to harmony, as dissonance, it will wound more particularly certain poetic minds; and I do not think it scandalous to consider every offense against morality, against moral beauty, as a kind of offense against universal rhythm and prosody.

It is that admirable, that immortal instinct for the beautiful which makes us consider the earth and its spectacles as a revelation, as something in correspondence with Heaven. The insatiable thirst for everything that lies beyond, and that life reveals, is the most living proof of our immortality.

It is at the same time by poetry and *through* poetry, by and *through* music that the soul glimpses the splendors beyond the tomb; and when an exquisite poem brings us to the verge of tears, those tears are not the proof of excessive pleasure; they are rather evidence of an aroused melancholy, of a condition of nerves, of a nature which has been exiled amid the imperfect and which would like to take possession immediately, on this very earth, of a revealed paradise.

Thus, the principle of poetry is precisely and simply human aspiration toward a superior beauty, and the manifestation of this principle is in an enthusiasm, an excitation of the soul—an enthusiasm altogether independent of passion which is the intoxication of the heart, and of truth which is the food of reason. For passion is *natural*, too natural not to introduce an offensive, discordant tone into the domain of pure beauty, too familiar and too violent not to scandalize the pure Desires, the gracious Melancholies and the noble Despairs which inhabit the supernatural regions of poetry.

This extraordinary elevation, this exquisite delicacy, this

accent of immortality which Edgar Poe demands of the Muse, far from making him less attentive to the technique of execution, have impelled him constantly to sharpen his genius as a technician. Many people, especially those who have read the strange poem called *The Raven*, would be shocked if I analyzed the article in which our poet, apparently innocently, but with a slight impertinence which I cannot condemn, has explained in detail the method of construction which he used, the adaptation of the rhythm, the choice of a refrain—the shortest possible and the most suitable to a variety of applications, and at the same time the most representative of melancholy and despair, embellished with the most sonorous rhyme of all (nevermore)— the choice of a bird capable of imitating the human voice, but a bird—the raven—branded with a baneful and fatal character in popular imagination—the choice of the most poetic of all tones, the melancholy tone—of the most poetic sentiment, love for one dead, etc.—"And I shall not place the hero of my poem in poor surroundings," he says, "because poverty is commonplace and contrary to the idea of Beauty. His melancholy will be sheltered by a magnificently and poetically furnished room." The reader will detect in several of Poe's short stories curious symptoms of this inordinate taste for beautiful forms, especially for beautiful forms that are strange, for ornate surroundings and oriental sumptuousness.

I said that this article seemed marred by a slight impertinence. Confirmed advocates of inspiration would be sure to find in it blasphemy and profanation; but I believe that it is for them especially that the article has been written. Just as certain writers feign carelessness, aiming at a masterpiece with their eyes closed, full of confidence in disorder, expecting that words thrown at the ceiling will fall back on the floor in the form of a poem, so Edgar Poe—one of the most inspired men I know—has made a pretense of hiding spontaneity, of simulating coolness and deliberation. "It will not be regarded as a breach of decorum on my part"—he says with an amusing pride which I do not consider in bad taste—"to show that no one point in its composition is referable either to accident or intuition—that the work proceeded, step by step, to its completion with the precision and rigid consequence of a mathematical problem." Only lovers of chance, I say, only fatalists of inspiration and fanatics of *free verse* can find this *attention to detail* odd. There are no insignificant details in matters of art.

As for free verse, I shall add that Poe attached an extreme importance to rhyme, and that in the analysis which he has made of the mathematical and musical pleasure which the mind derives from rhyme, he has introduced as much care, as much subtlety as in all the other subjects pertaining to the art of poetry. Just as he has shown that the refrain is capable of infinitely varied applications, so also he has sought to renew, to redouble the pleasure derived from rhyme by adding to it an unexpected element, the strange, which is the indispensable condiment, as it were, of all beauty. He often makes a happy use of repetitions of the same line or of several lines, insistent reiterations of phrases which simulate the obsessions of melancholy or of a fixed idea—of a pure and simple refrain introduced in several different ways—of a variant refrain which feigns carelessness and inadvertence—of rhymes redoubled and tripled and also of a kind of rhyme which introduces into modern poetry, but with more precision and purpose, the surprises of Leonine verse.

It is obvious that the value of all these means can be proved only through application; and a translation of poetry so studied, so concentrated, can be a fond dream, but only a dream. Poe wrote little poetry; he has sometimes expressed regret at not being able to devote himself, not more often, but exclusively, to this type of work which he considered the most noble. But his poetry always creates a powerful effect. It is not the ardent outpouring of Byron, it is not the soft, harmonious, distinguished melancholy of Tennyson for whom, it may be said in passing, he had an almost fraternal admiration. It is something profound and shimmering like a dream, mysterious and perfect like crystal. I do not need to add, I presume, that American critics have often disparaged his poetry; very recently I found in a dictionary of American biography an article in which it was adjudged esoteric, in which it was feared that this muse in learned garb might create a school in the proud country of utilitarian morality, and in which regret was expressed that Poe had not applied his talents to the expression of moral truths in place of spending them in quest of a bizarre ideal, of lavishing in his verses a mysterious, but sensual voluptuousness.

We are all familiar with that kind of sharp riposte. The

reproaches that bad critics heap upon good poets are the same in all countries. In reading this article it seemed to me that I was reading the translation of one of those numerous indictments brought by Parisian critics against those of our poets who are most fond of perfection. Our favorites are easy to guess and every lover of pure poetry will understand me when I say that in the eyes of our antipoetic race Victor Hugo would be less admired if he were perfect, and he has succeeded in having all his lyric genius forgiven only by introducing forcibly and brutally into his poetry what Edgar Poe considered the major modern heresy—*the teaching of a lesson.*

FYODOR M. DOSTOEVSKI [1821–81], Russian novelist, journalist, and short-story writer, was well-read in foreign literatures. In one issue of his magazine *Time* (*Wremia*) (I, 230), Dostoevski introduced to Russian readers three of Poe's tales—"The Tell-Tale Heart," "The Black Cat," and "The Devil in the Belfry"—with the prefatory essay reprinted below. Dostoevski valued especially Poe's psychological insight, realism of detail, "capricious" fancy, and unbounded American imagination. The appeal of Poe for Russian readers culminated in the 1900's with the translation of his complete works by Konstantin Balmont, who hailed "the mad Edgar" as "our elder brother."

Three Tales of Edgar Poe

FYODOR M. DOSTOEVSKI

Two or three stories by Edgar Poe have already been translated and published in Russian magazines. Here we present to our readers three more. What a strange, though enormously talented writer, that Edgar Poe! His work can hardly be labeled as purely fantastic, and in so far as it falls into this category, its fantasticalness is a merely external one, if one may say so. He admits, for instance, that an Egyptian mummy that had lain five thousand years in a pyramid, was recalled into life with the help of galvanism. Or he presumes that a dead man, again by means of galvanism, tells the state of his mind, and so on, and so on. Yet

From *Wremia*, 1861, translated by Vladimir Astrov.

such an assumption alone does not make a story really fantastic. Poe merely supposes the outward possibility of an unnatural event, though he always demonstrates logically that possibility and does it sometimes even with astounding skill; and this premise once granted, he in all the rest proceeds quite realistically. In this he differs essentially from the fantastic as used for example by Hoffmann. The latter personifies the forces of Nature in images, introduces in his tales sorceresses and specters, and seeks his ideals in a far-off utterly unearthly world, and not only assumes this mysterious magical world as superior but seems to believe in its real existence. . . . Not so Edgar Poe. Not fantastic should he be called but capricious. And how odd are the vagaries of his fancy and at the same time how audacious! He chooses as a rule the most extravagant reality, places his hero in a most extraordinary outward or psychological situation, and, then, describes the inner state of that person with marvellous acumen and amazing realism. Moreover, there exists one characteristic that is singularly peculiar to Poe and which distinguishes him from every other writer, and that is the vigor of his imagination. Not that his fancy exceeds that of all other poets, but his imagination is endowed with a quality which in such magnitude we have not met anywhere else, namely the power of details. Try, for instance, yourselves to realize in your mind anything that is very unusual or has never before occurred, and is only conceived as possible, and you will experience how vague and shadowy an image will appear before your inner eye. You will either grasp more or less general traits of the inward image or you will concentrate upon the one or the other particular, fragmentary feature. Yet Edgar Poe presents the whole fancied picture or events in all its details with such stupendous plasticity that you cannot but believe in the reality or possibility of a fact which actually never has occurred and even never could happen. Thus he describes in one of his stories a voyage to the moon, and his narrative is so full and particular, hour by hour following the imagined travel, that you involuntarily succumb to the illusion of its reality. In the same way he once told in an American newspaper the story of a balloon that crossed the ocean from Europe to the New World, and his tale was so circumstantial, so accurate, so filled with unexpected, accidental happenings, in short was so realistic and truthful that at least for a couple of hours everybody was convinced of the reported fact and only later investigation proved it to be entirely invented. The same power of imagination, or rather combining power, characterizes his stories of the Purloined Letter, of the murder committed by an orangutan, of the discovered treasure, and so on.

Poe has often been compared with Hoffmann. As we have said before, we believe such a comparison to be false. Hoffmann is a much greater poet. For he possesses an ideal, however wrong sometimes, yet an ideal full of purity and of inherent human beauty. You find this ideal embodied even oftener in Hoffmann's nonfantastic creations, such as "Meister Martin" or the charming and delightful "Salvator Rosa," to say nothing of his masterpiece, "Kater Murr." In Hoffmann, true and ripe humor, powerful realism as well as malice, are welded with a strong craving for beauty and with the shining light of the ideal. Poe's fantasticalness, as compared with that, seems strangely "material," if such expression may be allowed. Even his most unbounded imagination betrays the true American. To acquaint our readers with this capricious talent we present meanwhile three of his tales.

To ALGERNON CHARLES SWINBURNE [1837–1909], Poe was "that wonderful and exquisite poet . . . the only one (as yet) among her [America's] men of genius who has won not merely English but European fame." The following letter to Sara Sigourney Rice is testimony to the spreading recognition of Poe throughout Europe.

Letter to Sara Sigourney Rice

ALGERNON CHARLES SWINBURNE

November 9 [1875]

Dear Madam

I have heard with much pleasure of the memorial at length raised to your illustrious fellow-citizen. The genius of Edgar

Published in the New York *Daily Tribune*, November 27, 1875, p. 4; facsimile in *Edgar Allan Poe, A Memorial Volume*, Sara S. Rice, ed. (Baltimore, 1877), pp. 69–72.

Poe has won on this side of the Atlantic such wide and warm recognition that the sympathy which I cannot hope fitly or fully to express in adequate words is undoubtedly shared at this moment by hundreds as far as the news may have spread throughout not England only but France as well; where as I need not remind you the most beautiful and durable of monuments has been reared to the genius of Poe by the laborious devotion of a genius equal and akin to his own; and where the admirable translation of his prose works by a fellow-poet, whom also we have now to lament before his time, is even now being perfected by a careful and exquisite version of his poems, with illustrations full of the subtle and tragic force of fancy which impelled and moulded the original song; a double homage due to the loyal and loving cooperation of one of the most remarkable younger poets and one of the most powerful leading painters in France—M. Mallarmé and M. Manet.

It is not for me to offer any tribute here to the fame of your great countryman, or to dilate with superfluous and intrusive admiration on the special quality of his strong and delicate genius, so sure of aim and faultless of touch in all the better and finer part of work he has left us. I would only, in conveying to the members of the Poe Memorial Committee my sincere acknowledgment of the honour they have done me in recalling my name on such an occasion, take leave to express my firm conviction that widely as the fame of Poe has already spread, and deeply as it is already rooted in Europe, it is even now growing wider and striking deeper as time advances; the surest presage that time, the eternal enemy of small and shallow reputations, will prove in this case also the constant and trusty friend and keeper of a true poet's full-grown fame.

I remain Dear Madam
Yours very truly,
A. C. Swinburne

STÉPHANE MALLARMÉ [1842–98], French poet, translator of Poe's poems, teacher of English for thirty years in French *lycées,* and friend of well-known writers, artists, and musicians, became the leader of that group of young poets known as the *Symbolistes,* who gathered weekly at the famous "Tuesdays" held at his home in Paris. The following tribute to Poe is the improved definitive version (1883) of the sonnet written in 1876 for the dedication of Poe's tomb in Baltimore (cf. *Edgar Allan Poe: A Memorial Volume,* S. S. Rice, ed., Baltimore, 1877). Beginning with a line now famous for its tight condensation of meaning and implication, the theme of the poem runs generally as follows:

By Eternity changed at last into what he essentially Is, the Poet with naked sword rouses up the epoch of his contemporaries, overwhelmed with horror to realize that they had never understood that death was triumphant in that strange voice.

Hearing, of old, that angel bestow a purer meaning upon the words of the tribe, they started up like the detestable Hydra, bawling out that his words were but a wizard's spell imbibed dishonorably from the draught of some dark brew.

If, out of the conflict of earth and heaven,—O grief!—our thoughts carve no bas-relief with which to adorn Poe's shining tomb—

Then, calm block of stone, here fallen from obscure disaster, may at least this granite forever thrust its barrier against dark flights of Blasphemy scattered throughout the years to come. (Translated by Doris G. Carlson.)

Le Tombeau d'Edgar Poe

STÉPHANE MALLARMÉ

Tel qu'en Lui-même enfin l'éternité le change,
Le Poëte suscite avec un glaive nu
Son siècle épouvanté de n'avoir pas connu
Que la mort triomphait dans cette voix étrange!

Eux, comme un vil sursaut d'hydre oyant jadis l'ange
Donner un sens plus pur aux mots de la tribu
Proclamèrent très haut le sortilège bu
Dans le flot sans honneur de quelque noir mélange.

From *Edgar Allan Poe: A Memorial Volume,* S. S. Rice, ed., Baltimore: Turnbull, 1877.

Du sol et de la nue hostiles, ô grief!
Si notre idée avec ne sculpte un bas-relief
Dont la tombe de Poe éblouissante s'orne,

Calme bloc ici-bas chu d'un désastre obscur,
Que ce granit du moins montre à jamais sa borne
Aux noirs vols du Blasphème épars dans le futur.

In a letter to Sara S. Rice, Mallarmé translated the earlier version of his sonnet into English, with a few notes on the meaning of key words. But as his translation is neither idiomatic nor reliable, it is not reproduced here.

In his autobiography HENRY JAMES [1843–1916] describes how he thrilled to his playmates' recitals of "The Raven," "Lenore," and "Annabel Lee," and their reading of "The Pit and the Pendulum," "The Gold Bug," and "The Murders in the Rue Morgue." Perhaps this juvenile introduction to Poe explains James's later association of Poe's writings with a "decidedly primitive stage of reflection" and his allusion to Poe's "very valueless verses," later changed to "very superficial verses," with the further admission to Andrew Lang that "I suppose I made a mistake" (or words to that effect). In *The Golden Bowl* (1904), on the other hand, he recalls "a wonderful tale . . . which was a thing to show, by the way, what imagination Americans *could* have—the story of the shipwrecked Gordon Pym. . . ." The following early comments, however, are most often quoted to represent James's view of Poe.

Comments

HENRY JAMES

For American readers, furthermore, Baudelaire is compromised by his having made himself the apostle of our own Edgar Poe. He translated, very carefully and exactly, all of Poe's prose writings, and, we believe, some of his very valueless verses. With all due respect to the very original genius of the author of

This review of *Les Fleurs du Mal* first appeared in *The Nation*, April 27, 1876. Reprinted in "Baudelaire" in *French Poets and Novelists* (New York and London: Macmillan, 1878), p. 76.

the "Tales of Mystery," it seems to us that to take him with more than a certain degree of seriousness is to lack seriousness one's self. An enthusiasm for Poe is the mark of a decidedly primitive stage of reflection. Baudelaire thought him a profound philosopher, the neglect of whose golden utterances stamped his native land with infamy. Nevertheless, Poe was much the greater charlatan of the two, as well as the greater genius. [1876]

There was but little literary criticism in the United States at the time Hawthorne's earlier works were published; but among the reviewers Edgar Poe perhaps held the scales the highest. He, at any rate, rattled them loudest, and pretended, more than any one else, to conduct the weighing-process on scientific principles. Very remarkable was this process of Edgar Poe's, and very extraordinary were his principles; but he had the advantage of being a man of genius, and his intelligence was frequently great. His collection of critical sketches of the American writers flourishing in what M. Taine would call his *milieu* and *moment,* is very curious and interesting reading, and it has one quality which ought to keep it from ever being completely forgotten. It is probably the most complete and exquisite specimen of *provincialism* ever prepared for the edification of men. Poe's judgments are pretentious, spiteful, vulgar; but they contain a great deal of sense and discrimination as well, and here and there, sometimes at frequent intervals, we find a phrase of happy insight imbedded in a patch of the most fatuous pedantry. He wrote a chapter upon Hawthorne, and spoke of him, on the whole, very kindly; and his estimate is of sufficient value to make it noticeable that he should express lively disapproval of the large part allotted to allegory in his tales—in defence of which, he says, "however, or for whatever object employed, there is scarcely one respectable word to be said . . . The deepest emotion," he goes on, "aroused within us by the happiest allegory *as* allegory, is a very, *very* imperfectly satisfied sense of the writer's ingenuity in overcoming a difficulty we should have preferred his not having attempted to overcome. . . . One thing is clear, that if allegory ever establishes a fact, it is by dint of overturning a fiction"; and Poe has furthermore the courage

From *Hawthorne* (New York: Harper, 1879).

to remark that the *Pilgrim's Progress* is a "ludicrously overrated book." Certainly, as a general thing, we are struck with the ingenuity and felicity of Hawthorne's analogies and correspondences; the idea appears to have made itself at home in them easily. Nothing could be better in this respect than *The Snow Image* (a little masterpiece), or *The Great Carbuncle,* or *Doctor Heidegger's Experiment,* or *Rappaccini's Daughter.* But in such things as *The Birth-Mark* and *The Bosom-Serpent* we are struck with something stiff and mechanical, slightly incongruous, as if the kernel had not assimilated its envelope.

THOMAS WENTWORTH HIGGINSON [1823–1911], author, critic, and Unitarian minister, is best known in literature as the "discoverer" of Emily Dickinson and subsequently her friend and correspondent. In the following essay from his *Short Studies of American Authors* (1888), he gives a colorful and interesting first-hand account of Poe's reading of "Al Aaraaf" at the Boston Lyceum in 1845, to an audience at first mystified and then spellbound. Quite representative of the period are Higginson's faintly disguised moral judgments on Poe, whom he compares unfavorably with Hawthorne, both as a writer and a person, though remarking, "how wonderful remains the power of Poe's imaginative tales, and how immense is the ingenuity of his puzzles and disentanglements."

Poe

THOMAS WENTWORTH HIGGINSON

It happens to us but few times in our lives to come consciously into the presence of that extraordinary miracle we call genius. Among the many literary persons whom I have happened to meet, at home or abroad, there are not half a dozen who have left an irresistible sense of this rare quality; and, among these few, Poe stands next to Hawthorne in the vividness of personal impression he produced. I saw him but once, and it was on that celebrated occasion, in 1845, when he startled Boston by substituting his boyish production, "Al Aaraaf," for the more serious

First printed in *Literary World,* March 15, 1879.

poem which he was to have delivered before the Lyceum. There was much curiosity to see him, for his prose-writings had been eagerly read, at least among college students, and his poems were just beginning to excite still greater attention. After a rather solid and very partisan address by Caleb Cushing, then just returned from his Chinese embassy, the poet was introduced. I distinctly recall his face, with its ample forehead, brill.ant eyes, and narrowness of nose and chin; an essentially ideal face, not noble, yet anything but coarse; with the look of over-sensitiveness which when uncontrolled may prove more debasing than coarseness. It was a face to rivet one's attention in any crowd; yet a face that no one would feel safe in loving. It is not perhaps strange that I find or fancy in the portrait of Charles Baudelaire, Poe's French admirer and translator, something of the traits that are indelibly associated with that one glimpse of Poe.

I remember that when introduced he stood with a sort of shrinking before the audience and then began in a thin, tremulous, hardly musical voice, an apology for his poem, and a deprecation of the expected criticism of a Boston audience; reiterating this in a sort of persistent, querulous way, which did not seem like satire, but impressed me at the time as nauseous flattery. It was not then known, nor was it established for long after—even when he had himself asserted it—that the poet was himself born in Boston; and no one can ever tell, perhaps, what was the real feeling behind the apparently sycophantic attitude. When, at the end, he abruptly began the recitation of his rather perplexing poem, the audience looked thoroughly mystified. The verses had long since been printed in his youthful volume, and had re-appeared within a few days, if I mistake not, in Wiley & Putnam's edition of his poems; and they produced no very distinct impression on the audience until Poe began to read the maiden's song in the second part. Already his tones had been softening to a finer melody than at first, and when he came to the verse:

> Ligeia! Ligeia,
>   My beautiful one!
> Whose harshest idea
>   Will to melody run,

O! is it thy will
  On the breezes to toss?
Or capriciously still
  Like the lone albatross
Incumbent on night
  (As she on the air)
To keep watch with delight
  On the harmony there?

his voice seemed attenuated to the finest golden thread; the
audience became hushed, and, as it were, breathless; there
seemed no life in the hall but his; and every syllable was accen-
tuated with such delicacy, and sustained with such sweetness
as I never heard equaled by other lips. When the lyric ended,
it was like the ceasing of the gipsy's chant in Browning's "Flight
of the Duchess"; and I remember nothing more, except that in
walking back to Cambridge my comrades and I felt that we had
been under the spell of some wizard. Indeed, I feel much the
same in the retrospect to this day.

The melody did not belong, in this case, to the poet's voice
alone; it was already in the words. His verse, when he was willing to give it natural utterance, was like that of Coleridge in
rich sweetness, and like that was often impaired by theories of
structure and systematic experiments in meter. Never in American literature, I think, was such a fountain of melody flung into
the air as when "Lenore" first appeared in the *Pioneer;* and
never did fountain so drop downward as when Poe rearranged
it in its present form. The irregular measure had a beauty as
original as that of "Christabel," and the lines had an ever-vary-
ing, ever-lyrical cadence of their own until their author himself
took them and cramped them into couplets. What a change from

Peccavimus!
But rave not thus!
And let the solemn song
Go up to God so mournfully that *she* may feel no wrong!

to the amended version, portioned off in regular lengths, thus:

Peccavimus! but rave not thus! and let a Sabbath song
Go up to God so solemnly, the dead may feel no wrong.

Or worse yet, when he introduced that tedious jingle of slightly varied repetition which reached its climax in lines like these:

Till the fair and gentle Eulalie became my blushing bride.
Till the yellow-haired young Eulalie became my smiling
bride.

This trick, caught from Poe, still survives in our literature; made more permanent, perhaps, by the success of his "Raven." This poem, which made him popular, seems to me far inferior to some of his earlier and slighter effusions; as those exquisite verses "To Helen" which are among our American classics, and have made

The glory that was Greece
And the grandeur that was Rome,

a permanent phrase in our language.

Poe's place in purely imaginative prose-writing is as unquestionable as Hawthorne's. He even succeeded, which Hawthorne did not, in penetrating the artistic indifference of the French mind; and it was a substantial triumph, when we consider that Baudelaire put himself or his friends to the trouble of translating even the prolonged platitudes of "Eureka," and the wearisome narrative of "Arthur Gordon Pym." Neither Poe nor Hawthorne has ever been fully recognized in England; and yet no Englishman of our time, except possibly De Quincey, has done any prose imaginative work to be named with theirs. But in comparing Poe with Hawthorne, we see that the genius of the latter has hands and feet as well as wings, so that all his work is solid as masonry, while Poe's is broken and disfigured by all sorts of inequalities and imitation and stucco; he not disdaining, for want of true integrity, to disguise and falsify, to claim knowledge that he did not possess, to invent quotations and references, and even, as Griswold showed, to manipulate and exaggerate puffs of himself. I remember the chagrin with which I looked through Tieck, in my student-days, to find the "Journey into the Blue Distance" to which Poe refers in the "House of Usher"; and how one of the poet's intimates laughed me to scorn for being deceived by any of Poe's citations; saying that he hardly knew a word of German.

But making all possible deductions, how wonderful remains

the power of Poe's imaginative tales, and how immense is the
ingenuity of his puzzles and disentanglements. The conundrums
of Wilkie Collins never renew their interest after the answer is
known; but Poe's can be read again and again. It is where
spiritual depths are to be touched that he shows his weakness;
where he attempts it, as in "William Wilson," it seems exceptional; where there is the greatest display of philosophic form
he is often most trivial, whereas Hawthorne is often profoundest
when he has disarmed you by his simplicity. The truth is that
Poe lavished on things comparatively superficial those great intellectual resources which Hawthorne reverently husbanded and
used. That there is something behind even genius to make or
mar it, this is the lesson of the two lives.

Poe makes one of his heroes define another as "that *monstrum horrendum,* an unprincipled man of genius." It is in the
malice and fury of his own critical work that his low moral tone
most betrays itself. No atmosphere can be more belittling than
that of his "New York Literati"; it is a mass of vehement dog-
matism and petty personalities; opinions warped by private feeling, and varying from page to page. He seemed to have absolutely no standard of critical judgment, though it is true that
there was very little anywhere in America, during those acri-
monious days, when the most honorable head might be covered
with insult or neglect, while any young poetess who smiled
sweetly on Poe or Griswold or Willis might find herself placed
among the muses. Poe complimented and rather patronized
Hawthorne; but found him only "peculiar and *not* original"; saying of him, "He has not half the material for the exclusiveness
of literature that he has for its universality," whatever that may
mean; and finally he tried to make it appear that Hawthorne
had plagiarized from himself. He returned again and again to
the attack on Longfellow as a willful plagiarist, denouncing the
trivial resemblance between his "Midnight Mass for the Dying
Year" and Tennyson's "Death of the Old Year," as "belonging
to the most barbarous class of literary piracy (Works, ed. 1853,
III, 325). To make this attack was "to throttle the guilty" (III,
300); and while dealing thus ferociously with Longfellow, thus
condescendingly with Hawthorne, he was claiming a foremost
rank among American authors for obscurities now forgotten,
such as Mrs. Amelia B. Welby and Estelle Anne Lewis. No one

ever did more than Poe to lower the tone of literary criticism in this country; and the greater his talent, the greater the mischief.

As a poet he held for a time the place earlier occupied by Byron, and later by Swinburne, as the patron saint of all willful boys suspected of genius, and convicted at least of its infirmities. He belonged to the melancholy class of wasted men, like the German Hoffmann, whom perhaps of all men of genius he most resembled. No doubt, if we are to apply any standard of moral weight or sanity to literary men—a proposal which Poe would doubtless have ridiculed—it can only be in a very large and generous way. If a career has only a manly ring to it we can forgive many errors—as in reading, for instance, the autobiography of Benvenuto Cellini, carrying always his life in his hand amid a brilliant and reckless society. But the existence of a poor Bohemian, besotted when he has money, angry and vindictive when the money is spent, this is a dismal tragedy, for which genius only makes the footlights burn with more luster. There is a passage in Keats's letters, written from the haunts of Burns, in which he expresses himself as filled with pity for the poet's life; "he drank with blackguards, he was miserable; we can see horribly clear in the works of such a man his life, as if we were God's spies." Yet Burns's sins and miseries left his heart unspoiled, and this cannot be said of Poe. After all, the austere virtues—the virtues of Emerson, Hawthorne, Whittier—are the best soil for genius.

I like best to think of Poe as associated with his gifted betrothed, Sarah Helen Whitman, whom I saw sometimes in her later years. She had outlived her early friends and loves and hopes, and perhaps her literary fame, such as it was; she had certainly outlived her recognized ties with Poe, and all but his memory. There she dwelt in her little suite of rooms, bearing youth still in her heart and in her voice, and on her hair also, and in her dress. Her dimly-lighted parlor was always decked, here and there, with scarlet; and she sat, robed in white, her back always to the light, with a discreetly-tinted shadow over her still thoughtful and noble face. She seemed a person embalmed while still alive; it was as if she might dwell forever there, prolonging into an indefinite future the tradition of a poet's love; and when we remembered that she had been Poe's betrothed, that his kisses had touched her lips, that she still believed in him and was his defender, all criticism might well, for her sake, be disarmed, and her saintly life atone for his stormy and sad career.

———————

WALT WHITMAN [1819–92], like Higginson and many others, praises the craftsmanship and criticizes the lack of moral principle in Poe's verses. That which excited and impressed Baudelaire seems downright pathological to Whitman, except as he confessed that "Poe's genius has yet conquered a special recognition for itself, and I too have come to fully admit it, and appreciate it and him" and "Even my own objections draw me to him at last, and those very points, with his sad fate, will doubtless always make him dearer to young and fervid minds." The report in the *Star*, probably written by Whitman, also had a heading: "Walt Whitman at the Poe Funeral—*Conspicuous Absence of the Popular Poets*—" followed by these lines: "About the most significant part of the Poe reburial ceremonies yesterday—which only a crowded and remarkably magnetic audience of the very best class of young people, women preponderating, prevented from growing tedious—was the marked absence from the spot of every popular poet and author, American and foreign. Only Walt Whitman was present." These lines are omitted in the *Critic* version, June 3, 1882. (All variants have been collated in *The Collected Writings of Walt Whitman: Prose Works*, 1892, I, 230–32, New York: New York University Press, 1961, v. 3, pt. 1.)

Edgar Poe's Significance

WALT WHITMAN

Jan. 1, 1880.—In diagnosing this disease called humanity—to assume for the nonce what seems a chief mood of the personality and writings of my subject—I have thought that poets, somewhere or other on the list, present the most mark'd indications. Comprehending artists in a mass, musicians, painters, actors, and so on, and considering each and all of them as radiations or flanges of that furious whirling wheel, poetry, the centre and axis of the whole, where else indeed may we so well investigate the causes, growths, tally-marks of the time—the age's matter and malady?

From *Specimen Days, Complete Prose Works*, 1892.

By common consent there is nothing better for man or woman than a perfect and noble life, morally without flaw, happily balanced in activity, physically sound and pure, giving its due proportion, and no more, to the sympathetic, the human emotional element—a life, in all these, unhasting, unresting, untiring to the end. And yet there is another shape of personality dearer far to the artist-sense (which likes the play of strongest lights and shades), where the perfect character, the good, the heroic, although never attain'd, is never lost sight of, but through failures, sorrows, temporary downfalls, is return'd to again and again, and while often violated, is passionately adhered to as long as mind, muscles, voice, obey the power we call volition. This sort of personality we see more or less in Burns, Byron, Schiller, and George Sand. But we do not see it in Edgar Poe. (All this is the result of reading at intervals the last three days a new volume of his poems—I took it on my rambles down by the pond, and by degrees read it all through there.) While to the character first outlined the service Poe renders is certainly that entire contrast and contradiction which is next best to fully exemplifying it.

Almost without the first sign of moral principle, or of the concrete or its heroisms, or the simpler affections of the heart, Poe's verses illustrate an intense faculty for technical and abstract beauty, with the rhyming art to excess, an incorrigible propensity toward nocturnal themes, a demoniac undertone behind every page—and, by final judgment, probably belong among the electric lights of imaginative literature, brilliant and dazzling, but with no heat. There is an indescribable magnetism about the poet's life and reminiscences, as well as the poems. To one who could work out their subtle retracing and retrospect the latter would make a close tally no doubt between the author's birth and antecedents, his childhood and youth, his physique, his so-call'd education, his studies and associates, the literary and social Baltimore, Richmond, Philadelphia, and New York, of those times—not only the places and circumstances in themselves, but often, very often, in a strange spurning of, and reaction from them all.

The following from a report in the Washington "Star" of November 16, 1875, may afford those who care for it something further of my point of view toward this interesting figure and

influence of our era. There occurr'd about that date in Baltimore
a public reburial of Poe's remains, and dedication of a monument over the grave.

"Being in Washington on a visit at the time, 'the old gray'
went over to Baltimore, and though ill from paralysis, consented
to hobble up and silently take a seat on the platform, but refused to make any speech, saying, 'I have felt a strong impulse
to come over and be here to-day myself in memory of Poe, which
I have obey'd, but not the slightest impulse to make a speech,
which, my dear friends, must also be obeyed.' In an informal
circle, however, in conversation after the ceremonies, Whitman
said: 'For a long while, and until lately, I had a distaste for Poe's
writings. I wanted, and still want for poetry, the clear sun shining, and fresh air blowing—the strength and power of health,
not of delirium, even amid the stormiest passions—with always
the background of the eternal moralities. Noncomplying with
these requirements, Poe's genius has yet conquer'd a special recognition for itself, and I too have come to fully admit it, and
appreciate it and him.

" 'In a dream I once had, I saw a vessel on the sea, at midnight, in a storm. It was no great full-rigg'd ship, nor majestic
steamer, steering firmly through the gale, but seem'd one of those
superb little schooner yachts I had often seen lying anchor'd,
rocking so jauntily, in the waters around New York, or up Long
Island sound—now flying uncontroll'd with torn sails and broken
spars through the wild sleet and winds and waves of the night.
On the deck was a slender, slight, beautiful figure, a dim man,
apparently enjoying all the terror, the murk, and the dislocation
of which he was the centre and the victim. That figure of my
lurid dream might stand for Edgar Poe, his spirit, his fortunes,
and his poems—themselves all lurid dreams.' "

Much more may be said, but I most desired to exploit the
idea put at the beginning. By its popular poets the calibres of
an age, the weak spots of its embankments, its sub-currents,
(often more significant than the biggest surface ones), are un-
erringly indicated. The lush and the weird that have taken such
extraordinary possession of Nineteenth century verse-lovers—
what mean they? The inevitable tendency of poetic culture
to morbidity, abnormal beauty—the sickliness of all technical

thought or refinement in itself—the abnegation of the perennial and democratic concretes at first hand, the body, the earth and sea, sex and the like—and the substitution of something for them at second or third hand—what bearings have they on current pathological study?

———————

WILLIAM BUTLER YEATS [1865–1939], in writing to thank W. T. Horton for a copy of Poe illustrated by Horton, remarks that he likes best the illustration for "The Raven." This letter, then, understandably focuses on that poem, with the "vulgarity" charge that later came to a climax in Huxley's attack on "Ulalume." Yeats's admiration for Poe's lyric poetry was expressed more forcefully, and without qualification, in his message to the Poe Centenary commemoration at the University of Virginia, January 1909. Yeats's statement then that Poe "is so certainly the greatest of American poets, and always and for all lands a great lyric poet" is known to many; few have read his letter of September 3, 1899.

Letter to W. T. Horton

WILLIAM BUTLER YEATS

Sept. 3rd, 1899   Coole Park

My dear Horton, I have been a long time without writing to thank you for your Poe.[2] I like the Raven on the head of Pallas about best. I like next the drawing on page 18—a really admirable grotesque. I do not know why you or indeed anybody should want to illustrate Poe however. His fame always puzzles me. I have to acknowledge that even after one allows for the difficulties of a critic who speaks a foreign language, a writer who has had so much influence on Baudelaire and Villiers de L'Isle Adam has some great merit. I admire a few lyrics of his extremely and a few pages of his prose, chiefly in his critical essays,

From *Letters of W. B. Yeats,* Allan Wade, ed. (New York, 1955).

[1] From a typewritten copy.

[2] *The Raven* and *The Pit and the Pendulum.* By E. A. Poe. London: Leonard Smithers, 1899.

which are sometimes profound. The rest of him seems to me vulgar and commonplace and the Pit and the Pendulum and the Raven do not seem to me to have permanent literary value of any kind. Analyse the Raven and you find that its subject is a commonplace and its execution a rhythmical trick. Its rhythm never lives for a moment, never once moves with an emotional life. The whole thing seems to me insincere and vulgar. Analyse the Pit and the Pendulum and you find an appeal to the nerves by tawdry physical affrightments, at least so it seems to me who am yet puzzled at the fame of such things. No, your book is the *Pilgrim's Progress.* You could do that in a fine ancient spirit, full of a sincere naivety.

. . . .

WILLIAM BUTLER YEATS

II. 1900-1948

EDWIN ARLINGTON ROBINSON [1869–1935] composed this sonnet in 1894. It epitomizes the late nineteenth-century Gothic-Romantic view of Poe. The first stanza especially has much in common with Whitman's dream image: Poe is the lost, lonely "wild stranger" peering through the darkness of the night. From the second stanza it would appear that Robinson, like Whitman, responded more deeply to the poems than to the tales of Poe. This sonnet is omitted from Robinson's collected poems.

For a Copy of Poe's Poems

EDWIN ARLINGTON ROBINSON

Like a wild stranger out of wizard-land
 He dwelt a little with us, and withdrew;
 Bleak and unblossomed were the ways he knew,
Dark was the glass through which his fine eye scanned
Life's hard perplexities; and frail his hand,
 Groping in utter night for pleasure's clue.
 These wonder-songs, fantastically few,
He left us . . . but we cannot understand.

Lone voices calling for a dimmed ideal
 Mix with the varied music of the years
 And take their place with sorrows gone before:
Some are wide yearnings ringing with a real
 And royal hopelessness, some are thin tears,
 Some are the ghosts of dreams, and one—Lenore.

Born in Louisiana, J. BRANDER MATTHEWS [1852–1929] was a critic, essayist, editor, and novelist, and later became professor of literature at Columbia. A specialist in drama and the craft of writing, he exerted extraordinary influence as a writer and critic. Holding that Poe refrained from exploiting mystery and horror for its own sake or for mere suspense and curiosity as in Balzac and the early Gothic writers, Matthews defines in the following essay the unique and superior quality of Poe's detective stories.

From *Lippincott's Magazine,* August 1906.

Poe and the Detective Story

J. BRANDER MATTHEWS

I

In one of those essays which were often as speculative and suggestive as he claimed, the late John Addington Symonds called attention to three successive phases of criticism, pointing out that the critics had first set up as judges, delivering opinions from the bench and never hesitating to put on the black cap; that then they had changed into showmen, dwelling chiefly on the beauties of the masterpieces they were exhibiting; and that finally, and only very recently, they had become natural historians, studying "each object in relation to its antecedents and its consequences" and making themselves acquainted "with the conditions under which the artist grew, the habits of his race, the opinions of his age, his physiological and psychological peculiarities." And Symonds might have added that it is only in this latest phase, when the critics have availed themselves of the methods of the comparative biologists, that they are concerned with the interesting problems connected with the origin of the several literary species.

All over the world today devoted students are working at the hidden history of the lyric, for example, and of certain subdivisions of this species, such as the elegy, as it flowered long ago in Greece and as it has flourished in most of the literatures of modern Europe. To the "natural historian" of literary art, these subdivisions of a species are becoming more and more interesting, as he perceives more clearly how prone the poets have always been to work in accord with the pattern popular in their own time and to express themselves freely in the form they found ready to their hands. The student of the English drama is delighted when he can seize firmly the rise and fall of the tragedy of blood for one example, of the comedy of humors for another, and of sentimental comedy for a third; just as the investigator into the history of fiction is pleased to be able to trace the transformations of the pastoral, of the picaresque romance, and of the later short story.

The beginnings of a species, or of a subspecies, are obscure

From *Scribner's Magazine*, Sept. 1907, XLII, 287–93.

more often than not; and they are rarely to be declared with certainty. "Nothing is more difficult than to discover who have been in literature the first inventors" of a new form, so M. Jules Lemaître once asserted, adding that innovations have generally been attempted by writers of no great value, and not infrequently by those who failed in those first efforts, unable to profit by their own originality. And it is natural enough that a good many sighting shots should be wasted on a new target before even an accomplished marksman could plump his bullet in the bull's-eye. The historical novel as we know it now must be credited to Scott, who preluded by the rather feeble "Waverly," before attaining the more boldly planned "Rob Roy" and "Guy Mannering." The sea tale is to be ascribed to Cooper, whose wavering faith in its successful accomplishment is reflected in the shifting of the successive episodes of the "Pilot" from land to water and back again to land; and it was only when he came to write the "Red Rover" that Cooper displayed full confidence in the form he was the first to experiment with. But the history of the detective story begins with the publication of the "Murders in the Rue Morgue," a masterpiece of its kind, which even its author was unable to surpass; and Poe, unlike most other originators, rang the bell the very first time he took aim.

II

The detective story which Poe invented sharply differentiates itself from the earlier tales of mystery, and also from the later narratives in which actual detectives figure incidentally. Perhaps the first of these tales of mystery is Walpole's "Castle of Otranto," which appears to us now clumsy enough, with its puerile attempts to excite terror. The romances of Mrs. Radcliffe are scarcely more solidly built—indeed, the fatigue of the sophisticated reader of to-day when he undertakes the perusal of these old-fashioned and long-winded chronicles may be ascribed partly to the flimsiness of the foundation which is supposed to support the awe-inspiring superstructure. Godwin's "Caleb Williams" is far more firmly put together; and its artful planning called for imagination as well as mere invention. In the "Edgar Huntley" of Charles Brockden Brown the veil of doubt skilfully shrouds the unsuspected and unsuspecting murderer who did the evil deed in his sleep—anticipating the somnambulist hero of Wilkie Collins' "Moonstone."

The disadvantages of this mystery-mongering have been pointed out by Poe with his wonted acuteness in his criticism of "Barnaby Rudge." After retelling the plot of Dickens' contorted narrative, and after putting the successive episodes into their true sequence, Poe asserted that "the thesis of the novel may thus be regarded as based upon curiosity," and he declared that "every point is so arranged as to perplex the reader and whet his desire for elucidation." He insisted "that the secret be well kept is obviously necessary," because if it leaks out "against the author's will, his purposes are immediately at odds and ends." Then he remarked that although "there can be no question that . . . many points . . . which would have been comparatively insipid even if given in full detail in a natural sequence, are endued with the interest of mystery; but neither can it be denied that a vast many more points are at the same time deprived of all effect, and become null, through the impossibility of comprehending them without the key." In other words, the novelist has chosen to sacrifice to the fleeting interest which is evoked only by wonder the more abiding interest which is aroused by the clear perception of the interplay of character and motive. Poe suggested that even "Barnaby Rudge"—in spite of its author's efforts to keep secret the real springs of action which controlled the characters—if taken up a second time by a reader put into possession of all that had been concealed, would be found to possess quadruple brilliance, "a brilliance unprofitably sacrificed at the shrine of the keenest interest of mere mystery."

Dickens was not the last novelist of note to be tempted and to fall into this snare. In the "Disciple," and again in "André Cornélis," M. Paul Bourget was lured from the path of psychologic analysis into the maze of mystery-mongering; but he had the tact to employ his secrets to excite interest only in the beginning of what were, after all, studies from life, each of them setting forth the struggle of a man with the memory of his crime. In "The Wreckers" Stevenson and his young collaborator attempted that "form of police novel or mystery story which consisted in beginning your yarn anywhere but at the beginning, and finishing it anywhere but at the end." They were attracted by its "peculiar interest when done, and the peculiar difficulties that attend its execution." They were "repelled by that appearance of insincerity and shallowness of tone which seems its inevitable drawback," because "the mind of the reader always bent to pick up clews receives no impression of reality or life, rather of an airless, elaborate mechanism; and the book remains enthralling, but insignificant, like a game of chess, not a work of human art." They hoped to find a new way of handling the old tale of mystery, so that they might get the profit without paying the price. But already in his criticism of "Barnaby Rudge" had Poe showed why disappointment was unavoidable, because the more artfully the dark intimations of horror are held out, the more certain it is that the anticipation must surpass the reality. No matter how terrific the circumstances may be which shall appear to have occasioned the mystery, "still they will not be able to satisfy the mind of the reader. He will surely be disappointed."

Even Balzac, with all his mastery of the novelist's art, lost more than he gained when he strove to arouse the interest of his readers by an appeal to their curiosity. His mystery-mongering is sometimes perilously close to blatant sensationalism and overt charlatanry; and he seems to be seeking the bald effect for its own sake. In the "Chouans," and again in the "Ténébreuse Affaire," he has complicated plots and counterplots entangled almost to confusion, but the reader "receives no impression of reality or life" even if these novels cannot be dismissed as empty examples of "airless, elaborate mechanism."

The members of the secret police appearing in these stories have all a vague likeness to Vidocq, whose alleged memoirs were published in 1828, a few years before the author of the "Human Comedy" began to deal with the scheming of the underworld. Balzac's spies and his detectives are not convincing, despite his utmost effort; and we do not believe in their preternatural acuteness. Even in the conduct of their intrigues we are lost in a murky mistiness. Balzac is at his best when he is arousing the emotions of recognition; and he is at his worst when he sinks to evoking the emotions of surprise.

III

In the true detective story as Poe conceived it in the "Murders in the Rue Morgue," it is not in the mystery itself that the author seeks to interest the reader, but rather in the successive steps whereby his analytic observer is enabled to solve a problem that might well be dismissed as beyond human elucidation.

Attention is centred on the unravelling of the tangled skein rather than on the knot itself. The emotion aroused is not mere surprise, it is recognition of the unsuspected capabilities of the human brain; it is not a wondering curiosity as to an airless mechanism, but a heightening admiration for the analytic acumen capable of working out an acceptable answer to the puzzle propounded. In other words, Poe, while he availed himself of the obvious advantages of keeping a secret from his readers and of leaving them guessing as long as he pleased, shifted the point of attack and succeeded in giving a human interest to his tale of wonder.

And by this shift Poe transported the detective story from the group of tales of adventure into the group of portrayals of character. By bestowing upon it a human interest, he raised it in the literary scale. There is no need now to exaggerate the merits of this feat or to suggest that Poe himself was not capable of loftier efforts. Of course the "Fall of the House of Usher," which is of imagination all compact, is more valid evidence of his genius than the "Murders in the Rue Morgue," which is the product rather of his invention, supremely ingenious as it is. Even though the detective story as Poe produced it is elevated far above the barren tale of mystery which preceded it and which has been revived in our own day, it is not one of the loftiest of literary forms, and its possibilities are severely limited. It suffers to-day from the fact that in the half century and more since Poe set the pattern it has been vulgarized, debased, degraded by a swarm of imitators who lacked his certainty of touch, his instinctive tact, his intellectual individuality. In their hands it has been bereft of its distinction and despoiled of its atmosphere.

Even at its best, in the simple perfection of form that Poe bestowed on it, there is no denying that it demanded from its creator no depth of sentiment, no warmth of emotion, and no large understanding of human desire. There are those who would dismiss it carelessly, as making an appeal not far removed from that of the riddle and of the conundrum. There are those again who would liken it rather to the adroit trick of a clever conjurer. No doubt, it gratifies in us chiefly that delight in difficulty conquered, which is a part of the primitive play impulse potent in us all, but tending to die out as we grow older, as we lessen in energy, and as we feel more deeply the tragi-comedy of existence. But inexpensive as it may seem to those of us who look to literature for enlightenment, for solace in the hour of need, for stimulus to stiffen the will in the never-ending struggle of life, the detective tale, as Poe contrived it, has merits of its own as distinct and as undeniable as those of the historical novel, for example, or of the sea tale. It may please the young rather than the old, but the pleasure it can give is ever innocent; and the young are always in the majority.

IV

In so far as Poe had any predecessor in the composing of a narrative, the interest of which should reside in the application of human intelligence to the solution of a mystery, this was not Balzac, although the American romancer was sufficiently familiar with the "Human Comedy" to venture an unidentified quotation from it. Nor was this predecessor Cooper, whom Balzac admired and even imitated, although Leatherstocking in tracking his redskin enemies revealed the tense observation and the faculty of deduction with which Poe was to endow his Dupin. The only predecessor with a good claim to be considered a progenitor is Voltaire, in whose "Zadig" we can find the method which Poe was to apply more elaborately. The Goncourts perceived this descent of Poe from Voltaire when they recorded in their "Journal" that the strange tales of the American poet seemed to them to belong to "a new literature, the literature of the twentieth century, scientifically miraculous story-telling by A + B, a literature at once monomaniac and mathematical, Zadig as district attorney, Cyrano de Bergerac as a pupil of Arago."

Voltaire tells us that Zadig by study gained "a sagacity which discovered to him a thousand differences where other men saw only uniformity"; and he describes a misadventure which befell Zadig when he was living in the kingdom of Babylon. One day the chief eunuch asked if he had seen the Queen's dog. "It is a female, isn't it?" returned Zadig; "a spaniel, and very small; she littered not long ago; she is lame of the left fore foot; and she has very long ears." "So you have seen her?" cried the eunuch. "No," Zadig answered; "I have never seen her; and I never even knew that the Queen had a dog."

About the same time the handsomest horse in the king's

stables escaped; and the chief huntsman, meeting Zadig, inquired if he had not seen the animal. And Zadig responded: "It is the horse that gallops the best; he is five feet high; his shoe is very small; his tail is three and a half feet long; the knobs of his bit are of twenty-three carat gold; and he is shod with eleven-penny silver." And the chief huntsman asked, "Which way did he go?" To which Zadig replied: "I have not seen him; and I have never heard anything about him."

The chief eunuch and the chief huntsman naturally believed that Zadig had stolen the queen's dog and the king's horse; so they had him arrested and condemned, first to the knout, and afterward to exile for life in Siberia. And then both the missing animals were recovered; so Zadig was allowed to plead his case. He swore that he had never seen either the dog of the queen nor the horse of the king. This is what had happened: He had been walking toward a little wood and he had seen on the sand the track of an animal, and he judged that it had been a dog. Little furrows scratched in the low hillocks of sand between the footprints showed him that it was a female whose teats were pendent, and who therefore must have littered recently. As the sand was less deeply marked by one foot than by the three others, he had perceived the queen's dog to be lame.

As for the larger quadruped, Zadig, while walking in a narrow path in the wood, had seen the prints of a horse's shoes, all at an equal distance; and he had said to himself that here was a steed with a perfect stride. The path was narrow, being only seven feet wide, and here and there the dust had been flicked from the trees on either hand, and so Zadig had made sure that the horse had a tail three and a half feet long. The branches crossed over the path at the height of five feet, and as leaves had been broken off, the observer had decided that the horse was just five feet high. As to the bit, this must be of gold, since the horse had rubbed it against a stone, which Zadig had recognized as a touchstone and on which he had assayed the trace of precious metal. And from the marks left by the horse's shoes on another kind of stone Zadig had felt certain that they were made of eleven-penny silver.

Huxley has pointed out that the method of Zadig is the method which has made possible the incessant scientific discovery of the last century. It is the method of Wellington at Assaye, assuming that there must be a ford at a certain place on the river, because there was a village on each side. It is the method of Grant at Vicksburg, examining the knapsacks of the Confederate soldiers slain in a sortie to see if these contained rations, which would show that the garrison was seeking to break out because the place was untenable. It is also the method of Poe in the "Gold Bug" and in the "Murders in the Rue Morgue."

In his application of this method, not casually, playfully, and with satiric intent, as Voltaire had applied it, but seriously and taking it as the mainspring of his story, Poe added an ingenious improvement of his own devising. Upon the preternaturally acute observer who was to control the machinery of the tale, the American poet bestowed a companion of only an average alertness and keenness; and to this commonplace companion the romancer confided the telling of the story. By this seemingly simple device Poe doubled the effectiveness of his work, because this unobservant and unimaginative narrator of the unravelling of a tangled skein by an observant and imaginative analyst naturally recorded his own admiration and astonishment as the wonder was wrought before his eyes, so that the admiration and astonishment were transmitted directly and suggestively to the readers of the narrative.

In the "Gold Bug" the wonder worker is Legrand, and in both the "Murders in the Rue Morgue" and the "Purloined Letter" he is M. Dupin; and in all three tales the telling of the story is entrusted to an anonymous narrator, serving not only as a sort of Greek chorus to hint to the spectators the emotions they ought to feel, but also as the describer of the personality and peculiarities of Legrand and Dupin, who are thus individualized, humanized, and related to the real world. If they had not been accepted by the narrator as actual beings of flesh and blood, they might otherwise retain the thinness and the dryness of disembodied intelligences working in a vacuum.

This device of the transmitting narrator is indisputably valuable; and, properly enough, it reappears in the one series of detective tales which may be thought by some to rival Poe's. The alluring record of the investigations of Mr. Sherlock Holmes is the work of a certain Dr. Watson, a human being but little more clearly characterized than the anonymous narrators who have preserved for us the memory of Legrand and Dupin. But

Poe here again exhibited a more artistic reserve than any of his imitators, in so far as he refrained from the undue laudation of the strange intellectual feats which are the central interest of these three tales. In the "Gold Bug" he even heightens his suspense by allowing the narrator to suggest that Legrand might be of unsound mind; and in the "Murders in the Rue Morgue" the narrator, although lost in astonishment at the acuteness of Dupin, never permits his admiration to become fulsome; he holds himself in, as though fearing that overpraise might provoke a denial. Moreover, Poe refrained from all exhibitions of Dupin's skill merely for its own sake—exhibitions only dazzling the spectators and not furthering his immediate purpose.

Nothing could be franker than Sir Conan Doyle's acknowledgment of his indebtedness. "Edgar Allan Poe, who, in his carelessly prodigal fashion, threw out the seeds from which so many of our present forms of literature have sprung, was the father of the detective tale, and covered its limits so completely that I fail to see how his followers can find any fresh ground which they can confidently call their own. For the secret of the thinness and also of the intensity of the detective story is that the writer is left with only one quality, that of intellectual acuteness, with which to endow his hero. Everything else is outside the picture and weakens the effect. The problem and its solution must form the theme, and the character drawing is limited and subordinate. On this narrow path the writer must walk, and he sees the footmarks of Poe always in front of him. He is happy if he ever finds the means of breaking away and striking out on some little side-track of his own."

The deviser of the adventures of Sherlock Holmes hit on a happy phrase when he declared that "the problem and its solution must form the theme." This principle was violated by Dumas, who gave us the solution before the problem, when he showed how d'Artagnan used the method of Zadig to deduce all the details of the duel on horseback, in the "Vicomte de Bragelonne," after the author had himself described to us the incidents of that fight. But when he was thus discounting his effect Dumas probably had in mind, not Poe, but Cooper, whose observant redskins he mightily admired and whom he frankly imitated in the "Mohicans of Paris."

V

Although Poe tells these three stories in the first person, as if he was himself only the recorder of the marvellous deeds of another, both Legrand and Dupin are projections of his own personality; they are characters created by him to be endowed with certain of his own qualifications and peculiarities. They were called into being to be possessed of the inventive and analytical powers of Poe himself. "To be an artist, first and always, requires a turn for induction and analysis"—so Mr. Stedman has aptly put it; and this turn for induction and analysis Poe had far more obviously than most artists. When he was a student he excelled in mathematics; in all his other tales he displays the same power of logical construction; and he delighted in the exercise of his own acumen, vaunting his ability to translate any cipher that might be sent to him and succeeding in making good his boast. In the criticism of "Barnaby Rudge," and again in the explanation of the Maelzel chess-player, Poe used for himself the same faculty of divination, the same power of seizing the one clue needful, however tangled amid other threads, which he had bestowed upon Legrand and Dupin.

If we may exclude the "Marie Rogêt" narrative in which Poe was working over an actual case of murder, we find him only three times undertaking the "tale of ratiocination," to use his own term; and in all three stories he was singularly happy in the problem he invented for solution. For each of the three he found a fit theme, wholly different from that employed in either of the others. He adroitly adjusted the proper accessories, and he created an appropriate atmosphere. With no sense of strain, and no awkwardness of manner, he dealt with episodes strange indeed, but so simply treated as to seem natural, at least for the moment. There is no violence of intrigue or conjecture; indeed Poe strives to suggest a background of the commonplace against which his marvels may seem the more marvellous. In none of his stories is Poe's consummate mastery of the narrative art, his ultimate craftsmanship, his certain control of all the devices of the most accomplished story-teller, more evident than in these three.

And yet they are but detective stories, after all; and Poe himself, never prone to underestimate what he had written, spoke of them lightly and even hinted that they had been over-praised. Probably they were easy writing—for him—and there-fore they were not so close to his heart as certain other of his tales over which he had toiled long and more laboriously. Prob-ably also he felt the detective story to be an inferior form. How-ever superior his stories in this kind might be, he knew them to be unworthy of comparison with his more imaginative tales, which he had filled with a thrilling weirdness and which attained a soaring elevation far above any height to be achieved by ingenious narratives setting forth the solving of a puzzle.

It is in a letter to Philip Pendleton Cooke, written in 1846, that Poe disparaged his detective stories and declared that they "owe most of their popularity to being something in a new key. I do not mean to say that they are not ingenious—but people think them more ingenious than they are—on account of their method and *air* of method. In the 'Murders in the Rue Morgue,' for instance, where is the ingenuity of unravelling a web which you yourself (the author) have woven for the express purpose of unravelling? The reader is made to confound the ingenuity of the supposititious Dupin with that of the writer of the story." Here, surely, Poe is overmodest; at least he overstates the case against himself. The ingenuity of the author obviously lies in his invention of a web which seemingly cannot be unravelled and which nevertheless one of the characters of the tale, Le-grand or Dupin, succeeds in unravelling at last. This ingenuity may be, in one way, less than that required to solve an actual problem in real life; but it is also, in another way, more, for it had to invent its own puzzle and to put this together so that the secret seemed to be absolutely hidden, although all the facts needed to solve it were plainly presented to the reader.

In the same letter to Cooke, Poe remarked on the "wide di-versity and variety" of his tales when contrasted one with an-other; and he asserted that he did not consider any one better than another. "There is a vast variety of kinds, and in degree of value these kinds vary—but each tale is equally good *of its kind*." He added that "the loftiest kind is that of the highest imagina-tion." For this reason only he considered that "Ligeia" might be called the best of his stories. Now, after a lapse of threescore years, the "Fall of the House of Usher," with its "serene and sombre beauty," would seem to deserve the first place of all. And among the detective stories, standing on a lower plane as they do, because they were wrought by invention rather than by the interpreting imagination, the foremost position may be given to the "Murders in the Rue Morgue." In this tale Poe's invention is most ingenious and his subject is selected with the fullest understanding of the utmost possibilities of the detective story. At the core of it is a strange, mysterious, monstrous crime; and M. Anatole France was never wiser than when he declared the unfailing interest of mankind in a gigantic misdeed "because we find in all crimes that fund of hunger and desire on which we all live, the good as well as the bad." Before a crime such as this we seem to find ourselves peering into the contorted visage of primitive man, obeying no law but his own caprice.

The superiority of the poet who wrote the first detective story over all those who have striven to tread in the trail he blazed is obvious enough. It resides not only in his finer workmanship, his more delicate art, his finer certainty of execution, his more absolute knowledge of what it was best to do and of the way best to do this; it is to be seen not only in his command of verisimilitude, in his plausibility, in his faculty of enwrapping the figures of his narrative in the atmosphere most fit for them; it is not in any of these things or in all of them that Poe's supremacy is founded. The reason of that supremacy must be sought in the fact that, after all, Poe was of a truth a poet, and that he had the informing imagination of a poet, even though it was only the more prosaic side of the faculty divine which he chose to employ in these tales of ratiocination.

It is by their possession of poetry, however slight their portion might be, that Fitzjames O'Brien and M. Jean Richepin and Mr. Rudyard Kipling were kept from rank failure when they followed in Poe's footsteps and sought to imitate, or at least to emulate his more largely imaginative tales in the "Diamond Lens" of the Irish-American, in the "Morts Bizarres" of the Frenchman, and in half a dozen tales of the Anglo-Indian. But what tincture of poesy, what sweep of vision, what magic of style, is there in the attempts of the most of the others who have taken pattern by his detective stories? None, and less than none. Ingenuity of a kind there is in Gaboriau's longer fictions, and in those of Fortuné de Boisgobey, and in those of Wilkie Collins; but this ingenuity is never so simply employed, and it is often artificial and violent and mechanical. It exists for its own sake, with little relation to the admitted characteristics of our common humanity. It stands alone, and it is never accompanied by the apparent ease which adds charm to Poe's handling of his puzzles.

Consider how often Gaboriau puts us off with a broken-backed narrative, taking up his curtain on a promising problem, presenting it to us in aspects of increasing difficulty, only at last to confess his impotence by starting afresh and slowly detailing the explanatory episodes which happened before the curtain rose. Consider how frequently Fortuné de Boisgobey failed to play fair. Consider how juiceless was the documentary method of Wilkie Collins, how mechanical and how arid, how futilely complicated, how prolonged, and how fatiguing. Consider all the minor members of the sorry brood hatched out of the same egg, how cheap and how childish the most of them are. Consider all these; and we are forced to the conclusion that if the writing of a good detective story is so rare and so difficult, if only one of Poe's imitators has been able really to rival his achievement, if this single success has been the result of an acceptance of Poe's formula and of a close adherence to Poe's practice, then, what Poe wrought is really unique; and we must give him the guerdon of praise due to an artist who has accomplished the first time of trying that which others have failed to achieve even after he had shown them how.

GEORGE BERNARD SHAW [1856–1950], like Baudelaire fifty years earlier, saw Poe as "the finest of fine artists" condemned with Whitman to suffer and die in an America dead to its Revolutionary heritage. To Shaw, Poe was not only "the greatest journalistic critic of his time" but supreme as a poet, and though limited by his "aloofness from the common people," was "the most legitimate, the most classical, of modern writers."

Edgar Allan Poe

GEORGE BERNARD SHAW

There was a time when America, the Land of the Free, and the birthplace of Washington, seemed a natural fatherland for Edgar Allan Poe. Nowadays the thing has become inconceivable: no young man can read Poe's works without asking incredulously what the devil he is doing in *that* galley. America has been found out; and Poe has not; that is the situation. How did he live there, this finest of fine artists, this born aristocrat of letters? Alas! he did not live there: he died there, and was duly explained away as a drunkard and a failure, though it remains an open question whether he really drank as much in his whole lifetime as a modern successful American drinks, without comment, in six months.

If the Judgment Day were fixed for the centenary of Poe's birth, there are among the dead only two men born since the Declaration of Independence whose plea for mercy could avert a prompt sentence of damnation on the entire nation; and it is extremely doubtful whether those two could be persuaded to pervert eternal justice by uttering it. The two are, of course, Poe and Whitman; and there is between them the remarkable difference that Whitman is still credibly an American, whereas even the Americans themselves, though rather short of men of genius, omit Poe's name from their Pantheon, either from a sense that it is hopeless for them to claim so foreign a figure, or from simple Monroeism. One asks, has the America of Poe's day passed away, or did it ever exist?

Probably it never existed. It was an illusion, like the respectable Whig Victorian England of Macaulay. Karl Marx stripped the whitewash from that sepulchre; and we have ever since been struggling with a conviction of social sin which makes every country in which industrial capitalism is rampant a hell to us. For let no American fear that America, on that hypothetic Judgment Day, would perish alone. America would be damned in very good European company, and would feel proud and happy, and contemptuous of the saved. She would not even plead the influence of the mother from whom she has inherited

From the *Nation* (London), January 16, 1909.

all her worst vices. If the American stands today in scandalous preeminence as an anarchist and a ruffian, a liar and a braggart, an idolater and a sensualist, that is only because he has thrown off the disguises of Catholicism and feudalism which still give Europe an air of decency, and sins openly, impudently, and consciously, instead of furtively, hypocritically, and muddle-headedly, as we do. Not until he acquires European manners does the American anarchist become the gentleman who assures you that people cannot be made moral by Act of Parliament (the truth being that it is only by Acts of Parliament that men in large communities can be made moral, even when they want to); or the American ruffian hand over his revolver and bowie knife to be used for him by a policeman or soldier; or the American liar and braggart adopt the tone of the newspaper, the pulpit, and the platform; or the American idolater write authorized biographies of millionaires; or the American sensualist secure the patronage of all the Muses for his pornography.

Howbeit, Poe remains homeless. There is nothing at all like him in America: nothing, at all events, visible across the Atlantic. At that distance we can see Whistler plainly enough, and Mark Twain. But Whistler was very American in some ways: so American that nobody but another American could possibly have written his adventures and gloried in them without reserve. Mark Twain, resembling Dickens in his combination of public spirit and irresistible literary power with a congenital incapacity for lying and bragging, and a congenital hatred of waste and cruelty, remains American by the local color of his stories. There is a further difference. Both Mark Twain and Whistler are as Philistine as Dickens and Thackeray. The appalling thing about Dickens, the greatest of the Victorians, is that in his novels there is nothing personal to live for except eating, drinking, and pretending to be happily married. For him the great synthetic ideals do not exist, any more than the great preludes and toccatas of Bach, the symphonies of Beethoven, the paintings of Giotto and Mantegna, Velasquez and Rembrandt. Instead of being heir to all the ages, he came into a comparatively small and smutty literary property bequeathed by Smollett and Fielding. His criticism of Fechter's Hamlet, and his use of a speech of Macbeth's to illustrate the character of Mrs. Macstinger, shew how little Shakespear meant to him. Thackeray is even worse:

the notions of painting he picked up at Heatherley's school were further from the mark than Dickens' ignorance; he is equally in the dark as to music; and though he did not, when he wished to be enormously pleasant and jolly, begin, like Dickens, to describe the gorgings and guzzlings which make Christmas our annual national disgrace, that is rather because he never does want to be enormously pleasant and jolly than because he has any higher notions of personal enjoyment. The truth is that neither Dickens nor Thackeray would be tolerable were it not that life is an end in itself and a means to nothing but its own perfection; consequently any man who describes life vividly will entertain us, however uncultivated the life he describes may be. Mark Twain has lived long enough to become a much better philosopher than either Dickens or Thackeray: for instance, when he immortalized General Funston by scalping him, he did it scientifically, knowing exactly what he meant right down to the foundation in the natural history of human character. Also, he got from the Mississippi something that Dickens could not get from Chatham and Pentonville. But he wrote A Yankee at the Court of King Arthur just as Dickens wrote A Child's History of England. For the ideal of Catholic chivalry he had nothing but derision; and he exhibited it, not in conflict with reality, as Cervantes did, but in conflict with the prejudices of a Philistine compared to whom Sancho Panza is an Admirable Crichton, an Abelard, even a Plato. Also, he described Lohengrin as "a shivaree," though he liked the wedding chorus; and this shews that Mark, like Dickens, was not properly educated; for Wagner would have been just the man for him if he had been trained to understand and use music as Mr. Rockefeller was trained to understand and use money. America did not teach him the language of the great ideals, just as England did not teach it to Dickens and Thackeray. Consequently, though nobody can suspect Dickens or Mark Twain of lacking the qualities and impulses that are the soul of such grotesque makeshift bodies as Church and State, Chivalry, Classicism, Art, Gentility, and the Holy Roman Empire; and nobody blames them for seeing that these bodies were mostly so decomposed as to have become intolerable nuisances, you have only to compare them with Carlyle and Ruskin, or with Euripides and Aristophanes, to see how, for want of a language of art and a body of philosophy, they were so much more interested in the fun and pathos of personal adventure than in the comedy and tragedy of human destiny.

Whistler was a Philistine, too. Outside the corner of art in which he was a virtuoso and a propagandist, he was a Man of Derision. Important as his propaganda was, and admired as his work was, no society could assimilate him. He could not even induce a British jury to award him substantial damages against a rich critic who had "done him out of his job"; and this is certainly the climax of social failure in England.

Edgar Allan Poe was not in the least a Philistine. He wrote always as if his native Boston was Athens, his Charlottesville University Plato's Academy, and his cottage the crown of the heights of Fiesole. He was the greatest journalistic critic of his time, placing good European work at sight when the European critics were waiting for somebody to tell them what to say. His poetry is so exquisitely refined that posterity will refuse to believe that it belongs to the same civilization as the glory of Mrs. Julia Ward Howe's lilies or the honest doggerel of Whittier. Tennyson, who was nothing if not a virtuoso, never produced a success that will bear reading after Poe's failures. Poe constantly and inevitably produced magic where his greatest contemporaries produced only beauty. Tennyson's popular pieces, The May Queen and The Charge of the Six Hundred, cannot stand hackneying: they become positively nauseous after a time. The Raven, The Bells, and Annabel Lee are as fascinating at the thousandth repetition as at the first.

Poe's supremacy in this respect has cost him his reputation. This is a phenomenon which occurs when an artist achieves such perfection as to place himself *hors concours*. The greatest painter England ever produced is Hogarth, a miraculous draughtsman and an exquisite and poetic colorist. But he is never mentioned by critics. They talk copiously about Romney, the Gibson of his day; freely about Reynolds; nervously about the great Gainsborough; and not at all about Rowlandson and Hogarth, missing the inextinguishable grace of Rowlandson because they assume that all caricatures of this period are ugly, and avoiding Hogarth instinctively as critically unmanageable. In the same way, we have given up mentioning Poe: that is why the Americans forgot him when they posted up the names of their great in their Pantheon. Yet his is the first—almost the only name that the real connoisseur looks for.

But Poe, for all his virtuosity, is always a poet, and never a mere virtuoso. Poe put forward his Eureka, the formulation of his philosophy, as the most important thing he had done. His poems always have the universe as their background. So have the figures in his stories. Even in his tales of humor, which we shake our heads at as mistakes, they have this elemental quality. Toby Dammit himself, though his very name turns up the nose of the cultured critic, is more impressive and his end more tragic than the serious inventions of most story-tellers. The short-sighted gentleman who married his grandmother is no common butt of a common purveyor of the facetious: the grandmother has the elegance and free mind of Ninon de l'Enclos, the grandson the *tenue* of a marquis. This story was sent by Poe to Horne, whose Orion he had reviewed as poetry ought to be reviewed, with a request that it might be sold to an English magazine. The English magazine regretted that the deplorable immorality of the story made it for ever impossible in England!

In his stories of mystery and imagination Poe created a world-record for the English language: perhaps for all the languages. The story of the Lady Ligeia is not merely one of the wonders of literature: it is unparalleled and unapproached. There is really nothing to be said about it: we others simply take off our hats and let Mr. Poe go first. It is interesting to compare Poe's stories with William Morris'. Both are not merely stories: they are complete works of art, like prayer carpets; and they are, in Poe's phrase, stories of imagination. They are masterpieces of style: what people call Macaulay's style is by comparison a mere method. But they are more different than it seems possible for two art works in the same kind to be. Morris will have nothing to do with mystery. "Ghost stories," he used to say, "have all the same explanation: the people are telling lies." His Sigurd has the beauty of mystery as it has every other sort of beauty, being, as it is, incomparably the greatest English epic; but his stories are in the open from end to end, whilst in Poe's stories the sun never shines.

Poe's limitation was his aloofness from the common people. Grotesques, negroes, madmen with delirium tremens, even gorillas, take the place of ordinary peasants and courtiers, citizens and soldiers, in his theatre. His houses are haunted houses, his woods enchanted woods; and he makes them so real that reality itself cannot sustain the comparison. His kingdom is not of this world.

Above all, Poe is great because he is independent of cheap attractions, independent of sex, of patriotism, of fighting, of sentimentality, snobbery, gluttony, and all the rest of the vulgar stock-in-trade of his profession. This is what gives him his superb distinction. One vulgarized thing, the pathos of dying children, he touched in Annabel Lee, and devulgarized it at once. He could not even amuse himself with detective stories without purifying the atmosphere of them until they became more edifying than most of Hymns, Ancient and Modern. His verse sometimes alarms and puzzles the reader by fainting with its own beauty; but the beauty is never the beauty of the flesh. You never say to him as you have to say uneasily to so many modern artists: "Yes, my friend, but these are things that men and women should *live* and not write about. Literature is not a keyhole for people with starved affections to peep through at the banquets of the body." It never became one in Poe's hands. Life cannot give you what he gives you except through fine art; and it was his instinctive observance of this distinction, and the fact that it did not beggar him, as it would beggar most writers, that makes him the most legitimate, the most classical, of modern writers.

It also explains why America does not care much for him, and why he has hardly been mentioned in England these many years. America and England are wallowing in the sensuality which their immense increase of riches has placed within their reach. I do not blame them: sensuality is a very necessary and healthy and educative element in life. Unfortunately, it is ill distributed; and our reading masses are looking on at it and thinking about it and longing for it, and having precarious little holiday treats of it, instead of sharing it temperately and continuously, and ceasing to be preoccupied with it. When the distribution is better adjusted and the preoccupation ceases, there will be a noble reaction in favor of the great writers like Poe, who begin just where the world, the flesh, and the devil leave off.

N. VACHEL LINDSAY [1879–1931], American poet who toured the South as a troubadour, living by sales of his poems and drawings, was born in Illinois of parents with an Indiana and Kentucky background. Before he was fourteen, he had read Poe's "complete works, criticism and all." He became "a kind of literary outcast" in the Springfield High School, because he "championed Poe and his view." One of the better verse tributes to Poe, the following poem sees Poe not simply as the amusing "jester" and "jingle man" but also as an entertaining "wizard" whose magic hides a sensibility tormented by the neglect of a complacent, materialistic America.

The Wizard in the Street

(*Concerning Edgar Allan Poe*)

N. VACHEL LINDSAY

Who now will praise the Wizard in the street
With loyal songs, with humors grave and sweet—
This Jingle-man, of strolling players born,
Whom holy folk have hurried by in scorn,
This threadbare jester, neither wise nor good,
With melancholy bells upon his hood?

The hurrying great ones scorn his Raven's croak,
And well may mock his mystifying cloak
Inscribed with runes from tongues he has not read
To make the ignoramus turn his head.
The artificial glitter of his eyes
Has captured half-grown boys. They think him wise.
Some shallow player-folk esteem him deep,
Soothed by his steady wand's mesmeric sweep.

The little lacquered boxes in his hands
Somehow suggest old times and reverenced lands.
From them doll-monsters come, we know not how:
Puppets, with Cain's black rubric on the brow.
Some passing jugglers, smiling, now concede
That his best cabinet-work is made, indeed
By bleeding his right arm, day after day,
Triumphantly to seal and to inlay.
They praise his little act of shedding tears;
A trick, well learned, with patience, thro' the years.

From *Village Magazine*, 1910, and *Collected Poems*, 1923.

I love him in this blatant, well-fed place.
Of all the faces, his the only face
Beautiful, tho' painted for the stage,
Lit up with song, then torn with cold, small rage,
Shames that are living, loves and hopes long dead,
Consuming pride, and hunger, real, for bread.

Here by the curb, ye Prophets thunder deep:
"What Nations sow, they must expect to reap,"

Or haste to clothe the race with truth and power,
With hymns and shouts increasing every hour.

Useful are you. There stands the useless one
Who builds the Haunted Palace in the sun.
Good tailors, can you dress a doll for me
With silks that whisper of the sounding sea?
One moment, citizens,—the weary tramp
Unveileth Psyche with the agate lamp.
Which one of you can spread a spotted cloak
And raise an unaccounted incense smoke
Until within the twilight of the day
Stands dark Ligeia in her disarray,
Witchcraft and desperate passion in her breath
And battling will, that conquers even death?

And now the evening goes. No man has thrown
The weary dog his well-earned crust or bone.
We grin and hie us home and go to sleep,
Or feast like kings till midnight, drinking deep.
He drank alone, for sorrow, and then slept,
And few there were that watched him, few that wept.
He found the gutter, lost to love and man.
Too slowly came the good Samaritan.

————————

In 1892 PAUL VALÉRY [1871–1945], in a letter to André Gide, expressed
unbounded admiration for Poe: "Poe . . . is the only writer—without any
fault. He never makes a false move—he is not guided by instinct—but
with lucidity and to advantage, he creates form out of the void." At twenty
Valéry discovered *Eureka*, which impressed him deeply as an original epic

of intellectual speculation, without parallel in his scientific, philosophical, or literary experience. Somewhat to his regret, he did not write an essay on *Eureka* until thirty years later when "Au sujet d'Eurêka" appeared as a preface to Baudelaire's translation (1921) of that work. The first half, reprinted here, concludes by regarding Poe's essay as essentially an "abstract poem," or as he described it in 1924, a "poème cosmogonique moderne," belonging to cosmogony as one of the oldest of literatures, a literature of myth and fable. Considering it as science, Valéry accepts Poe's fundamental conception of matter as "profound and sovereign," neither proved nor disproved by discoveries since 1847. Although not without some irony and skepticism, especially as to Poe's solipsism, finalism, and naive use of analogy, Valéry associates Poe's coherence theory of truth with Einstein's theory of relativity, and draws significant distinctions between classical notions of cause, category, and determinism, on the one hand, and Poe's views of causality and of consciousness and potentiality as inherent in matter. The influence of Poe on Valéry was not, as T. S. Eliot later maintained, a matter of poetic technique alone.

On Poe's "Eureka"

PAUL VALÉRY

I was twenty and believed in majesty of thought. I found it a strange torture to be, and not to be. At times I could feel infinite forces within me. They disappeared when faced with problems, and the weakness of my effective powers filled me with despair. I was moody, quick, tolerant in appearance, fundamentally hard, extreme in contempt, absolute in admiration, easy to impress, impossible to convince. I put my faith in a few ideas which had come to me. I regarded their conformity with the being which gave them birth as a certain indication of their universal value. Since they appeared so distinctly to my mind, they also appeared invincible; convictions born of desire are always the strongest.

I guarded these shadowy ideas as my secrets of state. I was ashamed of their strangeness; I feared they were absurd; I even knew they were absurd, but not entirely so. They were vain in themselves, but powerful by virtue of the remarkable force with which my confidence endowed me. My jealous watch over this mystery of weakness filled me with a sort of vigour.

I had ceased to write verse, and had almost ceased to read.

From *Variety* (I, 123–37), 1927, translation by Malcolm Cowley of "Au sujet d'Eurêka." Preface to *Eurêka*, translated by Baudelaire, 1921; *Variété* I, 1923.

Novels and poems, in my opinion, were only impure and half-unconscious applications of a few properties inherent in the great secrets I hoped some day to reveal—basing this hope on the unremitting assurance that they must necessarily exist. As for philosophers, I had read them very little, and was irritated by that little, because they never answered any of the questions which tormented me. They filled me only with boredom; never with the feeling that they were communicating some verifiable power. I thought it useless, moreover, to speculate about abstractions without first defining them. And yet can one do otherwise? The only hope for a philosophy is to render itself impersonal. We must await this great step toward the time of the world's end.

I had dipped into a few mystics. It is impossible to speak ill of their works, for all one discovers there is what one brings.

I was at this point when *Eureka* fell into my hands.

My studies under my dull and woebegone professors had led me to believe that science is not love; that its fruits are perhaps useful, but its foliage very spiny and its bark terribly rough. I reserved mathematics for a type of boringly exact minds, incommensurable with my own.

Literature, on the other hand, had often shocked me by its lack of discipline, connexion, and necessity in handling ideas. Frequently its object is trifling. French poetry ignores, or even fears, all the tragedies and epics of the intellect. On the few occasions when it ventures into this territory, it becomes sad and dull beyond measure. Neither Lucretius nor Dante was French. We have no poets of the intelligence. Perhaps our feeling for the separation of literary *genres*—in other words, for the independence of the different movements of the mind—is such that we can suffer nothing which combines them. Those things which can exist without singing we cannot endow with song. But our poetry, during the last hundred years, has shown such a rare power of renewal that perhaps the future will not be slow to grant it some of those works which are grand in their style, noble in their severity, and dominate both the senses and the intellect.

In a few moments *Eureka* had introduced me to Newton's law, the name of Laplace, the hypothesis which he proposed, and the very existence of speculations and researches which were never mentioned to adolescents—for fear, I suppose, that we might be interested, instead of measuring the astonishing length of the hour with yawns and dreams. In those days, whatever was likely to stimulate the intellectual appetite was placed among the arcana. It was a time when fat textbooks of physics did not whisper a word about the law of gravity, or Carnot's principle, or the conservation of energy; instead they were addicted to Magdeburg hemispheres, three-branched faucets, and the tenuous theories to which they were laboriously inspired by the problem of the siphon.

And yet, would it be wasting the time of study to make young minds suspect the origins, high destinies, and living virtue of those computations and very arid theorems which pedagogues inflict on them without logical order, and even with a rather remarkable incoherence?

These sciences now taught so coldly were founded and developed by men with a passionate interest in their work. *Eureka* made me feel some of this passion.

I confess that I was greatly astonished and only partially pleased by the preposterous claims and ambitions of the author, the solemn tone of his preamble, and the extraordinary discussion of method with which the volume opens. These first pages, however, gave indication of a central idea, although it was enveloped in a mystery which suggested partly a certain powerlessness, partly a deliberate reserve, and partly the reluctance of an enthusiastic soul to reveal its most precious secrets. . . . And all this did not leave me cold.

To attain what he calls *the truth,* Poe invokes what he calls *consistency.* It is not easy to give an exact definition of this consistency. The author has not done so, although he must have had a clear conception of its meaning.

According to him, the *truth* which he seeks can only be grasped by immediate adherence to an intuition of such nature that it renders present, and in some sort perceptible to the mind, the reciprocal dependence of the parts and properties of the system under consideration. This reciprocal dependence extends to the successive phases of the system; causality becomes symmetrical. To a point of view which embraced the totality of the universe, a cause and its effect might be taken one for the other; they could be said to exchange their rôles.

Two remarks at this point. The first I shall merely indicate, for it would lead us far, both the reader and myself. The doctrine of final causes plays a capital part in Poe's system. This doctrine is no longer fashionable, and I have neither the strength nor the desire to defend it. But we must agree that the notions of cause and adaptation lead almost inevitably to this conclusion (and I do not speak of the immense difficulties, and hence of the temptations, offered by certain facts, such as the existence of instincts, etc.). The simplest course is to dismiss the problem. Our only way of solving it is through pure imagination, and this can better be applied to other tasks.

Let us pass to the second remark. In Poe's system, consistency is both the source of the discovery and the discovery itself. This is an admirable conception: an example and application of reciprocal adaptation. The universe is formed on a plan the profound symmetry of which is present, as it were, in the inner structure of our minds. Hence, the poetic instinct will lead us blindly to the truth.

One frequently meets with analogous ideas among the mathematicians. They come to regard their discoveries not as "creations" of their mathematical faculties, but rather as something captured from a treasure composed of pre-existent and natural forms, a treasure which becomes accessible only through a rare conjecture of disciplined effort, sensibility, and desire.

All the consequences developed in *Eureka* are not deduced with the exactness, nor led up to with the degree of clarity, which one might desire. There are shadows and lacunæ. There are interventions which the author hardly explains. There is a God.

For the spectator of the dramas and comedies of the intellect, nothing is more interesting than to see the ingenuity, the insistency, the trickery and anxiety of an inventor at grips with his own invention. He is admirably familiar with all its defects. He inevitably wishes to display all its beauties, exploit its advantages, conceal its poverty, and at any cost make it the image of his ideal. A merchant adorns his merchandise. A woman changes her appearance before a mirror. Preachers, philosophers, politicians, and, in general, all men whose function is to expound uncertain things, are always a mixture of sincerity and silences (and this is the most favourable assumption). What they do not wish to consider, they do not wish us to see. . . .

The fundamental idea of *Eureka* is none the less a profound and sovereign idea.

It would not be exaggerating its importance to recognize, in his theory of consistency, a fairly definite attempt to describe the universe by its *intrinsic properties.* The following proposition can be found toward the end of *Eureka:* "Each law of nature depends at all points on all the other laws." This might easily be considered, if not as a formula, at least as the expression of a tendency toward generalized relativity.

That this tendency approaches recent conceptions becomes evident when one discovers, in the *poem* under discussion, an affirmation of the *symmetrical* and reciprocal relationship of matter, time, space, gravity, and light. I emphasize the word symmetrical, for *it is, in reality, a formal symmetry which is the essential characteristic of Einstein's universe.* Herein lies the beauty of his conception.

But Poe does not confine himself to the physical constituents of phenomena. He introduces life and consciousness into his plan. At this point how many thoughts occur to the mind! The time is past when one could distinguish easily between the material and the spiritual. Formerly all discussion was based on a complete knowledge of "matter," which it was thought could be limited by definition. In a word, everything depended on *appearance.*

The appearance of matter is that of a dead substance, a *potentiality* which becomes *activity* only through the intervention of something exterior and entirely foreign to its nature. From this definition, inevitable consequences used to be drawn. But matter has changed. Our old conception of its nature was derived from pure observation; experiments have led to an opposite notion. The whole of modern physics, which has created, as it were, *relays* for our senses, has persuaded us that our former definition had neither an absolute nor a speculative value. We find that matter is strangely diverse and infinitely surprising; that it is formed of transformations which continue and are lost in minuteness, even in the abysses of minuteness; we learn that perpetual motion is perhaps realized. In matter an eternal fever rages.

At present we no longer know what a fragment of any given body may or may not contain or produce, now or in the future. The very idea of matter is distinguished as little as you will from that of energy. Everything is stirred by deeper and deeper agitations, rotations, exchanges, radiations. Our own eyes, our hands, our nerves, are made of such stuff; and the appearance of death or sleep which matter at first presents, as well as its passivity and surrender to external forces, are conceptions built up in our senses, like those shadows obtained by a certain superposition of lights.

All this can be resumed in the statement that the properties of matter seem to depend only on the category of size in which we place the observer. But in this case the classical attributes of matter—its lack of spontaneity, its essential difference from movement, and the continuity or homogeneity of its texture— become merely superficial, and can no longer be absolutely contrasted with such concepts as life, sensibility, or thought. Once we depart from the category of size in which rough observations are made, all former definitions prove incorrect. We are certain that unknown properties and forces are exerted in the *infra-world,* since we have discovered a few of these which our senses were not made to perceive. But we can neither enumerate them, nor even assign a definite number to the increasing plurality of chapters in the science of physics.

We cannot even be certain that the whole body of our concepts is not illusory, when transported into those domains which limit and support our own. To speak of iron or hydrogen is to presuppose entities—the existence and permanence of which can only be inferred from very limited and comparatively brief experiments. Moreover, there is no reason to believe that our space, our time, and our causality preserve any meaning whatsoever in those domains where the existence of our bodies is *impossible.* And certainly, the man who attempts to imagine the inner reality of things can do so only by adapting the ordinary categories of his mind. But the more he extends his researches, and, in some degree, the more he increases his powers of recording phenomena, the further he travels from what might be called the *optimum* of his perceptions. Determinism is lost among inextricable systems, with billions of variables, where the mind's eye can no longer trace the operation of laws and come to rest on some permanent fact. Whereas the imagination was once employed in giving final form to a truth which the senses had led one to infer, and the power of logic had woven into a single piece—now, when discontinuity becomes the rule, this imagination must confess its impotence. And when the *means* become the objects of our judgments, we are ceasing to consider events in themselves. Our knowledge is tending toward power, and has turned aside from a coordinated contemplation of things; prodigies of mathematical subtlety are required to restore a little unity to our world. We mention first principles no longer, and physical laws have become mere instruments, always capable of being perfected. They no longer govern the world, but are involved in the weakness of our minds; we can no longer rely on their simplicity; always, like a persistent point, there is some unresolved decimal which brings us back to a feeling of incompleteness, a sense of the inexhaustible.

One can see, from these remarks, that Poe's intuitions as to the general nature of the physical, moral, and metaphysical universe are neither proved nor disproved by the extremely numerous and important discoveries which have been made since 1847. Certain of his views could even be incorporated, without excessive difficulty, into fairly recent conceptions. When he measures the duration of his Cosmos by the time necessary to realize all possible combinations of the elements, one thinks of Boltzmann's theories and of his estimates of probability as applied to the kinetic theory of gas. Carnot's principle is also foreshadowed in *Eureka,* as is the representation of this principle by the mechanics of diffusion; the author seems to have been a precursor of those bold spirits who would rescue the universe from its certain death by means of an infinitely brief passage through an infinitely improbable state.

Since a complete analysis of *Eureka* is not my present intention, I shall hardly mention the use which Poe makes of the nebular hypothesis. When Laplace advanced this theory, his object was limited. He proposed only to reconstruct the development of the solar system. To this end he assumed the existence of a gaseous mass in the process of cooling. The core of the mass had already reached a high degree of condensation, and the whole rotated on an axis passing through its centre of gravity. He assumed the existence of this gravity, as well as the invariability of mechanical laws, and made it his sole task to explain the direction of rotation of the planets and their satellites, the slight eccentricity of their orbits, and the relatively small degree of inclination. Under these conditions, being subjected to centrifugal force and the process of cooling, matter would flow from the poles toward the equator of the mass, and at the points where gravity and centrifugal acceleration balanced each other, would be disposed in a zone. Thus a nebulous ring was formed; it would soon be broken, and the fragments of this ring would finally coalesce to form a planet.

The reader of *Eureka* will see how Poe has extended the application both of the nebular hypothesis and the law of gravity. On these mathematical foundations he has built an abstract poem, one of the rare modern examples of a total explanation of the material and spiritual universe, a *cosmogony*. It belongs to a department of literature remarkable for its persistence and astonishing in its variety; cosmogony is one of the oldest of all literary forms.

. . . .

DAVID HERBERT LAWRENCE [1885–1930] included in his most influential critical book, *Studies in Classic American Literature* (1923), an expanded version of an article on Poe which had originally appeared in *The English Review*, April 1919. In this highly suggestive and influential essay, Lawrence analyzes Poe's "love stories"—"Ligeia" and "The Fall of the House of Usher." As a scientist rather than as an artist, Poe wrote these "ghastly stories" of the disintegration of the soul of modern neurotic man, including Poe's own soul, thus performing, in Lawrence's view, one of the bitterest and most necessary tasks. Conscious, wilful, probing analysis of another person, the insistence on "oneness" in love (as in Poe's own marriage), whether through sensual or spiritual love, violates the intrinsic isolation or integrity of that other.

Edgar Allan Poe

DAVID HERBERT LAWRENCE

Poe has no truck with Indians or Nature. He makes no bones about Red Brothers and Wigwams.

He is absolutely concerned with the disintegration-processes of his own psyche. As we have said, the rhythm of American art-activity is dual.

1. A disintegrating and sloughing of the old consciousness.
2. The forming of a new consciousness underneath.

Fenimore Cooper has the two vibrations going on together.

From *Studies in Classic American Literature,* 1923.

Poe has only one, only the disintegrative vibration. This makes him almost more a scientist than an artist.

Moralists have always wondered helplessly why Poe's "morbid" tales need have been written. They need to be written because old things need to die and disintegrate, because the old white psyche has to be gradually broken down before anything else can come to pass.

Man must be stripped even of himself. And it is a painful, sometimes a ghastly, process.

Poe had a pretty bitter doom. Doomed to seethe down his soul in a great continuous convulsion of disintegration, and doomed to register the process. And then doomed to be abused for it, when he had performed some of the bitterest tasks of human experience, that can be asked of a man. Necessary tasks, too. For the human soul must suffer its own disintegration, *consciously*, if ever it is to survive.

But Poe is rather a scientist than an artist. He is reducing his own self as a scientist reduces a salt in a crucible. It is an almost chemical analysis of the soul and consciousness. Whereas in true art there is always the double rhythm of creating and destroying.

This is why Poe calls his things "tales." They are a concatenation of cause and effect.

His best pieces, however, are not tales. They are more. They are ghastly stories of the human soul in its disruptive throes.

Moreover, they are "love" stories.

Ligeia and *The Fall of the House of Usher* are really love stories.

Love is the mysterious vital attraction which draws things together, closer, closer together. For this reason sex is the actual crisis of love. For in sex the two blood-systems, in the male and female, concentrate and come into contact, the merest film intervening. Yet if the intervening film breaks down, it is death.

So there you are. There is a limit to everything. There is a limit to love.

The central law of all organic life is that each organism is intrinsically isolate and single in itself.

The moment its isolation breaks down, and there comes an actual mixing and confusion, death sets in.

This is true of every individual organism, from man to amœba.

But the secondary law of all organic life is that each organism only lives through contact with other matter, assimilation, and contact with other life, which means assimilation of new vibrations, nonmaterial. Each individual organism is vivified by intimate contact with fellow organisms: up to a certain point.

So man. He breathes the air into him, he swallows food and water. But more than this. He takes into him the life of his fellow men, with whom he comes into contact, and he gives back life to them. This contact draws nearer and nearer, as the intimacy increases. When it is a whole contact, we call it love. Men live by food, but die if they eat too much. Men live by love, but die, or cause death, if they love too much.

There are two loves: sacred and profane, spiritual and sensual.

In sensual love, it is the two blood-systems, the man's and the woman's, which sweep up into pure contact, and *almost* fuse. Almost mingle. Never quite. There is always the finest imaginable wall between the two blood-waves, through which pass unknown vibrations, forces, but through which the blood itself must never break, or it means bleeding.

In spiritual love, the contact is purely nervous. The nerves in the lovers are set vibrating in unison like two instruments. The pitch can rise higher and higher. But carry this too far, and the nerves begin to break, to bleed, as it were, and a form of death sets in.

The trouble about man is that he insists on being master of his own fate, and he insists on *oneness*. For instance, having discovered the ecstasy of spiritual love, he insists that he shall have this all the time, and nothing but this, for this is life. It is what he calls "heightening" life. He wants his nerves to be set vibrating in the intense and exhilarating unison with the nerves of another being, and by this means he acquires an ecstasy of vision, he finds himself in glowing unison with all the universe.

But as a matter of fact this glowing unison is only a temporary thing, because the first law of life is that each organism is isolate in itself, it must return to its own isolation.

Yet man has tried the glow of unison, called love, and he *likes* it. It gives him his highest gratification. He wants it. He wants it all the time. He wants it and he will have it. He doesn't want to return to his own isolation. Or if he must, it is only as a prowling beast returns to its lair to rest and set out again.

This brings us to Edgar Allan Poe. The clue to him lies in the motto he chose for *Ligeia,* a quotation from the mystic Joseph Glanvill: "And the will therein lieth, which dieth not. Who knoweth the mysteries of the will, with its vigour? For God is but a great will pervading all things by nature of its intentness. Man doth not yield himself to the angels, nor unto death utterly, save only through the weakness of his feeble will."

It is a profound saying: and a deadly one.

Because if God is a great will, then the universe is but an instrument.

I don't know what God is. But He is not simply a will. That is too simple. Too anthropomorphic. Because a man wants his own will, and nothing but his will, he needn't say that God is the same will, magnified *ad infinitum.*

For me, there may be one God, but He is nameless and unknowable.

For me, there are also many gods, that come into me and leave me again. And they have very various wills, I must say.

But the point is Poe.

Poe had experienced the ecstasies of extreme spiritual love. And he wanted those ecstasies and nothing but those ecstasies. He wanted that great gratification, the sense of flowing, the sense of unison, the sense of heightening of life. He had experienced this gratification. He was told on every hand that this ecstasy of spiritual, nervous love was the greatest thing in life, was life itself. And he had tried it for himself, he knew that for him it *was* life itself. So he wanted it. And he *would have* it. He set up his will against the whole of the limitations of nature.

This is a brave man, acting on his own belief, and his own experience. But it is also an arrogant man, and a fool.

Poe was going to get the ecstasy and the heightening, cost what it might. He went on in a frenzy, as characteristic American women nowadays go on in a frenzy, after the very same thing: the heightening, the flow, the ecstasy. Poe tried alcohol, and any drug he could lay his hands on. He also tried any human being he could lay his hands on.

His grand attempt and achievement was with his wife; his cousin, a girl with a singing voice. With her he went in for the intensest flow, the heightening, the prismatic shades of ecstasy. It was the intensest nervous vibration of unison, pressed higher and higher in pitch, till the blood-vessels of the girl broke, and the blood began to flow out loose. It was love. If you call it love.

Love can be terribly obscene.

It is love that causes the neuroticism of the day. It is love that is the prime cause of tuberculosis.

The nerves that vibrate most intensely in spiritual unisons are the sympathetic ganglia of the breast, of the throat, and the hind brain. Drive this vibration over-intensely, and you weaken the sympathetic tissues of the chest—the lungs—or of the throat, or of the lower brain, and the tubercles are given a ripe field.

But Poe drove the vibrations beyond any human pitch of endurance.

Being his cousin, she was more easily keyed to him.

Ligeia is the chief story. Ligeia! A mental-derived name. To him the woman, his wife, was not Lucy. She was Ligeia. No doubt she even preferred it thus.

Ligeia is Poe's love-story, and its very fantasy makes it more truly his own story.

It is a tale of love pushed over a verge. And love pushed to extremes is a battle of wills between the lovers.

Love is become a battle of wills.

Which shall first destroy the other, of the lovers? Which can hold out longest, against the other?

Ligeia is still the old-fashioned woman. Her will is still to submit. She wills to submit to the vampire of her husband's consciousness. Even death.

"In stature she was tall, somewhat slender, and, in her latter days, even emaciated. I would in vain attempt to portray the majesty, the quiet ease, of her demeanour, or the incomprehensible lightness and elasticity of her footfall. . . . I was never made aware of her entrance into my closed study, save by the dear music of her low sweet voice, as she placed her marble hand upon my shoulder."

Poe has been so praised for his style. But it seems to me a meretricious affair. "Her marble hand" and "the elasticity of her footfall" seem more like chair-springs and mantelpieces than a human creature. She never was quite a human creature to him. She was an instrument from which he got his extremes of sensation. His *machine à plaisir,* as somebody says.

All Poe's style, moreover, has this mechanical quality, as his poetry has a mechanical rhythm. He never sees anything in terms of life, almost always in terms of matter, jewels, marble, etc.,—or in terms of force, scientific. And his cadences are all managed mechanically. This is what is called "having a style."

What he wants to do with Ligeia is to analyse her, till he knows all her component parts, till he has got her all in his consciousness. She is some strange chemical salt which he must analyse out in the test-tubes of his brain, and then—when he's finished the analysis—*E finita la commedia!*

But she won't be quite analysed out. There is something, something he can't get. Writing of her eyes, he says: "They were, I must believe, far larger than the ordinary eyes of our own race"—as if anybody would want eyes "far larger" than other folks'. "They were even fuller than the fullest of the gazelle eyes of the tribe of the valley of Nourjahad"—which is blarney. "The hue of the orbs was the most brilliant of black and, far over them, hung jetty lashes of great length"—suggests a whiplash. "The brows, slightly irregular in outline, had the same tint. The 'strangeness,' however, which I found in the eyes, was of a nature distinct from the formation, or the colour, or the brilliancy of the features, and must, after all, be referred to the *expression*."—Sounds like an anatomist anatomizing a cat—"Ah, word of no meaning! behind whose vast latitude of mere sound we entrench our ignorance of so much of the spiritual. The expression of the eyes of Ligeia! How for long hours have I pondered upon it! How have I, through the whole of a midsummer night, struggled to fathom it! What was it—that something more profound than the well of Democritus—which lay far within the pupils of my beloved! What *was* it? I was possessed with a passion to discover. . . ."

It is easy to see why each man kills the thing he loves. To *know* a living thing is to kill it. You have to kill a thing to know it satisfactorily. For this reason, the desirous consciousness, the SPIRIT, is a vampire.

One should be sufficiently intelligent and interested to know a good deal *about* any person one comes into close contact with. *About* her. Or *about* him.

But to try to *know* any living being is to try to suck the life out of that being.

Above all things, with the woman one loves. Every sacred instinct teaches one that one must leave her unknown. You know your woman darkly, in the blood. To try to *know* her mentally is to try to kill her. Beware, oh woman, of the man who wants to *find out what you are*. And, oh men, beware a thousand times more of the woman who wants to *know* you, or *get* you, what you are.

It is the temptation of a vampire fiend, is this knowledge.

Man does so horribly want to master the secret of life and of individuality *with his mind*. It is like the analysis of protoplasm. You can only analyse *dead* protoplasm, and know its constituents. It is a death-process.

Keep KNOWLEDGE for the world of matter, force, and function. It has got nothing to do with being.

But Poe wanted to know—wanted to know what was the strangeness in the eyes of Ligeia. She might have told him it was horror at his probing, horror at being vamped by his consciousness.

But she wanted to be vamped. She wanted to be probed by his consciousness, to be KNOWN. She paid for wanting it, too.

Nowadays it is usually the man who wants to be vamped, to be KNOWN.

Edgar Allan probed and probed. So often he seemed on the verge. But she went over the verge of death before he came over the verge of knowledge. And it is always so.

He decided, therefore, that the clue to the strangeness lay in the mystery of will. "And the will therein lieth, which dieth not . . ."

Ligeia had a "gigantic volition." . . . "An intensity in thought, action, or speech was possibly, in her, a result, or at least an index" (he really meant indication) "of that gigantic volition which, during our long intercourse, failed to give other and more immediate evidence of its existence."

I should have thought her long submission to him was chief and ample "other evidence."

"Of all the women whom I have ever known, she, the outwardly calm, the ever-placid Ligeia, was the most violently a prey to the tumultuous vultures of stern passion. And of such passion I could form no estimate, save by the miraculous expansion of those eyes which at once so delighted and appalled me—by the almost magical melody, modulation, distinctness, and placidity of her very low voice—and by the fierce energy (rendered doubly effective by contrast with her manner of utterance) of the wild words which she habitually uttered."

Poor Poe, he had caught a bird of the same feather as himself. One of those terrible cravers, who crave the further sensation. Crave to madness or death. "Vultures of stern passion" indeed! Condors.

But having recognized that the clue was in her gigantic volition, he should have realized that the process of this loving, this craving, this knowing, was a struggle of wills. But Ligeia, true to the great tradition and mode of womanly love, by her will kept herself submissive, recipient. She is the passive body who is explored and analysed into death. And yet, at times, her great female will must have revolted. "Vultures of stern passion!" With a convulsion of desire she desired his further probing and exploring. To any lengths. But then, "tumultuous vultures of stern passion." She had to fight with herself.

But Ligeia wanted to go on and on with the craving, with the love, with the sensation, with the probing, with the knowing, on and on to the end.

There is no end. There is only the rupture of death. That's where men, and women, are "had." Man is always sold, in his search for final KNOWLEDGE.

"That she loved me I should not have doubted; and I might have been easily aware that, in a bosom such as hers, love would have reigned no ordinary passion. But in death only was I fully impressed with the strength of her affection. For long hours, detaining my hand, would she pour out before me the overflowing of a heart whose more than passionate devotion amounted to idolatry." (Oh, the indecency of all this endless intimate talk!) "How had I deserved to be so blessed by such confessions?" (Another man would have felt himself cursed.) "How had I deserved to be so cursed with the removal of my beloved in the hour of her making them? But upon this subject I cannot bear to dilate. Let me say only that in Ligeia's more than womanly abandonment to a love, alas! all unmerited, all unworthily bestowed, I at length recognized the principle of her longing, with so wildly earnest a desire, for the life which was now fleeing so rapidly away. It is this wild longing—it is this eager vehemence of desire for life—*but* for life, that I have no power to portray, no utterance capable of expressing."

Well, that is ghastly enough, in all conscience.

"And from them that have not shall be taken away even that which they have."

"To him that hath life shall be given life, and from him that hath not life shall be taken away even that life which he hath."

Or her either.

These terribly conscious birds, like Poe and his Ligeia, deny the very life that is in them; they want to turn it all into talk, into *knowing*. And so life, which will *not* be known, leaves them.

But poor Ligeia, how could she help it? It was her doom. All the centuries of the SPIRIT, all the years of American rebellion against the Holy Ghost, had done it to her.

She dies, when she would rather do anything than die. And when she dies the clue, which he only lived to grasp, dies with her.

Foiled!

Foiled!

No wonder she shrieks with her last breath.

On the last day Ligeia dictates to her husband a poem. As poems go, it is rather false, meretricious. But put yourself in Ligeia's place, and it is real enough, and ghastly beyond bearing.

> Out—out are all the lights—out all!
> And over each quivering form
> The curtain, a funeral pall,
> Comes down with the rush of a storm,
> While the angels, all pallid and wan,
> Uprising, unveiling, affirm
> That the play is the tragedy, 'Man,'
> And its hero, the Conqueror Worm.

Which is the American equivalent for a William Blake poem. For Blake, too, was one of these ghastly, obscene "Knowers."

" 'O God!' half shrieked Ligeia, leaping to her feet and extending her arms aloft with a spasmodic movement, as I made an end of these lines—'O God! O Divine Father! shall these things be undeviatingly so? Shall this conqueror be not once conquered? Are we not part and parcel in Thee? Who—who knoweth the mysteries of the will with its vigour? Man doth not yield him to the angels, *nor unto death utterly,* save only through the weakness of his feeble will.' "

So Ligeia dies. And yields to death at least partly. *Anche troppo.*

As for her cry to God—has not God said that those who sin against the Holy Ghost shall not be forgiven?

And the Holy Ghost is within us. It is the thing that prompts us to be real, not to push our own cravings too far, not to submit to stunts and high-falutin, above all, not to be too egoistic and wilful in our conscious self, but to change as the spirit inside us bids us change, and leave off when it bids us leave off, and laugh when we must laugh, particularly at ourselves, for in deadly earnestness there is always something a bit ridiculous. The Holy Ghost bids us never be too deadly in our earnestness, always to laugh in time, at ourselves and everything. Particularly at our sublimities. Everything has its hour of ridicule—everything.

Now Poe and Ligeia, alas, couldn't laugh. They were frenziedly earnest. And frenziedly they pushed on this vibration of consciousness and unison in consciousness. They sinned against the Holy Ghost that bids us all laugh and forget, bids us know our own limits. And they weren't forgiven.

Ligeia needn't blame God. She had only her own will, her "gigantic volition" to thank, lusting after more consciousness, more beastly KNOWING.

Ligeia dies. The husband goes to England, vulgarly buys or rents a gloomy, grand old abbey, puts it into some sort of repair, and furnishes it with exotic, mysterious, theatrical splendour. Never anything open and real. This theatrical "volition" of his. The bad taste of sensationalism.

Then he marries the fair-haired, blue-eyed Lady Rowena Trevanion, of Tremaine. That is, she would be a sort of Saxon-Cornish blue-blood damsel. Poor Poe!

"In halls such as these—in a bridal chamber such as this—I passed, with the Lady of Tremaine, the unhallowed hours of the first month of our marriage—passed them with but little disquietude. That my wife dreaded the fierce moodiness of my temper—that she shunned me and loved me but little—I could not help perceiving, but it gave me rather pleasure than otherwise. I loathed her with a hatred belonging more to demon than to man. My memory flew back (oh, with what intensity of regret!) to Ligeia, the beloved, the august, the beautiful, the entombed. I revelled in recollections of her purity . . ." etc.

Now the vampire lust is consciously such.

In the second month of the marriage the Lady Rowena fell ill. It is the shadow of Ligeia hangs over her. It is the ghostly Ligeia who pours poison into Rowena's cup. It is the spirit of Ligeia, leagued with the spirit of the husband, that now lusts in the slow destruction of Rowena. The two vampires, dead wife and living husband.

For Ligeia has not yielded unto death *utterly*. Her fixed, frustrated will comes back in vindictiveness. She could not have her way in life. So she, too, will find victims in life. And the husband, all the time, only uses Rowena as a living body on which to wreak his vengeance for his being thwarted with Ligeia. Thwarted from the final KNOWING her.

And at last from the corpse of Rowena, Ligeia rises. Out of her death, through the door of a corpse they have destroyed between them, reappears Ligeia, still trying to have her will, to have more love and knowledge, the final gratification which is never final, with her husband.

For it is true, as William James and Conan Doyle and the rest allow, that a spirit can persist in the after-death. Persist by its own volition. But usually, the evil persistence of a thwarted will, returning for vengeance on life. Lemures, vampires.

It is a ghastly story of the assertion of the human will, the will-to-love and the will-to-consciousness, asserted against death itself. The pride of human conceit in KNOWLEDGE.

There are terrible spirits, ghosts, in the air of America.

Eleanora, the next story, is a fantasy revealing the sensational delights of the man in his early marriage with the young and tender bride. They dwelt, he, his cousin and her mother, in the sequestered Valley of Many-coloured Grass, the valley of prismatic sensation, where everything seems spectrum-coloured. They looked down at their *own images* in the River of Silence, and drew the god Eros from that wave: out of their own self-consciousness, that is. This is a description of the life of introspection and of the love which is begotten by the self in the self, the self-made love. The trees are like serpents worshipping the sun. That is, they represent the phallic passion in its poisonous or mental activity. Everything runs to consciousness: serpents worshipping the sun. The embrace of love, which should bring darkness and oblivion, would with these lovers be a daytime thing bringing more heightened consciousness, visions, spectrum-visions, prismatic. The evil thing that daytime love-making is, and all sex-palaver.

In *Berenice* the man must go down to the sepulchre of his beloved and pull out her thirty-two small white teeth, which he carries in a box with him. It is repulsive and gloating. The teeth are the instruments of biting, of resistance, of antagonism. They often become symbols of opposition, little instruments or entities of crushing and destroying. Hence the dragon's teeth in the myth. Hence the man in *Berenice* must take possession of the irreducible part of his mistress. "*Toutes ses dents étaient des idées,*" he says. Then they are little fixed ideas of mordant hate, of which he possesses himself.

The other great story linking up with this group is *The Fall of the House of Usher*. Here the love is between brother and sister. When the self is broken, and the mystery of the recognition of *otherness* fails, then the longing for identification with the beloved becomes a lust. And it is this longing for identification, utter merging, which is at the base of the incest problem. In psychoanalysis almost every trouble in the psyche is traced to an incest-desire. But it won't do. Incest-desire is only one of the modes by which men strive to get their gratification of the intensest vibration of the spiritual nerves, without any resistance. In the family, the natural vibration is most nearly in unison. With a stranger, there is greater resistance. Incest is the getting of gratification and the avoiding of resistance.

The root of all evil is that we all want this spiritual gratification, this flow, this apparent heightening of life, this knowledge, this valley of many-coloured grass, even grass and light prismatically decomposed, giving ecstasy. We want all this *without resistance*. We want it continually. And this is the root of all evil in us.

We ought to pray to be resisted, and resisted to the bitter end. We ought to decide to have done at last with craving.

The motto to *The Fall of the House of Usher* is a couple of lines from Béranger.

> *Son cœur est un luth suspendu;*
> *Sitôt qu'on le touche il résonne.*

We have all the trappings of Poe's rather overdone, vulgar

fantasy. "I reined my horse to the precipitous brink of a black and lurid tarn that lay in unruffled lustre by the dwelling, and gazed down—but with a shudder even more thrilling than before—upon the remodelled and inverted images of the grey sedge, and the ghastly tree-stems, and the vacant and eye-like windows." The House of Usher, both dwelling and family, was very old. Minute fungi overspread the exterior of the house, hanging in festoons from the eaves. Gothic archways, a valet of stealthy step, sombre tapestries, ebon black floors, a profusion of tattered and antique furniture, feeble gleams of encrimsoned light through latticed panes, and over all "an air of stern, deep, and irredeemable gloom"—this makes up the interior.

The inmates of the house, Roderick and Madeline Usher, are the last remnants of their incomparably ancient and decayed race. Roderick has the same large, luminous eye, the same slightly arched nose of delicate Hebrew model, as characterized Ligeia. He is ill with the nervous malady of his family. It is he whose nerves are so strung that they vibrate to the unknown quiverings of the ether. He, too, has lost his self, his living soul, and becomes a sensitized instrument of the external influences; his nerves are verily like an æolian harp which must vibrate. He lives in "some struggle with the grim phantasm, Fear," for he is only the physical, post-mortem reality of a living being.

It is a question how much, once the true centrality of the self is broken, the instrumental consciousness of man can register. When man becomes selfless, wafting instrumental like a harp in an open window, how much can his elemental consciousness express? The blood as it runs has its own sympathies and responses to the material world, quite apart from seeing. And the nerves we know vibrate all the while to unseen presences, unseen forces. So Roderick Usher quivers on the edge of material existence.

It is this mechanical consciousness which gives "the fervid facility of his impromptus." It is the same thing that gives Poe his extraordinary facility in versification. The absence of real central or impulsive being in himself leaves him inordinately, mechanically sensitive to sounds and effects, associations of sounds, associations of rhyme, for example—mechanical, facile, having no root in any passion. It is all a secondary, meretricious process. So we get Roderick Usher's poem, *The Haunted Palace,* with its swift yet mechanical subtleties of rhyme and rhythm, its vulgarity of epithet. It is all a sort of dream-process, where the association between parts is mechanical, accidental as far as passional meaning goes.

Usher thought that all vegetable things had sentience. Surely all material things have a *form* of sentience, even the inorganic: surely they all exist in some subtle and complicated tension of vibration which makes them sensitive to external influence and causes them to have an influence on other external objects, irrespective of contact. It is of this vibration or inorganic consciousness that Poe is master: the sleep-consciousness. Thus Roderick Usher was convinced that his whole surroundings, the stones of the house, the fungi, the water in the tarn, the very reflected image of the whole, was woven into a physical oneness with the family, condensed, as it were, into one atmosphere —the special atmosphere in which alone the Ushers could live. And it was this atmosphere which had moulded the destinies of his family.

But while ever the soul remains alive, it the moulder and not the moulded. It is the souls of living men that subtly impregnate stones, houses, mountains, continents, and give these their subtlest form. People only become subject to stones after having lost their integral souls.

In the human realm, Roderick had one connection: his sister Madeline. She, too, was dying of a mysterious disorder, nervous, cataleptic. The brother and sister loved each other passionately and exclusively. They were twins, almost identical in looks. It was the same absorbing love between them, this process of unison in nerve-vibration, resulting in more and more extreme exaltation and a sort of consciousness, and a gradual breakdown into death. The exquisitely sensitive Roger, vibrating without resistance with his sister Madeline, more and more exquisitely, and gradually devouring her, sucking her life like a vampire in his anguish of extreme love. And she asking to be sucked.

Madeline died and was carried down by her brother into the deep vaults of the house. But she was not dead. Her brother roamed about in incipient madness—a madness of unspeakable terror and guilt. After eight days they were suddenly startled by a clash of metal, then a distinct, hollow metallic, and clangorous, yet apparently muffled, reverberation. Then Roderick Usher, gibbering, began to express himself: *"We have put her living in the tomb!* Said I not that my senses were acute! I *now* tell you that I heard her first feeble movements in the hollow coffin. I heard them—many, many days ago—yet I dared not— *I dared not speak."*

It is the same old theme of "each man kills the thing he loves." He knew his love had killed her. He knew she died at last, like Ligeia, unwilling and unappeased. So, she rose again upon him. "But then without those doors there *did* stand the lofty and enshrouded figure of the lady Madeline of Usher. There was blood upon her white robes, and the evidence of some bitter struggle upon every portion of her emaciated frame. For a moment she remained trembling and reeling to and fro upon the threshold, then, with a low moaning cry, fell heavily inward upon the person of her brother, and in her violent and now final death-agonies bore him to the floor a corpse, and a victim to the terrors he had anticipated."

It is lurid and melodramatic, but it is true. It is a ghastly psychological truth of what happens in the last stages of this beloved love, which cannot be separate, cannot be isolate, cannot listen in isolation to the isolate Holy Ghost. For it is the Holy Ghost we must live by. The next era is the era of the Holy Ghost. And the Holy Ghost speaks individually inside each individual: always, forever a ghost. There is no manifestation to the general world. Each isolate individual listening in isolation to the Holy Ghost within him.

The Ushers, brother and sister, betrayed the Holy Ghost in themselves. They would love, love, love, without resistance. They would love, they would merge, they would be as one thing. So they dragged each other down into death. For the Holy Ghost says you must *not* be as one thing with another being. Each must abide by itself, and correspond only within certain limits.

The best tales all have the same burden. Hate is as inordinate as love, and as slowly consuming, as secret, as underground, as subtle. All this underground vault business in Poe only symbolizes that which takes place *beneath* the consciousness. On top, all is fair-spoken. Beneath, there is awful murderous extremity of burying alive. Fortunato, in *The Cask of Amontillado,* is buried alive out of perfect hatred, as the lady Madeline of Usher is buried alive out of love. The lust of hate is the inordinate desire to consume and unspeakably possess the soul of the hated one, just as the lust of love is the desire to possess, or to be possessed by, the beloved, utterly. But in either case the result is the dissolution of both souls, each losing itself in transgressing its own bounds.

The lust of Montresor is to devour utterly the soul of Fortunato. It would be no use killing him outright. If a man is killed outright his soul remains integral, free to return into the bosom of some beloved, where it can enact itself. In walling-up his enemy in the vault, Montresor seeks to bring about the indescribable capitulation of the man's soul, so that he, the victor, can possess himself of the very being of the vanquished. Perhaps this can actually be done. Perhaps, in the attempt, the victor breaks the bonds of his own identity, and collapses into nothingness, or into the infinite. Becomes a monster.

What holds good for inordinate hate holds good for inordinate love. The motto, *Nemo me impune lacessit,* might just as well be *Nemo me impune amat.*

In *William Wilson* we are given a rather unsubtle account of the attempt of a man to kill his own soul. William Wilson the mechanical, lustful ego succeeds in killing William Wilson the living self. The lustful ego lives on, gradually reducing itself towards the dust of the infinite.

In the *Murders in the Rue Morgue* and *The Gold Bug* we have those mechanical tales where the interest lies in the following out of a subtle chain of cause and effect. The interest is scientific rather than artistic, a study in psychologic reactions.

The fascination of murder itself is curious. Murder is not just killing. Murder is a lust to get at the very quick of life itself, and kill it—hence the stealth and the frequent morbid dismemberment of the corpse, the attempt to get at the very quick of the murdered being, to find the quick and to possess it. It is curious that the two men fascinated by the art of murder, though in different ways, should have been De Quincey and Poe, men so different in ways of life, yet perhaps not so widely different in nature. In each of them is traceable that strange lust for extreme love and extreme hate, possession by mystic violence of the other soul, or violent deathly surrender of the soul in the self:

an absence of manly virtue, which stands alone and accepts limits.

Inquisition and torture are akin to murder: the same lust. It is a combat between inquisitor and victim as to whether the inquisitor shall get at the quick of life itself, and pierce it. Pierce the very quick of the soul. The evil will of man tries to do this. The brave soul of man refuses to have the life-quick pierced in him. It is strange: but just as the thwarted will can persist evilly, after death, so can the brave spirit preserve, even through torture and death, the quick of life and truth. Nowadays society is evil. It finds subtle ways of torture, to destroy the life-quick, to get at the life-quick in a man. Every possible form. And still a man can hold out, if he can laugh and listen to the Holy Ghost. —But society is evil, evil, and love is evil. And evil breeds evil, more and more.

So the mystery goes on. La Bruyère says that all our human unhappiness *viennent de ne pouvoir être seuls.* As long as man lives he will be subject to the yearning of love or the burning of hate, which is only inverted love.

But he is subject to something more than this. If we do not live to eat, we do not live to love either.

We live to stand alone, and listen to the Holy Ghost. The Holy Ghost, who is inside us, and who is many gods. Many gods come and go, some say one thing and some say another, and we have to obey the God of the innermost hour. It is the multiplicity of gods within us make up the Holy Ghost.

But Poe knew only love, love, love, intense vibrations and heightened consciousness. Drugs, women, self-destruction, but anyhow the prismatic ecstasy of heightened consciousness and sense of love, of flow. The human soul in him was beside itself. But it was not lost. He told us plainly how it was, so that we should know.

He was an adventurer into vaults and cellars and horrible underground passages of the human soul. He sounded the horror and the warning of his own doom.

Doomed he was. He died wanting more love, and love killed him. A ghastly disease, love. Poe telling us of his disease: trying even to make his disease fair and attractive. Even succeeding.

Which is the inevitable falseness, duplicity of art, American art in particular.

WILLIAM CARLOS WILLIAMS [1883–1963], in *In the American Grain* (1925), devotes an essay to Poe as one with a distinctively American mind, shaped by a sense of "locality." Poe, he maintains, was not a macabre or eccentric genius, in the European style. On the contrary, according to Williams, "His greatness is that he turned his back and faced inland. . . ." Poe was a "new De Soto," who made an "immaculate" attack on imitation, makeshifts, and self-deception. In his poetry he was concerned with the soul, in his tales with form. He had a lean style and insisted on method, rather than rhapsodizing over nature. "Poe gives the sense, for the first time in America, that literature is serious."

Edgar Allan Poe

WILLIAM CARLOS WILLIAMS

Poe was not "a fault of nature," "a find for French eyes," ripe but unaccountable, as through our woollyheadedness we've sought to designate him, but a genius intimately shaped by his locality and time. It is to save our faces that we've given him a crazy reputation, a writer from whose classic accuracies we have not known how else to escape.

The false emphasis was helped by his Parisian vogue and tonal influence on Baudelaire, but the French mind was deeper hit than that. Poe's work strikes by its scrupulous originality, *not* "originality" in the bastard sense, but in its legitimate sense of solidity which goes back to the ground, a conviction that he *can* judge within himself. These things the French were *ready* to perceive and quick to use to their advantage: a new point from which to readjust the trigonometric measurements of literary form.

It is the New World, or to leave that for the better term, it is a *new locality* that is in Poe assertive; it is America, the first great burst through to expression of a reawakened genius of *place*.

Poe gives the sense for the first time in America, that literature is *serious*, not a matter of courtesy but of truth.

The aspect of his critical statements as a whole, from their hundred American titles to the inmost structure of his sentences, is that of a single gesture, not avoiding the trivial, to sweep all worthless chaff aside. It is a movement, first and last to clear the GROUND.

From *In the American Grain*, 1925.

There is a flavor of provincialism that is provincialism in the plainness of his reasoning upon elementary grammatical, syntactical, and prosodic grounds which awakened Lowell's derision. But insistence upon primary distinctions, that seems coldly academic, was in this case no more than evidence of a strong impulse to begin at the beginning. Poe was unsophisticated, when contrasted with the puerile sophistications of a Lowell. It is a *beginning* he has in mind, a juvenescent *local* literature. By this he avoids the clownish turn of trying to join, contrary to every reasonable impulse, a literature (the English) with which he had no actual connection and which might be presumed, long since, to have passed that beginning which to the *new* condition was requisite.

But Mr. Lowell's comment had to be answered:

Here comes Poe with his Raven, like Barnaby Rudge—
Three fifths of him genius, and two fifths sheer fudge;
Who talks like a book of iambs and pentameters
In a way to make all men of common sense damn meters
Who has written some things far the best of their kind;
But somehow the heart seems squeezed out by the mind.

It brings a technical retort from Poe upon the grounds that, "We may observe here that *profound* ignorance on any particular topic is always sure to manifest itself by some allusion to 'common sense' as an all-sufficient instructor." Then he tears L.'s versification to pieces, adding, "Mr. L. should not have meddled with the anapestic rhythm: it is exceedingly awkward in the hands of one who knows nothing about it, and who *will* persist in fancying that he can write it by ear." But, previously, he had nailed the matter in a different vein. Lowell "could not do a better thing than to take the advice of those who mean him well, and leave prose, with satiric verse, to those who are better able to manage them; while he contents himself with that class of poetry for which, and for which alone, he seems to have an especial vocation—the poetry of *sentiment*." But Poe might have added finally, in his own defense, what he says elsewhere, concerning the accusation in L.'s last two lines: "The *highest* order of the imaginative intellect is always preeminently mathematical—"

The whole passage is noteworthy not only for the brilliance

of such a statement as that, but also because of its use of the provincial "we" (*Mr. Griswold and the Poets*): "That we are not a poetical people has been asserted so often and so roundly, both at home and abroad that the slander, through mere dint of repetition, has come to be received as truth. Yet nothing can be farther removed from it. The mistake is but a portion, or corollary, of the old dogma, that the calculating faculties are at war with the ideal; while, in fact, it may be demonstrated that the two divisions of mental power are never to be found in perfection apart. The highest order of the imaginative intellect is always preëminently mathematical; and the converse."

"The idiosyncrasy of our political position has stimulated into early action whatever practical talent we possessed. Even in our national infancy we evinced a degree of utilitarian ability which put to shame the mature skill of our forefathers. While yet in leading strings we proved ourselves adepts in all the arts and sciences which promoted the *comfort* of the animal man. But the arena of exertion, and of consequent distinction, into which our first and most obvious wants impelled us, has been regarded as the field of our deliberate choice. Our necessities have been taken for our propensities. Having been forced to make railroads, it has been deemed impossible that we should make verse. Because it suited us to construct an engine in the first instance, it has been denied that we could compose an epic in the second. Because we are not all Homers in the beginning, it has been somewhat rashly taken for granted that we shall be all Jeremy Benthams to the end."

"But this is purest insanity . . ."

In the critical note upon *Francis Marryat*, the distinction between "nationality in letters," which Poe carefully slights, and the preëminent importance, in letters as in all other branches of imaginative creation, of the *local*, which is his constant focus of attention, is to be noted.

Poe was NOT, it must be repeated, a Macabre genius, *essentially* lost upon the grotesque and the arabesque. If we have appraised him a morass of "lolling lilies," *that* is surface only.

The local causes shaping Poe's genius were two in character: the necessity for a fresh beginning, backed by a native vigor of extraordinary proportions,—with the corollary, that all "colonial imitation" must be swept aside. This was the conscious force which rose in Poe as innumerable timeless insights resulting, by his genius, in firm statements on the character of form, profusely illustrated by his practices; and, *second* the immediate effect of the locality upon the first, upon his nascent impulses, upon his original thrusts; tormenting the depths into a surface of bizarre designs by which he's known and which are *not at all* the major point in question.

Yet BOTH influences were determined by the locality, which, in the usual fashion, finds its mind swayed by the results of its stupidity rather than by a self-interest bred of greater wisdom. As with all else in America, the value of Poe's genius TO OUR-SELVES must be *uncovered* from our droppings, or at least uncovered from the "protection" which it must have raised about itself to have survived in any form among us—where everything is quickly trampled.

Poe "saw the end"; unhappily he saw his own despair at the same time, yet he continued to attack, with amazing genius seeking to discover, and discovering, points of firmness by which to STAND and grasp, against the slipping way they had of holding on in his locality. Either the New World must be mine as I will have it, or it is a worthless bog. There can be no concession. His attack was *from the center out.* Either I exist or I do not exist and no amount of pap which I happen to be lapping can dull me to the loss. It was a doctrine, anti-American. Here everything was makeshift, everything was colossal, in profusion. The frightened hogs or scared birds feeding on the corn— It left, in 1840, the same mood as ever dominant among us. Take what you can get. What you lack, copy. It was a population puffed with braggadocio, whom Poe so beautifully summarizes in many of his prose tales. To such men, all of them, the most terrible experience in the world is to be shown up. This Poe did, in his criticisms, with venomous accuracy. It was a gesture to BE CLEAN. It was a wish to HAVE the world or leave it. It was the truest instinct in America demanding to be satisfied, and an end to makeshifts, self deceptions and grotesque excuses. And yet the grotesque inappropriateness of the life about him forced itself in among his words.

One is forced on the conception of the New World as a woman. Poe was a new De Soto. The rest might be content with little things, not he.

"Rather the ice than their way."

His attack upon the difficulty which faced him was brilliantly conceived, faultlessly maintained and successful. The best term is perhaps: immaculate.

What he wanted was connected with no particular place; therefore it *must* be where he *was.*

"We have at length arrived at that epoch when our literature may and must stand on its own merits, or fall through its own defects. We have snapped asunder the leading-strings of our British Grandmama, and, better still, we have survived the first hours of our novel freedom,—the first licentious hours of hobbledehoy braggadocio and swagger. *At last,* then, we are in a condition to be criticized—even more, to be neglected; . . ."

What Poe says gains power by his not diminishing his force for the slightness of the object; it is a sense of an inevitable, impartial tide. "We have *no* design to be bitter. We notice this book at all, only because it is an unusually large one of its kind, because it is lying here upon our table, and because, whether justly or unjustly, whether for good reason or for none, it has attracted some portion of the attention of the public." There is no softening for the department of names, old or new, but a sense of the evidence examined, as it lies on the page, by a faultless mechanism which he brings from the rear of his head for the trial.

Lowell, Bryant, etc., concerned poetry with literature, Poe concerned it with the soul; hence their differing conceptions of the use of language. With Poe, words were not hung by usage with associations, the pleasing wraiths of former masteries, this is the sentimental trap-door to beginnings. With Poe words were figures; an old language truly, but one from which he carried over only the most elemental qualities to his new purpose; which was, to find a way to tell his soul. Sometimes he used words so playfully his sentences seem to fly away from sense, the destructive! with the conserving abandon, foreshadowed, of a Gertrude Stein. The particles of language must be clear as sand. (See *Diddling.*)

This was an impossible conception for the gluey imagination of his day. Constantly he labored to detach SOMETHING from the inchoate mass—That's it:

His concern, the apex of his immaculate attack, was to

detach a "method" from the smear of common usage—it is the work of nine tenths of his criticism. He struck to lay low the *"niaiseries"* of form and content with which his world abounded. It was a machine-gun fire; even in the slaughter of banality he rises to a merciless distinction. (See *Rufus Dawes.*) He sought by stress upon construction to hold the loose-strung mass off even at the cost of an icy coldness of appearance; it was the first need of his time, an escape from the formless mass he hated. It is the very sense of a beginning, as *it is the impulse which drove him to the character of all his tales;* to get from sentiment to form, a backstroke from the swarming "population."

He has a habit, borrowed perhaps from algebra, of balancing his sentences in the middle, or of reversing them in the later clauses, a sense of play, as with objects, or numerals which he *has* in the original, disassociated, that is, from other literary habit; separate words which he feels and turns about as if he fitted them to his design with *some* sense of their individual quality: "those who belong properly to books, and to whom books, perhaps, do not quite so properly belong."

The strong sense of a beginning in Poe is in *no one* else before him. What he says, being thoroughly local in origin, has some chance of being universal in application, a thing they never dared conceive. Made to fit a *place* it will have that actual quality of *things* antimetaphysical——

About Poe there is—

No supernatural mystery—
No extraordinary eccentricity of fate——

He is American, understandable by a simple exercise of reason; a light in the morass—which *must* appear eerie, even to himself, by force of terrific contrast, an isolation that would naturally lead to drunkenness and death, logically and simply—by despair, as the very final evidence of a too fine seriousness and devotion.

It is natural that the French (foreigners, unacquainted with American conditions) should be attracted by the SURFACE of his genius and copy the wrong thing (but the expressive thing), the strange, the bizarre (the recoil) without sensing the actuality, of which that is the complement,—and we get for Poe a REPU-TATION for eccentric genius, maimed, the curious, the sick—at least the unexplainable crop-up, unrelated to his ground—which has become his inheritance.

. . . .

The fiery serpent that bit the children of Israel when they wandered through the wilderness was possibly the guinea worm, which enters the body as a water flea, develops, and ultimately, lies coiled under the skin, from one to six feet in length. It formerly was coaxed out by winding it on a stick little by little each day. Then the zoologist found that it seeks water in which to lay its eggs, and will naively crawl out if the affected leg or arm is simply submerged in water for a few hours.

The mysterious is so simple when revealed by science!

. . . .

On him is FOUNDED A LITERATURE—typical; an anger to sweep out the unoriginal, that became ill-tempered, a monomaniacal driving to destroy, to annihilate the copied, the slavish, the FALSE literature about him: this is the major impulse in his notes—darkening as he goes, losing the battle, as he feels himself going under—he emerges as the ghoulish, the driven back. It is the crudeness with which he was attacked in his own person, scoffed at—

He declares, maintains himself, pre-supposes himself and IS first rate. FIRST!—madly, valiantly battling for the right to BE first—to hold up his ORIGINALITY—

If a man—if an Orphicist—or SEER—or whatever else he may choose to call himself, while the rest of the world calls him an ass—if this gentleman have an idea which he does not understand himself, the best thing he can do is to say nothing about it; . . . but if he have any idea which is actually intelligible to himself, and if he sincerely wishes to render it intelligible to others, we then hold it as indisputable that he should employ those forms of speech which are the best adapted to further his object. He should speak to the people in that people's ordinary tongue. He should arrange words such as are habitually employed for the preliminary and introductory ideas to be conveyed—he should arrange them in collocations such as those in which we are accustomed to see those words arranged.

Meantime we earnestly ask if *bread-and-butter* be the vast IDEA in question—if *bread-and-butter* be any portion of this vast IDEA? for we have often observed that when a SEER has to speak of even so usual a thing as bread-and-butter, he can never be induced to mention it outright. . . .

The language of his essays is a remarkable HISTORY of the locality he springs from. There is no aroma to his words, rather a luminosity, that comes of a disassociation from anything else than thought and ideals; a coldly nebulous, side to side juxtaposition of the words as the ideas—It seems to fall back continuously to a bare surface exhausted by having reached no perch in tradition. Seldom a long or sensuous sentence, but with frequent reduplication upon itself as if holding itself up by itself.

Thought, thought, mass—and the sense of SOMETHING over the heads of the composite particles of the logic, the insignificance of the details, WHICH HE DID ACTUALLY achieve. A "childlike," simple, deductive reasoning IS his criticism—a sense of BEGINNING—of originality that presupposes an intrinsic WORTH in the reasoner—a sense of *stripped,* being clothed, nevertheless.

Unwilling to concede the necessity for any prop to his logical constructions, save the locality upon which originality is rested, he is the diametric opposite of Longfellow—to say the least. But Longfellow was the apotheosis of all that had preceded him in America, to this extent, that he brought over the *most* from "the other side." In *"Longfellow and Other Plagiarists,"* Poe looses himself to the full upon them. But what had they done? No more surely than five hundred architects are constantly practicing. Longfellow did it without genius, perhaps, but he did no more and no less than to bring the tower of the Seville Cathedral to Madison Square.

This is the expression of a "good" spirit. It is the desire to have "culture" for America by "finding" it, full blown—somewhere. But we had wandered too far, suffered too many losses for that. Such a conception could be no more than a pathetic reminiscence. It had NOTHING of the New World in it. Yet, it was bred of the wish to bring to the locality what it lacked.

What it lacked, really, was to be cultivated. So they build an unrelated copy upon it; this, as a sign of intelligence,—vigor. That is, to bring out its qualities, they cover them. Culture is still the effect of cultivation, to work with a thing until it be rare; as a golden dome among the mustard fields. It implies a solidity capable of cultivation. Its effects are marble blocks that lie perfectly fitted and aligned to express by isolate distinction the rising lusts which threw them off, regulated, in moving through the mass of impedimenta which is the world.

This is culture; in mastering them, to burst through the peculiarities of an environment. It is NOT culture to *oppress* a novel environment with the stale, if symmetrical, castoffs of another battle. They are nearly right when they say: Destroy the museums! But that is only the reflection, after all, of minds that fear to be slavish. Poe could look at France, Spain, Greece, and NOT be impelled to copy. He could do this BECAUSE he had the sense within him of a locality of his own, capable of cultivation.

Poe's use of the tags of other cultures than his own manages to be novel, interesting, useful, *unaffected*, since it succeeds in giving the impression of being not in the last dragged in by rule or pretence but of a fresh purpose such as I have indicated. There is nothing offensively "learned" there, nothing contemptuous, even in the witty tricks with bogus Latin which he plays on his illiterate public, which by *its* power, in turn, *permits* him an originality, *allows* him, even when he is satiric, an authenticity ——since he is not seeking to destroy but to assert, candidly, and to defend *his own*.

He was the first to realize that the hard, sardonic, truculent mass of the New World, hot, angry—was, in fact, not a thing to paint over, to smear, to destroy—for it WOULD not be destroyed, it was too powerful,—it smiled! That it is NOT a thing to be slighted by men. Difficult, its very difficulty was their strength. It was in the generous bulk of its animal crudity that their every fineness would be found safely imbedded.

Poe conceived the possibility, the sullen, volcanic inevitability of the *place*. He was willing to go down and wrestle with its conditions, using every tool France, England, Greece could give him,—but to use them to original purpose.

This is his anger against Longfellow.

The difficulty is in holding the mind down to the point of seeing the *beginning* difference between Poe and the rest. One cannot expect to see as wide a gap between him and the others as exists between the Greek and the Chinese. It is only in the conception of a *possibility* that he is most distinguished. His greatness is in that he turned his back and faced inland, to originality, with the identical gesture of a Boone.

And for *that* reason he is unrecognized. Americans have never recognized themselves. How can they? It is impossible until someone invent the ORIGINAL terms. As long as we are content to be called by somebody else's terms, we are incapable of being anything but our own dupes.

Thus Poe must suffer by his originality. Invent that which is new, even if it be made of pine from your own yard, and there's none to know what you have done. It is because there's no *name*. This is the cause of Poe's lack of recognition. He was American. He was the astounding, inconceivable growth of his locality. Gape at him they did, and he at them in amazement. Afterward with mutual hatred; he in disgust, they in mistrust. It is only that which is under your nose which seems inexplicable.

Here Poe emerges—in no sense the bizarre, isolate writer, the curious literary figure. On the contrary, in him American literature is anchored, in him alone, on solid ground.

In all he says there is a sense of him *surrounded* by his time, tearing at it, ever with more rancor, but always at battle, taking hold.

But Poe—differing from pioneers in other literatures, the great beginners—due to the nature of the people, *had first to lift his head through* a successful banality. This was a double impost. But he did it, NOT by despising, ignoring, slighting the work that preceded him but by attacking it. "Among all the pioneers of American literature, whether prose or poetical, there is *not one* (Note: In his own estimate even, he begins.) whose productions have not been much overrated by his countrymen."

"But originality, as it is one of the highest, is also one of the rarest of merits. In America it is especially, and very remarkably, rare—this through causes sufficiently well understood."

He abhorred the "excessively opportune."—Of course, he says, to write of the Indians, the forests, the great natural beauty of the New World will be attractive and make a hit—so he counsels writers to AVOID it, for reasons crystal clear and well chosen. (See *Fenimore Cooper*.) His whole insistence has been upon method, in opposition to a nameless rapture over nature. He admired Claude Lorrain. Instead of to hog-fill the copied style with a gross rural sap, he wanted a lean style, rapid as a hunter and with an aim as sure. One way, in the New World, men must go. Bust gut or acute wit. Find the ground, on your feet or on your belly. It is a fight. He counsels writers to *borrow nothing* from the scene, but to put all the weight of effort into the WRIT-ING. Put aside the GRAND scene and get to work to express yourself. Method, punctuation, grammar—

The local condition of literature FORCED Poe's hand. It is necessary to understand this if his names are to be grasped. By avoiding, of necessity, the fat country itself for its expression; to originate a style that does spring from the local conditions, not of trees and mountains, but of the "soul"—here starved, stricken by loss of liberty, ready to die—he is *forced in certain directions for his subjects.*

But this left him in difficulties. When he had narrowed himself down to a choice of method and subject, when all the meaningless lump of the lush landscape and all that that implies had been swept away, THEN, and only then will he begin to search for a subject. A voluntary lopping off of a NATURAL landscape, forced him into a field which he must have *searched* for, a field of cold logic, of invention, to which his work must still present a natural *appearance:* into his imaginative prose.

His criticism paves the way for what *must* be his prose—illustrating his favorite theory that the theory *includes the practice.*

No better means of transit from the criticism to the tales could be imagined than his discussion of the merits and demerits of Hawthorne as a prosist. He expresses his delight and surprise at finding Hawthorne's work of such excellence, but then he finds a fault:

"He has the purest style, the finest taste, the most available scholarship, the most delicate humor, the most touching pathos, the most radiant imagination, the most consummate ingenuity, and with these varied good qualities he has done well as a mystic. But is there any one of these qualities which would prevent his doing doubly as well in a career of honest, upright, sensible, prehensible, and comprehensible things? Let him mend his pen, get a bottle of visible ink, come out from the Old Manse, cut Mr. Alcott, hang (if possible) the Editor of *The Dial,* and throw out of the window to the pigs all his odd numbers of *The North American Review.*"

Hawthorne has no repugnance for handling what Poe purposely avoids, the contamination of the UNFORMED LUMP, the "*monstrum, horrendum, informe, ingens, cui lumen ademptum.*" And it is precisely here that lies Hawthorne's lack of importance to our literature when he is compared with Poe; what Hawthorne *loses* by his willing closeness to the life of his locality in its vague humors; his lifelike copying of the New England melancholy; his reposeful closeness to the town pump—Poe *gains* by abhorring; flying to the ends of the earth for "original" material—

By such a simple, logical twist does Poe succeed in being the more American, heeding more the local necessities, the harder structural imperatives—by standing off to SEE instead of forcing himself too close. Whereas Hawthorne, in his tales, by doing what everyone else in France, England, Germany was doing *for his own milieu,* is no more than copying their *method* with another setting; does not ORIGINATE; has not a *beginning* literature at heart that must establish its own rules, own framework,—Poe has realized by adopting a more elevated mien.

This feeling in Poe's tales, that is, the hidden, under, unapparent part, gives him the firmness of INSIGHT into the conditions upon which our literature must rest, always the same, a local one, surely, but not of sentiment or mood, as not of trees and Indians, but of original fibre, the normal toughness which fragility of mood presupposes, if it will be expressive of anything— It is the expression of Poe's clearness of insight into the true difficulty, and his soundness of judgment.

. . . .

To understand what Poe is driving at in his tales, one should read first NOT the popular, perfect—*Gold Bug, Murders in the Rue Morgue,* etc., which by their brilliancy detract from the observation of his deeper intent, but the less striking tales— in fact all, but especially those where his humor is less certain, his mood lighter, less tightly bound by the incident, where numerous illuminating *faults* are allowed to become expressive, *The Business Man, The Man That Was Used Up, Loss of Breath, BonBon, Diddling, The Angel of the Odd*—and others of his lesser Tales.

It should be noted how often certain things take place—how often there is death but not that only; it is the body broken apart, dismembered, as in *Loss of Breath—*

Then, as in *Hop Frog, The System of Dr. Tarr and Professor Fether* and the *Murders in the Rue Morgue—*the recurrent image of the ape. Is it his disgust with his immediate associates and his own fears, which cause this frequent use of the figure to create the emotion of extreme terror?—

> Your majesty cannot conceive of the *effect* produced, at a masquerade, by eight chained orang-outangs, imagined to be real ones by the most of the company; and rushing in with savage cries, among the crowd of delicately and gorgeously habited men and women. The contrast is inimitable.

Note, in *Silence—a Fable:* "sorrow and weariness and disgust with mankind and a longing for solitude."

Many colloquial words could be detached from Poe's usage if it were worthwhile, to show how the language he practices varies from English, but such an exercise would be of little value —*hipped, crack,* etc.—it does not touch bottom.

The Tales continue the theories of the criticism, carrying out what they propose:

(1) In choice of material, abstract. (2) In method, a logical construction that clips away, in great part, the "scenery" near at hand in order to let the real business of composition *show.* (3) A primitive awkwardness of diction, lack of polish, colloquialism that is, unexpectedly, especially in the dialogues, much in the vein of Mark Twain.

One feels that in the actual composition of his tales there must have been for him, as they embody it in fact, a fascination other than the topical one. The impulse that made him write them, that made him enjoy writing them—cannot have been the puerile one of amazement, but a deeper, logical enjoyment, in keeping with his own seriousness: it is that of PROVING even the most preposterous of his inventions plausible—that BY HIS METHOD he makes them WORK. They go: they *prove* him potent, they confirm his thought. And by the very extreme of their play, by so much the more do they hold up the actuality of that which he conceives.

If there ever had been another American to use his Greek,

Sanscrit, Hebrew, Latin, French, German, Italian and Spanish—
in the text—with anything like the unspoiled mastery of Poe, we
should have known, long since, what it meant to have a literature
of our own.

It is to have a *basis*, a local stanchion, by which to *bridge
over* the gap between present learning and the classical; that
asserts the continuity of the common virtues of style; that asserts
their aristocratic origin, or their democratic origin, the same, as
it has been pointed out recently, since an aristocracy is the
flower of a locality and so the *full* expression of a democracy.

Of his method in the Tales, the significance and the secret
is: authentic particles, a thousand of which spring to the mind
for quotation, taken apart and reknit with a view to emphasize,
enforce, and make evident, the *method*. Their quality of skill
in observation, their heat, local verity, being *overshadowed* only
by the detached, the abstract, the cold philosophy of their join-
ing together; a method springing so freshly from the local conditions which determine it, by their emphasis of firm crudity
and lack of coordinated structure, as to be worthy of most pains-
taking study— The whole period, America 1840, could be rebuilt,
psychologically (phrenologically) from Poe's "method."

. . . .

It is especially in the poetry where "death looked gigantically down" that the horror of the formless resistance which
opposed, maddened, destroyed him has forced its character into
the air, the wind, the blessed galleries of paradise, above a
morose, dead world, peopled by shadows and silence, and despair— It is the compelling force of his isolation.

The one earthly island he found where he might live in
something akin to the state he imagined, the love of his wife, had
to be single and inviolate. Failing of a more comprehensive
passion, which might have possessed him had the place been of
favorable omen, only in this narrow cell could he exist at all. Of
this the poems are the full effect. He is known as a poet, yet
there are but five poems, possibly three.

When she died, there was nothing left. In his despair he
had nowhere to turn. It is the very apotheosis of the place and
the time.

He died imploring from those about him a love he could not
possess, since his own love, as his poems, had been so mingled

in character with the iron revenge which completely surrounded him that it could not be repeated once its single object had been lost.

But here, in his poetry least of all, is there a mystery. It is but the accumulation of all that he has expressed, in the criticism, in the prose tales, but made as if so shaken with desire, that it has come off as a flame, destroying the very vial that contained it—and become, against his will almost it would seem, —himself.

It is not by a change in character but by its quickened motion that it has turned from mere heat into light—by its power of penetration that it has been brought to dwell upon love. By its acid power to break down truth that it has been *forced* upon love—

I mean that though in this his "method" has escaped him, yet his poems remain of the single stuff of his great "theory": to grasp the meaning, to understand, to reduce all things to method, to control, lifting himself to power—

And failing, truth turning to love, as if metamorphosed in his hands as he was about to grasp it—now the full horror of his isolation comes down—

In his prose he could still keep a firm hold, he still held the "arrangement" fast and stood above it, but in the poetry he was at the edge—there was nothing——

Here in poetry, where it is said "we approach the gods," Poe was caught, instead, in his time.

Now, defenseless, the place itself attacked him. Now the thinness of his coat, the terror of his isolation took hold.

Had he lived in a world where love throve, his poems might have grown differently. But living where he did, surrounded as he was by that world of unreality, a formless "population"— drifting and feeding—a huge terror possessed him.

His passion for the refrain is like an echo from a hollow. It is his own voice returning—

His imagery is of the desperate situation of his mind, thin as a flame to mount unsupported, successful for a moment in the love of—not so much his wife—but in the escape she filled for him with her frail person, herself afflicted as by "ghouls."

Disarmed, in his poetry the place itself comes through. This is the New World. It is this that it does, as if——

It is in this wraithlike quality of his poems, of his five poems, that Poe is most of the very ground, hard to find, as if we walked upon a cushion of light pressed thin beneath our feet, that insulates, satirises—while we lash ourselves up and down in a fury of impotence.

Poe stayed against the thin edge, driven to be heard by the battering racket about him to a distant screaming—the pure essence of his locality.

The best poem is *To One in Paradise*.

The publication in the early and middle 1920's of Poe biographies stimulated the writing of this fine essay by EDMUND WILSON [1895–   ]. Here he defines Poe as the "bridge" between the Romanticism of the early nineteenth century and the Symbolism of the later nineteenth, blaming a faulty historical sense for the prevailing notions that Poe was unrelated to the spirit of his time and had no connection with "reality." Poe is seen as a "thorough romantic" in his fiction and poetry, rendering deep psychological truths through terror, phantasmagoria, synaesthesia, and symbolism.

Poe at Home and Abroad

EDMUND WILSON

I

The recent revival of interest in Poe has brought to light a good deal of new information and supplied us for the first time with a serious interpretation of his personal career, but it has so far entirely neglected to explain why we should still want to read him. In respect to such figures as Poe, we Americans are still perhaps almost as provincial as those of their contemporaries who now seem to us ridiculous for having failed to recognize their genius. Today, we take their eminence for granted, but we still cannot help regarding them, not from the point of view of their real contributions to western culture, but primarily as fellow-Americans, whose activities we feel the necessity of ex-

From *New Republic*, Dec. 8, 1926; *The Shores of Light*, 1952.

plaining in terms of America and the circumstances of whose personal lives we are, as neighbors, in a position to investigate. Thus, at a date when "Edgar Poe" has figured in Europe for the last three-quarters of a century as a writer of the first importance, we in America are still preoccupied—though no longer in moral indignation—with his bad reputation as a citizen. Thus, Dr. J. W. Robertson, who perhaps started off the recent researches, five years ago published a book to show that Poe was a typical alcoholic. Thus, last year we saw the publication of Poe's correspondence with his foster-father. Thus, we are promised the early revelation of Poe's plagiarism of his plots from a hitherto unknown German source (as James Huneker has pointed out that Poe's later and most celebrated poems must certainly have owed a good deal to an obscure American poet named Thomas Holley Chivers). Thus, a Miss Mary E. Phillips has just published an enormous biography running to sixteen hundred and eighty-five pages—*Edgar Allan Poe, the Man*—a monument of uncritical devotion which it must have taken a lifetime to compile, stuffed with illustrations that include not only photographs of the little Scotch town from which Poe's foster-father came, of the librarian of the University of Virginia at the time when Poe was a student there and of the clock on the mantelpiece of Poe's cottage at Fordham, but also maps of New York, Richmond and Baltimore at the time when Poe lived in those cities; and containing embedded in its pudding-stone prose perhaps more miscellaneous facts about him than have ever before been assembled.

The ablest and the most important of recent American books on Poe, is, however, without any doubt, Mr. Joseph Wood Krutch's *Edgar Allan Poe: A Study in Genius*. Mr. Krutch has made an attempt to go beyond Doctor Robertson in diagnosing Poe's nervous malady, and his conclusions are by this time well known: he believes that Poe was driven in the first instance into seeking a position of literary eminence by a desire to compensate himself for the loss of social position of which his foster-father had deprived him; that, in consequence, perhaps of a "fixation" on his mother, he became sexually impotent and was forced, as a result of his inability to play a part in the normal world, to invent an abnormal world full of horror, repining and doom (the universally recognized concomitants, according to

Mr. Krutch, of sexual repression of this sort) in which he could take refuge; that his very intellectual activity, his love of working out cryptograms and crimes, had been primarily stimulated by the desire to prove himself logical when he felt he was going insane; and, finally, that his critical theory was merely a justification of his peculiar artistic practice, which was itself thus, in turn, a symptom of his disease. It must be said, in fairness to Mr. Krutch, that he does not fail to draw, at the end of his book, the conclusions about artists in general which follow from his particular conclusions. Mr. Krutch fully admits that, if what he says about Poe is true, it must also be true of "all imaginative works," which, in that case, should be regarded as the products of "unfulfilled desires" springing from "either idiosyncratic or universally human maladjustments to life." This does not, however, prevent Mr. Krutch from misunderstanding Poe's writings and seriously undervaluing them, nor even from complacently caricaturing them—as the modern school of social-psychological biography, of which Mr. Krutch is a typical representative, seems inevitably to tend to caricature the personalities of its subjects. We are nowadays being edified by the spectacle of some of the principal ornaments of the human race exhibited exclusively in terms of their most ridiculous manias, their most disquieting neuroses, and their most humiliating failures. Mr. Krutch has chosen for the frontispiece of what he calls a "study in genius" a daguerreotype of Poe taken in 1849, shortly before his death: it shows a pasty and dilapidated personage with untrimmed untidy hair, an uneven toothbrush mustache and large pouches under the eyes; the eyes themselves have a sad unfocussed stare; one eyelid is drooping; one hand is thrust into the coat-front with an air of feeble pretentiousness. The dignified solemnity of the figure is as ludicrous as a bad old-fashioned actor attempting to play *Hamlet*, and its visible disintegration unpleasantly suggests an alcoholic patient recently admitted to a cure. And something like this is the final impression left by Mr. Krutch's book. Mr. Krutch quotes with disapproval the statement of President Hadley of Yale, in explaining the refusal of the Hall of Fame to accept Poe among its immortals: "Poe wrote like a drunkard and a man who is not accustomed to pay his debts"; and yet Mr. Krutch himself, so interesting as a psychologist, is almost as unperceptive when he tells us, in effect, that Poe wrote like a dispossessed Southern gentleman and a man with a fixation on his mother.

For the rest, Mr. H. L. Mencken has written with admiration of Poe's destructive reviewing—that is, he has paid a tribute to an earlier practitioner of an art of his own; Mr. Van Wyck Brooks has examined Poe's work for evidences of the harshness and the sterility of a Puritan-pioneer society, and found it unsatisfactory as literature; and Mr. Lewis Mumford, in *The Golden Day*, seems to have taken his cue from Mr. Brooks when he finds in the hardness of Poe's effects the steel of the industrial age. It may, I believe, be said that no recent American critic, with the exception of Mr. Waldo Frank in his article on the Poe-Allan letters, has written with any real appreciation of Poe's absolute artistic importance.

II

One of the most striking features of all this American criticism of Poe is its tendency to regard him as a freak, having his existence somehow apart not merely from contemporary life but even from contemporary literature. "That his life happened to fall," writes Mr. Krutch, "between the years 1809 and 1849 is merely an accident, and he has no more in common with Whittier, Lowell, Longfellow or Emerson than he has with either the eighteenth or nineteenth centuries in England. . . . His works bear no conceivable relation, either external or internal, to the life of any people, and it is impossible to account for them on the basis of any social or intellectual tendencies or as the expression of the spirit of any age." Worse than this, we are always being told that Poe has no connection with "reality," that he writes exclusively of a "dream world" which has no point of contact with our own. The error of this second assertion immediately becomes apparent when we consider the falsity of the first. So far from having nothing in common with the spirit of the first half of the nineteenth century, Poe is certainly one of its most typical figures; that is to say, he is a thorough romantic, closely akin to his European contemporaries. Thus, his nightmarish vein of fantasy is very much like that of Coleridge; his poetry in its earlier phase derives from Shelley and Keats; his "dream fugues" resemble De Quincey's and his "prose poems," Maurice de Guérin's. His themes—which, as Baudelaire

says, are concerned with "the exception in the moral order"—
are in the tradition of Chateaubriand and Byron, and of the
romantic movement generally. It is, then, in terms of romanticism that we must look for reality in Poe. It shows a lack of
historical sense to expect of him the same sort of treatment of
life that we find in Dreiser or Sinclair Lewis and the recent preoccupation with which seems so to have misled our critics. From
this modern sociological point of view, the European writers
whom I have named above had no more connection with their
respective countries than had Poe with the United States. Their
settings and their dramatis personae, the images by which they
rendered their ideas, were as different as those of Poe from the
images of modern naturalism, and they used them for a different
kind of story-telling which conveyed a different kind of moral.

What, then, are the morals of Poe, the realities he tried to
express? The key is to be found in Baudelaire's phrase about
"the exception in the moral order." The exception in the moral
order was the predominant theme of the romantic movement.
It is absurd to complain, as our critics do, of Poe's indifference
to the claims of society, as if this indifference were something
abnormal: one of the principal features of romanticism was, not
merely an indifference to the claims of society, but an exalted
revolt against them. The favorite figure of the romantic writers
was the sympathetic individual considered from the point of
view of his non-amenability to law or convention. And in this,
Poe runs absolutely true to type: his heroes are the brothers of
Rolla and René; of Childe Harold, Manfred and Cain. Like
these latter, they are superior individuals who pursue extravagant fancies, plumb abysses of dissipation or yield to forbidden
passions (Poe made one or two experiments with the common
romantic theme of incest; but his specialties were a frigid sadism
and a curious form of adultery which never took place till the
woman whom the hero betrayed was dead). And, as in the case
of the other romantic heroes, their drama is the conflict of their
impulses with human or divine law. This impulse of the individual does not, however, in Poe, take often, as it does with the
other romantics, the form of a too generous passion overflowing
the canals of the world; but assumes rather the sinister character of what Poe called the "Imp of the Perverse." Yet this very
perversity of Poe, the kind of dizzy terror it engenders, due to
whatever nervous instability and whatever unlucky circum-

stances, have their poetry and their deep pathos—from those lines in one of the finest of his poems in which he tells how the doom of his later life appeared to him even in childhood as he gazed on "the cloud that took the form (When the rest of Heaven was blue) Of a demon in my view," to that terrible picture of the condemned man, "sick—sick unto death with that long agony," when "first [the candles] wore the aspect of charity, and seemed white slender angels who would save me; but then, all at once, there came a most deadly nausea over my spirit, and I felt every fibre in my frame thrill as if I had touched the wire of a galvanic battery, while the angel forms became meaningless specters, with heads of flame, and I saw that from them there would be no help. And then there stole into my fancy, like a rich musical note, the thought of what sweet rest there must be in the grave." And it is the lifelong "agony" of his moral experience that gives to Poe's *William Wilson* its superior sincerity and intensity over Stevenson's *Doctor Jekyll and Mr. Hyde*. In Stevenson, it is the virtuous half of the dual personality that destroys the divided man by exorcising the evil; but, in Poe, it is the evil half that does away with the good and that is even made to tell the whole story from its own point of view. Yet does not *William Wilson* bring home to us the horror of the moral transmutation more convincingly than the melodramatic fable of Doctor Jekyll and Mr. Hyde?

There is one special tragic theme of Poe's which deserves to be noted in this connection. Mr. Krutch says that Poe was impotent, and that, for this reason, though perhaps unconsciously, he chose to marry a girl of thirteen with whom it would be impossible for him to have regular conjugal relations. Mr. Krutch does not offer any proof of this, but we do not have to assume it to be true in order to agree with Mr. Krutch that Poe's marriage with Virginia Clemm was somehow unsatisfactory, and that it plays a strange role in his work. Virginia was Poe's first cousin, and it may be that, on this account, he had scruples about consummating the marriage. In any case, she became tubercular, and, twelve years after their marriage, died; while Poe himself grew neurotic, irritable and at last unbalanced. He was obsessed by desperate fantasies and seems, after her death, to have been almost insane. It is possible to follow Mr. Krutch in admitting that the atrocious sadism of many of Poe's later tales must have been due to some emotional repression. Though he undoubtedly adored Virginia, he seems at the same time to have wished her dead. He is always imagining, in his tales, long before her actual death, that a woman like Virginia has died and that her lover is free to love other women. But even here, the dead woman intervenes: in *Ligeia,* she reincarnates herself in the corpse of her successor, who has also died; in *Morella,* in her own daughter. And it is evidently this conflict of Poe's emotions which inspires, not merely these bizarre fancies, but also the unexplained feelings of remorse that so often haunt his heroes. After Virginia has actually died, the situation he has foreseen in the stories seems to be realized. He conducts flirtations with other women; but they are accompanied by "a wild inexplicable sentiment that resembles nothing so nearly as a consciousness of guilt." "I was never really insane," he writes to Mrs. Clemm just before his miserable death, "except on occasions when my heart was touched. I have been taken to prison once since I came here for getting drunk; but then I was not. It was about Virginia." The story of Poe and Virginia is a painful and rather unpleasant one; but it is perhaps worth discussing to this extent, for we recognize in it the actual relation which, viewed in the light of a romantic problem and transposed into romantic terms, fills Poe's writings with the ominous sense of a deadlock between the rebellious spirit, the individual will, on the one hand, and both its very romantic idealisms and its human bonds, on the other. "The whole realm of moral ideals," says Mr. Krutch, "is excluded [from Poe's work], not merely as morality *per se,* but also as artistic material used for the creation of conflicts and situations." What, then, does he suppose such stories as *Eleanora* and *Ligeia* are about? He goes on to say that horror is the only emotion which is "genuinely Poe's own" and that this "deliberately invents causes for itself," that "it is always a pure emotion without any rational foundation." How, he would no doubt ask, can anything describable as moral interest be found in the *Descent into the Maelström* or the *Case of M. Valdemar?* This question I propose to discuss in a moment.

III

Poe was, then, a typical romantic. But he was also something more. He contained the germs of a further development. By 1847, Baudelaire had begun to read Poe and had "experienced a strange commotion": when he had looked up the rest of Poe's writings in the files of American magazines, he found among them stories and poems which he had "thought vaguely and confusedly" of writing himself, and Poe became an obsession with him. He published in 1856 a volume of translations of Poe's tales; and from then on, the influence of Poe became one of the most important in French literature. M. Louis Seylaz has recently traced this influence in a book called *Edgar Poe et les Premiers Symbolistes Français*, in which he discusses the indebtedness to Poe of the French symbolist movement, from Baudelaire, through Verlaine, Rimbaud, Mallarmé (who translated Poe's poems), Villiers de L'Isle-Adam and Huysmans, to Paul Valéry in our own day (who has just written some interesting pages on Poe in a preface to a new edition of Baudelaire's *Les Fleurs du Mal*).

Let us inquire as to precisely in what this influence of Poe consisted that was felt so profoundly by the French through a whole half-century of their literature, yet which has so completely failed to impress itself upon the literature of Poe's own country that it is still possible for Americans to talk about him as if his principal claim to distinction were his title to be described as the "father of the short story." In the first place, says M. Valéry, Poe brought to the romanticism of the later nineteenth century a new aesthetic discipline. Perhaps more than any other writer, French or English, of the first half of the century, he had thought seriously and written clearly about the methods and aims of literature. He had formulated a critical theory, and he had supplied brilliant specimens of its practice. Even in poetry, by the time that Poe's influence had begun to be felt in France, it had been the ideals of naturalism that the post-romantic generation had tried to bring into play against the extravagance and the looseness of romanticism running to seed. But the American was now to provide them with a new and logical program that would aim to lop the overgrowths of romanticism and yet to achieve effects that can only be called romantic. What *were* these ultraromantic effects which had first been described by Poe and by what means did he propose to attain them?

"I *know*," writes Poe, "that indefiniteness is an element of the true music [of poetry]—I mean of the true musical expression . . . a suggestive indefiniteness of meaning with a view of bringing about a definiteness of vague and therefore of spiritual *effect.*" This is already the doctrine of symbolism. Poe had exemplified it in his own poems. Poe's poetry is rarely quite successful; but it is, none the less, of first-rate importance. He tells us rather pathetically, in his preface to his poems, apologizing for their imperfections, that "events not to be controlled" have prevented him "from making, at any time, any serious effort in what, under happier circumstances, would have been the field of my choice." The immaturity of his early verse, where he is imitating Shelley and Coleridge, is certainly not redeemed by the deliberate tricks of his later, which he seems to have borrowed from Chivers and which are always a little trashy. Yet all of Poe's poetry is interesting, because more than that of any other romantic (except perhaps Coleridge in *Kubla Khan*), it does approach the indefiniteness of music—that supreme goal of the symbolists. That is to say that, from the ordinary point of view, Poe's poetry is more nonsensical than that of any of the other romantics—and nonsensical in much the same way as, to the ordinary point of view, much of our best modern poetry appears. To note but a single instance: one of the characteristic traits of modern symbolism is a sort of psychological confusion between the impressions of the different senses. This confusion distinctly appears in Poe: thus we find him, in one of his poems, *hearing* the approach of the darkness; and, in the marvellous description in one of his tales of the fusing sensations that follow death, we read that "night arrived; and with its shadows a heavy discomfort. It oppressed my limbs with the oppression of some dull weight, and was palpable. There was also a moaning sound, not unlike the distant reverberation of surf, but more continuous, which, beginning with the first twilight, had grown in strength with the darkness. Suddenly lights were brought into the room . . . and issuing from the flame of each lamp, there flowed unbrokenly into my ears a strain of melodious monotone."

Poe's theory of short-story writing was similar to his theory of verse. "A skilful artist," he writes, "has constructed a tale. If wise, he has not fashioned his thought to accommodate his incidents; but having conceived, with deliberate care, a certain unique or single *effect* to be wrought out, he then invents such incidents—he then combines such events as may best aid him in establishing this preconceived effect." So the real significance of Poe's short stories does not lie in what they purport to relate. Many are confessedly dreams; and, as with dreams, though they seem absurd, their effect on our emotions is serious. And even those that pretend to the logic and the exactitude of actual narratives are, nevertheless, also dreams. The happenings in them differ from the mere macabre surprises and the astonishing adventures and voyages of such imitators of Poe as Conan Doyle. The descent into the maelström is a metaphor for the horror of the moral whirlpool into which, with some justification, Poe had, as we know from more explicit stories, a giddy apprehension of going down; the precariously delayed dissolution of M. Valdemar stands for that horror of living death that figures also in *Premature Burial,* which, arising from whatever blight, haunted Poe through all his later life. No one understood better than Poe that, in fiction and in poetry both, it is not what you say that counts, but what you make the reader feel (he always italicizes the word "effect"); no one understood better than Poe that the deepest psychological truth may be rendered through phantasmagoria. Even the realistic stories of Poe are, in fact, only phantasmagoria of a more circumstantial kind. Any realism of any age which does not convey some such truth is, of course, bound to be unsatisfactory. And today when a revolt is in progress against the literalness and the superficiality of the naturalistic movement that has come between Poe's time and ours, he ought to be of special interest.

"Poe's mentality was a rare synthesis," writes Mr. Padraic Colum. "He had elements in him that corresponded with the indefiniteness of music and the exactitude of mathematics." Is not this what modern literature is tending toward? It was Poe who sent out the bridge from the romanticism of the early nineteenth century to the symbolism of the later; and symbolism, as M. Seylaz points out, though scarcely any of its original exponents survive, now permeates literature. We must not, however, expect that Poe should be admired or understood in his capacity of suspension across this chasm by critics who are hardly aware that either of its banks exists.

GEORGE E. B. SAINTSBURY [1845–1933], an authority on French literature, was professor of rhetoric and English literature at Edinburgh [1895–1915]. In 1909 he wrote, "Thirty-three years ago, when I was endeavoring to make some opening in literature, I horrified and almost enraged a magazine editor of great note [Sir Leslie Stephen] by sending him an essay tending to show that Poe, with all his faults, was 'of the first order of poets.' I am of the same opinion to-day."

When it appeared originally in *The Dial* [1927], the following essay included an introductory section reviewing the new biographies by Krutch and Phillips. Here Saintsbury singles out for highest praise "To Helen," "For Annie," "Annabel Lee," and "Ulalume."

Edgar Allan Poe

GEORGE E. B. SAINTSBURY

I hope there is neither impertinence nor disqualification for my present business in confessing that my admiration for Poe does not rest upon [his] tales—or only on a very few of them. *Ligeia* and *The Fall of the House of Usher* satisfy me: though both would be better if they were shorter. But the pieces which attempt humour, like *Loss of Breath* and *Mummy*, almost make me an anti-Poeite, while those of pure horror are not much more to my taste. And for the "detective" kind, in which he can claim some fatherhood and an undoubted mastership, and for which the latest nineteenth and the earlier twentieth centuries have had so keen an appetite, I have no great affection. My pleasantest association with them is that, in early days, I remember English editions presenting us with a Gold *Beetle* instead of a Gold *Bug*. In its class *The Descent into the Maelstroom* is pretty faultless: and of the horrors, I used I think to prefer *The Cask of Amontillado*. This may have been partly because I liked Amontillado, but so I do still: and I did not find the other day when I re-read the story after many years, that I cared much for it. And even in the two excepted ones—perhaps owing to the fact that one of them contains one of his very best poems and the other not the worst—I find myself worried by the thought "Why is not this poetry?" Now one of the first laws or cautions of criticism is: "Never demand from any work something else than that which it presents itself as being, doing, offering. If you find that you can't help this, there is something really wrong either with the writer or with you." It must of course be left to third parties to decide which of these alternatives is here the case.

Not to neglect what is, in a curiously complicated way, something between poetry and prose—that is to say, drama—we must have a word or two on *Politian*. It is almost needless to say, though impossible to omit the saying, that this curious piece owes much to Professor Mabbott for elucidating its subject, castigating its text, and in other ways making the study of it more profitable and easier. But neither this nor any addition at all probable could much affect certain general conclusions about it. If we knew nothing about its date and authorship, most fairly acute and well-informed critics would put it down, now or at any future time as well as for the last half-century, as belonging to that singular period or division of English literature —ostensibly or formally theatrical—from which *The Cenci* shoots up like Ailsa Crag from the sea or the Wrekin from the flat country; which begins with Joanna Baillie and ends with Sir Henry Taylor, and the sea whereof may be allowed a few islets, the plain a hillock or two, like Milman's *Fazio* and Talfourd's *Ion*. It is perhaps a pity that Poe, who is in some ways so like his contemporary Beddoes, did not attempt the *Death's Jest-Book* vein; but as it is, one feels that he is not in his proper place. The few attempts at intermixed comedy are positively bad; Politian personally is weak Byron and water; while the whole (and let no one say "But it isn't a whole," for a few scenes will do) is nondramatic. You cannot imagine it acted with any success. Now a play may, I suppose, be bad to read and yet good to act; but I can't imagine its being good to read when it constantly suggests to the reader that it would be bad to act.

When Lowell,[1] or whoever it was, wrote "Mr. Poe *the poet*," the catch-sound of the words was no doubt, though not ill-naturedly, intentionally the object of the conjunction. But one

---

[1] There was almost less bad blood between the two than between Poe and any other notable man of letters in his time and country. They principally disagreed about matters of prosody, in which I venture to think that Poe was the nearer to the truth. But I have always been sorry that in more than one or two conversations which I had with Mr. Lowell when he was in England in the 'eighties, Poe, so far as I can recollect, was never mentioned.

might, without extravagance, take it seriously. To say that if Poe was not a poet he was nothing, would of course be extravagant. He is something more than a squadron-leader in the story-telling army: and I have myself, in books specially on the subject, done my little best to vindicate for him a higher place than has sometimes been allowed him, both in general and in metrical criticism. But his extreme inequality, arising in the main from insufficient education, injures his work in both respects; and, except in the points where it touches his poetry nearest, his tale-telling is at most "prime amid peers." As a poet he is absolutely alone. Lang gave him companions to a certain extent in William Morris and Gérard de Nerval; I have just suggested (again to a certain extent only) Beddoes; but none of these is exactly of the same variety of the same species of the same kind. Nothing, I think, is a better specimen passage of "Mr. Poe the poet's" poetry, on the smallest scale and neglecting the cumulative effect of his best pieces as a whole, than the famous couplet in *The Haunted Palace:*

> Banners, yellow, glorious, golden
> On its roof did float and flow.

I have said of this in its strictly technical aspect that the trochees themselves "float and flow and settle with the soft slowness of snowflakes." But there is a great deal more than this to be said. In the first place there is the extraordinary manipulation of the vowel-music—the contrast of the prominent sounds *a* and *e* once each and then a whole cascade of *o* in different forms of its sound, with the minor detail of the trisyllabic "glorious" ("glory-ous" may be left to whosoever likes it) and its subtle connection with the monosyllabic ending "flow." All that is "music" in a way no doubt: and the additional effect given by the pause at each word of the first line may be such perhaps. But then there is appeal to a quite new sense—the sense of *eyes* of the mind, which insists for itself on the banners, the roof they float from, their colour, and their motion as they flow. You don't want— unless you are the kind of creature for whom "movies" were made and whom they satisfy—any "illustration"; the words make you see the things as they make you hear the music accompany-ing. And then there comes the tug-of-war between the two critical views of Poe and even between the two sections of his admirers. There is something more which is not music nor picture, but is begotten in some uncanny, though by no means unholy, way by each on the other—the poetic effluence—the charm only perceptible to that *sense* of poetry which merciful nature has not withheld from myriads though it has only granted the power of production which satisfies it to a few.

Of course there is a certain kind of criticism which can amuse itself by shooting its arrows at the moon. For instance, I think I have seen objections taken to the pacification of Psyche in *Ulalume* by kissing her, on the ground that Psyche means soul and you can't kiss your—or any—soul. I am not myself so sure of the impossibility. Moreover, Poe addressed this Psyche as his "sister" and you certainly *can* kiss your own sister. Also, I should myself say that this classification of body and soul as brother and sister was not exactly an unpoetical one in itself. But criticism of this sort is better nonsuited than put to its trial on points. It is evidently a case of trying to light the blunt end of a match when chemical contact is required.

A few more short instances may be demanded. One might perhaps make a touchstone of the conclusion of *To Helen* (the first) by asking, "Is it as it stands—

> Ah! Psyche, from the regions which
> Are Holy Land—

the same as if it were written in continuous Alexandrine:

> Ah! Psyche, from the regions which are Holy Land?"

But that sample-item of what people are pleased, in this curious century of jargon, to call a *questionnaire* might be rather treacherous. It is better perhaps not to take any example from *The Raven:* and *The Bells* have always disappointed me. The piece does not seem as if Poe had ever heard real *old* bells, which indeed is possible: and if the excellent Mrs. Shew is to be believed, the subject was suggested to, not imagined by him, and started with rather childish stuff about "little silver bells" and "heavy iron bells." Poe in some of his moods would have been much more likely to shift the adjectives and might have made something of the shifting.

But the three summits of his range—actually it would seem the latest as well as the highest of his exploits of climbing—*For*

Annie, Ulalume, and *Annabel Lee*—are simply compact of "specimens," besides showing at its best what has not yet been dwelt on—his wonderful power of working "out and up," of *crescendo* and of producing an explosion after which there *must* be silence —a deliverance following which "there is namore to seyn." Although instances of the same method, they are not in the slightest degree replicas; each is entirely independent of the others.

Which of the three is "the best" it is unnecessary and probably unwise to inquire; perhaps there is not, except in mere quantity, any "better" or "best" in poetry: a thing is either poetry or it is not. It may be asked, "Is there no difference in intensity?" and perhaps there is: but all these are much on a par there. *For Annie* might, though one is loth to say it would, be improved by curtailment. You know, if you possess the faculty of knowing, that the thing is working up to some point and that point may seem to be unduly—at least unkindly—delayed. This delay, too, gives chance to the danger which proverbially attends the sublime. The line

I am better at length

and indeed the whole stanza which it concludes offer "the sons of Belial" one of those "glorious times" which they seldom miss enjoying. But the magnificence of the first with its concluding couplet—

And the fever called living
Is conquered at last—

should carry you over the second triumphantly to the first line of the third—

And I rest so composedly—

where the adverb is one of those single-word successes of which, considering the small bulk of his whole work in verse, Poe is so astonishingly full.

If the next half-dozen stanzas appeared alone one would certainly not care so much for them as at present: in a ferociously judicial mood you might even lift the blue pencil. But you have to put that down again very soon, with never the least subsequent temptation to take it up, some time before you come to those famous "Puritan pansies" which might induce the stoutest Cavalier to make a name-truce at least with Puritanism. And then after this gracious overture comes the main and never thenceforward failing *rise* of the piece—the introduction of Annie, and as it were the saturation of the poem with her presence and her actions and her name more and more to the end.

Observe, too, how the fellow, having got as it seemed the utmost out of word-fitness with "composedly," audaciously "does it again" in the same stanza with a repetition of that by the substitution of "contentedly"!

I suppose—indeed I may have already hinted at the proposition—that *Ulalume* is the prearranged and never-to-be-wholly-done-away-with battle-ground—the Belgium as it were of the Europe and not the Europe only of Poeian criticism. When Lang said fifty years ago that "it might require some moral courage to assert one's belief that the poem has an excuse for its existence," he was by no means speaking in mere irony and still less convicting that curious thing of imagination, "Victorianism," of one of its criminal follies. There were, at least in England, plenty of people who thought *Ulalume* quite deserving of existence: and I have seen within the last few months an expression of opinion already referred to, if not in the exact words, that she is not. For my own part, critical or not as the gods or the demons have made me, I cannot find speck or flaw in it, except that the name, capital for a poem, does not seem to me capital for a girl, and one other possible superfluity, of which presently. All the names, including Ulalume itself with the gloss I have given, and allowing the specialization in rhyme to Auber, suit: there ought to be a Mount Yaanek, if there is not. The singular motion, as of a heavy-laden charger strongly bitted, which he has put on his anapaestic metre; the streak of charm introduced into the dreariness by the presence of Psyche, the "sisterly" Psyche; the amazing stanza which concludes with what is a sort of motto-distich for Poe—

> Astarte's bediamonded crescent
> Distinct with its duplicate horn;

and any number of his marvellous single words, the most marvellous of which is the "immemorial" at the very heart and centre of the first stanza—all these things are there and a great deal more. If anybody says that it would be better without the last stanza, I don't know that I care to argue the point.

But if a critic need not be exactly a Zoïlus to suggest thinning in *For Annie* and lopping in *Ulalume,* he is lost if he even thinks of the shears in connection with *Annabel Lee.* I can imagine a very *very* poor creature saying, no doubt with perfect truth, that the verb "to covet" will only take an accusative after it and not like "grudge" or "envy" a sort of ablative in the literal sense of that word or dative in the technical as well. One would pat his head and say, "Yes! Yes!" It was perhaps a whim that made Poe wrench the metre a little, without any need or profit, by putting "chilling" at the end of a line. But these are almost beauty-spots—if in the miraculous rush and blaze of the whole thing they are anything at all—the rush that takes one's breath away and the blaze that dazzles one's sight. I am happy enough to have read a not inconsiderable proportion of the poetry which has been vouchsafed to the world in the two great ancient and a few modern languages, with a large amount of sometimes tolerable verse. Of the latter we need say no more, while giving it its own honour in the degree in which it may deserve it. Of the poetry there are many kinds: and in each kind there are degrees of glory. But in its own kind I know nothing that can beat, if I know anything that can equal, *Annabel Lee.* It begins quite quietly but with a motion of gathering speed and a sort of flicker of light and glow of heat: and these things quicken and brighten and grow till they finish in the last stanza, that incomparable explosion of rapturous regret that towers to the stars and sinks to the sea.

This, however, is no doubt terribly like fine writing, which is not my trade. Let us therefore conclude with perfectly plain prose. Some fifty years ago I was not allowed in England to call Poe "of the first order of poets"; fifty years after that I am able by kind permission of *The Dial* to call him so in his own country.

By what arguments this position was originally supported I cannot exactly say, for except the passage which Lang quoted I do not know what became of my rejected address. If I could not say with Landor that God is the only person of whom I would ask a thing twice, I certainly should not like to offer the same thing a second time, even to the most different person, after it had been once rejected. But I can sum up what has been

here said shortly enough. A poet of the first order must be able
to satisfy both the ears and the eyes of the mind; and beyond,
though through, this satisfaction he must give the indefinable
but by the right recipients unmistakable poetic "effluence," "emanation," or whatever you like to call it.

For me and for my house Poe does this.

In *The Bridge* [1930], HART CRANE [1899–1932] has the following passage
on Poe. In one of his letters, Crane remarked that in *In the American
Grain* William Carlos Williams placed "Poe and his 'character' in the same
position I had *symbolized* for him in 'The Tunnel' section." (*Letters,* 278.)
The latter part of the passage seems to question whether Poe, symbol of
the artist exploited by a hostile environment, could maintain his integrity
in the face of death and disintegration.

The Bridge

from "The Tunnel" section

HART CRANE

Whose head is swinging from the swollen strap?
Whose body smokes along the bitten rails,
Bursts from a smoldering bundle far behind
In back forks of the chasms of the brain—
Puffs from a riven stump far out behind
In interborough fissures of the mind . . . ?

And why do I often meet your visage here,
Your eyes like agate lanterns—on and on
Below the toothpaste and the dandruff ads?
—And did their riding eyes right through your side,
And did their eyes like unwashed platters ride?
And Death, aloft—gigantically down
Probing through you toward me, O Evermore!

From *Collected Poems* (New York: Liveright Publishing Corp., 1933), pp.
51–52.

And when they dragged your retching flesh,
Your trembling hands that night through Baltimore—
That last night on the ballot rounds, did you,
Shaking—did you deny the ticket, Poe?

———————

ALDOUS LEONARD HUXLEY [1894–1963]. It was inevitable that sooner or later a British critic would come forth with a blanket rejection of the French appreciation of Poe as a poet. Huxley's criticism of "the walloping dactylic metre" of "Ulalume" has been answered by the editors of the *Explicator* and by Professor Mabbott; the parody of the "too musical lusciousness" of the lines overlooks the state of mind of the speaker and the impressionistic nature of the poem.

Vulgarity in Literature

ALDOUS LEONARD HUXLEY

Eulalie, Ulalume, Raven and Bells, Conqueror Worm and Haunted Palace. . . . Was Edgar Allan Poe a major poet? It would surely never occur to any English-speaking critic to say so. And yet, in France, from 1850 till the present time, the best poets of each generation—yes, and the best critics, too; for, like most excellent poets, Baudelaire, Mallarmé, Paul Valéry are also admirable critics—have gone out of their way to praise him. Only a year or two ago M. Valéry repeated the now traditional French encomium of Poe, and added at the same time a protest against the faintness of our English praise. We who are speakers of English and not English scholars, who were born into the language and from childhood have been pickled in its literature —we can only say, with all due respect, that Baudelaire, Mallarmé and Valéry are wrong and that Poe is not one of our major poets. A taint of vulgarity spoils, for the English reader, all but two or three of his poems—the marvellous 'City in the Sea' and 'To Helen,' for example, whose beauty and crystal per-

Aldous Huxley, "Vulgarity in Literature," in *Music at Night and Other Essays*, pp. 267-78. Copyright 1930, 1958 by Aldous Huxley. Reprinted by permission of Harper & Row, Publishers.

fection make us realize, as we read them, what a very great artist perished on most of the occasions when Poe wrote verse. It is to this perished artist that the French poets pay their tribute. Not being English, they are incapable of appreciating those finer shades of vulgarity that ruin Poe for us, just as we, not being French, are incapable of appreciating those finer shades of lyrical beauty which are, for them, the making of La Fontaine.

The substance of Poe is refined; it is his form that is vulgar. He is, as it were, one of Nature's Gentlemen, unhappily cursed with incorrigible bad taste. To the most sensitive and high-souled man in the world we should find it hard to forgive, shall we say, the wearing of a diamond ring on every finger. Poe does the equivalent of this in his poetry; we notice the solecism and shudder. Foreign observers do not notice it; they detect only the native gentlemanliness in the poetical intention, not the vulgarity in the details of execution. To them, we seem perversely and quite incomprehensibly unjust.

It is when Poe tries to make it too poetical that his poetry takes on its peculiar tinge of badness. Protesting too much that he is a gentleman, and opulent into the bargain, he falls into vulgarity. Diamond rings on every finger proclaim the parvenu. Consider, for example, the first two stanzas of "Ulalume."

> The skies they were ashen and sober;
>   The leaves they were crisped and sere—
>   The leaves they were withering and sere;
> It was night in the lonesome October
>   Of my most immemorial year;
> It was hard by the dim lake of Auber,
>   In the misty mid region of Weir—
> It was down by the dank tarn of Auber
>   In the ghoul-haunted woodland of Weir.
>
> Here once, through an alley Titanic,
>   Of cypress, I roamed with my soul,
>   Of cypress, with Psyche my soul.
> These were days when my heart was volcanic
>   As the scoriac rivers that roll—
>   As the lavas that restlessly roll

Their sulphurous currents down Yaanek
In the ultimate clime of the pole—
That groan as they roll down Mount Yaanek
In the realms of the boreal pole.

These lines protest too much (and with what a variety of voices!) that they are poetical, and, protesting, are therefore vulgar. To start with, the walloping dactylic metre is all too musical. Poetry ought to be musical, but musical with tact, subtly and variously. Metres whose rhythms, as in this case, are strong, insistent and practically invariable offer the poet a kind of short cut to musicality. They provide him (my subject calls for a mixture of metaphors) with a ready-made, reach-me-down music. He does not have to create a music appropriately modulated to his meaning; all he has to do is to shovel the meaning into the moving stream of the metre and allow the current to carry it along on waves that, like those of the best hairdressers, are guaranteed permanent. Many nineteenth-century poets used these metrical short cuts to music, with artistically fatal results.

Then when nature around me is smiling
The last smile which answers to mine,
I do not believe it beguiling,
Because it reminds me of thine.

How can one take even Byron seriously, when he protests his musicalness in such loud and vulgar accents? It is only by luck or an almost superhuman poetical skill that these all too musical metres can be made to sound, through their insistent barrel-organ rhythms, the intricate, personal music of the poet's own meaning. Byron occasionally, for a line or two, takes the hard kink out of those dactylic permanent waves and appears, so to speak, in his own musical hair; and Hood, by an unparalleled prodigy of technique, turns even the reach-me-down music of "The Bridge of Sighs" into a personal music, made to the measure of the subject and his own emotion. Moore, on the contrary, is always perfectly content with the permanent wave; and Swinburne, that super-Moore of a later generation, was also content to be a permanent waver—the most accomplished, perhaps, in all the history of literature. The complexity of his ready-made musics and his technical skill in varying the number, shape and contour of his permanent waves are simply astonishing. But, like Poe and the others, he protested too much, he tried to be too poetical. However elaborately devious his short cuts to music may be, they are still short cuts—and short cuts (this is the irony) to poetical vulgarity.

A quotation and a parody will illustrate the difference between ready-made music and music made to measure. I remember (I trust correctly) a simile of Milton's:—

> Like that fair field
> Of Enna, where Proserpine gathering flowers,
> Herself a fairer flower, by gloomy Dis
> Was gathered, which cost Ceres all that pain
> To seek her through the world.

Rearranged according to their musical phrasing, these lines would have to be written thus:—

> Like that fair field of Enna,
>   where Proserpine gathering flowers,
> Herself a fairer flower,
>   by gloomy Dis was gathered,
> Which cost Ceres all that pain
> To seek her through the world.

The contrast between the lyrical swiftness of the first four phrases, with that row of limping spondees which tells of Ceres' pain, is thrillingly appropriate. Bespoke, the music fits the sense like a glove.

How would Poe have written on the same theme? I have ventured to invent his opening stanza.

> It was noon in the fair field of Enna,
>   When Proserpina gathering flowers—
>   Herself the most fragrant of flowers,
> Was gathered away to Gehenna
>   By the Prince of Plutonian powers;
> Was born down the windings of Brenner
>   To the gloom of his amorous bowers—
> Down the tortuous highway of Brenner
>   To the God's agapemonous bowers.

The parody is not too outrageous to be critically beside the point; and anyhow the music is genuine Poe. That permanent wave is unquestionably an *ondulation de chez Edgar*. The much too musical metre is (to change the metaphor once more) like a rich chasuble, so stiff with gold and gems that it stands unsupported, a carapace of jewelled sound, into which the sense, like some snotty little seminarist, irrelevantly creeps and is lost. This music of Poe's—how much less really musical it is than that which, out of his nearly neutral decasyllables, Milton fashioned on purpose to fit the slender beauty of Proserpine, the strength and swiftness of the ravisher and her mother's heavy, despairing sorrow!

Of the versification of "The Raven" Poe says, in his *Philosophy of Composition:* "My first object (as usual) was originality. The extent to which this has been neglected in versification is one of the most unaccountable things in the world. Admitting that there is little possibility of variety in mere *rhythm,* it is still clear that the possible varieties of metre and stanza are absolutely infinite—and yet, *for centuries, no man, in verse, has ever done or ever seemed to think of doing an original thing."* This fact, which Poe hardly exaggerates, speaks volumes for the good sense of the poets. Feeling that almost all strikingly original metres and stanzas were only illegitimate short cuts to a music which, when reached, turned out to be but a poor and vulgar substitute for individual music, they wisely stuck to the less blatantly musical metres of tradition. The ordinary iambic decasyllable, for example, is intrinsically musical enough to be just able, when required, to stand up by itself. But its musical stiffness can easily be taken out of it. It can be now a chasuble, a golden carapace of sound, now, if the poet so desires, a pliant, soft and, musically speaking, almost neutral material, out of which he can fashion a special music of his own to fit his thoughts and feelings in all their incessant transformations. Good landscape painters seldom choose a "picturesque" subject; they want to paint their own picture, not have it imposed on them by nature. In the thoroughly paintable little places of this world you will generally find only bad painters. (It's so easy to paint the thoroughly paintable.) The good ones prefer the unspectacular neutralities of the Home Counties to those Cornish coves and Ligurian fishing villages, whose picturesqueness is the delight of all those who have no pictures of their own to project on to the canvas. It is the same with poetry: good poets avoid what I may call, by analogy, 'musicesque' metres, preferring to create their own music out of raw materials as nearly as possible neutral. Only bad poets, or good poets against their better judgment, and by mistake, go to the Musicesque for their material. "For centuries no man, in verse, has ever done or ever seemed to think of doing an original thing." It remained for Poe and the other nineteenth-century metrists to do it; Procrustes-like, they tortured and amputated significance into fitting the ready-made music of their highly original metres and stanzas. The result was, in most cases, as vulgar as a Royal Academy Sunrise on Ben Nevis (with Highland Cattle) or a genuine hand-painted sketch of Portofino.

How could a judge so fastidious as Baudelaire listen to Poe's music and remain unaware of its vulgarity? A happy ignorance of English versification preserved him, I fancy, from this realization. His own imitations of mediaeval hymns prove how far he was from understanding the first principles of versification in a language where the stresses are not, as in French, equal, but essentially and insistently uneven. In his Latin poems Baudelaire makes the ghost of Bernard of Cluny write as though he had learned his art from Racine. The principles of English versification are much the same as those of mediaeval Latin. If Baudelaire could discover lines composed of equally stressed syllables in Bernard, he must also have discovered them in Poe. Interpreted according to Racinian principles, such verses as

> It was down by the dank tarn of Auber
> In the ghoul-haunted woodland of Weir

must have taken on, for Baudelaire, heaven knows what exotic subtlety of rhythm. We can never hope to guess what that ghoul-haunted woodland means to a Frenchman possessing only a distant and theoretical knowledge of our language.

Returning now to "Ulalume," we find that its too poetical metre has the effect of vulgarizing by contagion what would be otherwise perfectly harmless and refined technical devices. Thus, even the very mild alliterations in "the ghoul-haunted woodland of Weir" seem to protest too much. And yet an iambic verse beginning "Woodland of Weir, ghoul-haunted," would not sound in the least over-poetical. It is only in the dactylic environment that those two w's strike one as protesting too much.

And then there are the proper names. Well used, proper names can be relied on to produce the most thrilling musical-magical effects. But use them without discretion, and the magic evaporates into abracadabrical absurdity, or becomes its own mocking parody; the over-emphatic music shrills first into vulgarity and finally into ridiculousness. Poe tends to place his proper names in the most conspicuous position in the line (he uses them constantly as rhyme words), showing them off—these magical-musical jewels—as the *rastacouaire* might display the twin cabochon emeralds at his shirt cuffs and the platinum wrist watch, with his monogram in diamonds. These proper-name rhyme-jewels are particularly flashy in Poe's case because they are mostly dissyllabic. Now, the dissyllabic rhyme in English is poetically so precious and so conspicuous by its richness that, if it is not perfect in itself and perfectly used, it emphatically ruins what it was meant emphatically to adorn. Thus, sound and association make of "Thule" a musical-magical proper name of exceptional power. But when Poe writes,

> I have reached these lands but newly
> From an ultimate dim Thule,

he spoils the effect which the word ought to produce by insisting too much, and incompetently, on its musicality. He shows off his jewel as conspicuously as he can, but only reveals thereby the badness of its setting and his own Levantine love of display. For "newly" does not rhyme with "Thule"—or only rhymes on condition that you pronounce the adverb as though you were a Bengali, or the name as though you came from Whitechapel. The paramour of Goethe's king rhymed perfectly with the name of his kingdom; and when Laforgue wrote of that 'roi de Thulé, Immaculé' his *rime riche* was entirely above suspicion. Poe's rich rhymes, on the contrary, are seldom above suspicion. That dank tarn of Auber is only very dubiously a fit poetical companion for the tenth month, and though Mount Yaanek is, *ex hypothesi*, a volcano, the rhyme with volcanic is, frankly, impossible. On other occasions Poe's proper names rhyme not only well enough, but actually, in the particular context, much too well. Dead D'Elormie, in "The Bridal Ballad," is prosodically in order, because Poe had brought his ancestors over with the Conqueror (as he also imported the ancestors of that Guy de Vere who wept his tear over Lenore) for the express purpose of providing a richly musical-magical rhyme to "bore me" and "before me." Dead D'Elormie is first cousin to Edward Lear's aged Uncle Arly, sitting on a heap of Barley—ludicrous; but also (unlike dear Uncle Arly) horribly vulgar, because of the too musical lusciousness of his invented name and his display, in all tragical seriousness, of an obviously faked Norman pedigree. Dead D'Elormie is a poetical disaster.

———————

CONSTANCE M. ROURKE [1885–1941] was born in Cleveland, Ohio, and educated at the Sorbonne and Vassar, where she taught from 1910 to 1915. A specialist in popular culture, she edited the *Index of American Design* (1937) and *The Roots of American Culture* (1942), wrote biographies of Davy Crockett, Audubon, Charles Seeler, and several studies of the American cultural past. The following excerpt from her *American Humor: A Study of the National Character* (1931) is one of few attempts to see Poe in an American context. For Miss Rourke it is the native tradition of the popular comic story that explains Poe's fondness for the hoax (as in *Rodman, Pym*, "Hans Pfaall"), the comic fantasy, the burlesque ("King Pest"), and Poe's insistent first-person exploration of subconscious conflict ("William Wilson").

Edgar Allan Poe

CONSTANCE M. ROURKE

Of all American writers Poe has become a symbol for the type of genius which rises clear from its time, nourished mainly from hidden inner sources. Poe himself would have delighted in that theory, for he fostered the conviction that he ranged over only the rarest and most esoteric materials. But Poe came from that Scotch-Irish stock with its heritage of unsettlement from which were drawn the scouts and myth-makers and many strollers of the West; the theatrical strain that had been strong among them

From *American Humor*, 1931.

was his by birth; and he began to write at the end of the '20's when American myth-making was passing into its great popular diffusion. Essential foreign influences on Poe have been discovered, but in general the influences which weigh most with any writer are those which are akin to his own feeling and purposes. Poe drew upon German and French romanticism: but a homely romantic movement of native origin was making itself felt nearer at hand; and Poe both by temperament and environment was susceptible to the native forces.

The impact of popular comic story-telling in America must have reached Poe. At his foster-father's house Negro legends were surely current among the slaves; he must have heard the exploits of those adventurers by land and sea who drifted into the office of Allan and Company. Since this firm were agents for subscriptions to newspapers Poe no doubt had access to the current almanacs, which even in an early day were beginning to print compact stories of wild adventure. He may have seen tales of buccaneering and of buried treasure there, preparing him for *The Gold Bug*, or of hazards at sea, which suggested *Arthur Gordon Pym*. At the University of Virginia a few of his companions were accomplished in the western art of biting and gouging; probably story-telling was exhibited as another form of prowess. Poe himself gained a reputation as an amusing story-teller in these years. At Baltimore in 1831 and 1832 he could hardly have missed echoes of western story-telling, for Baltimore was a point of convergence for travelers from all that wide circle known as the Southwest; they came on horseback or by stage over the mountains, by boat from Savannah or New Orleans. Their appearance was striking: their talk and tales were caught fragmentarily by many observers. At the theaters the backwoodsman was being portrayed in the semblance of Crockett; and the new stage character was creating a highly novel sensation.

That broad grotesque myth-making which had to do with corn-crackers and country rapscallions Poe surely encountered, for in 1835 he reviewed Longstreet's *Georgia Scenes,* with enthusiasm. When Poe went to Philadelphia, always a center for the comic theater, the larger pattern of native figures must again have moved before him, and surely his association with Burton on the *Gentleman's Magazine* gave an impetus to his sense of native comedy, for though Burton's alliance with Brougham lay in the future, he had long been a comedian and had compiled comic joke-books and song-books. Poe possessed besides what Woodberry has called "a contemporaneous mind." He quickly turned to matters of current interest, exploration, treasure-hunting, mesmerism, Masonry, balloons, topics that crowded the newspapers and were being discussed by popular lecturers. He turned to comedy; as by instinct he turned to the hoax. His early *Journal of Julius Rodman* purported to give a literal account of a western journey and was essentially a hoax, as was his *Arthur Gordon Pym* with its studied effort to produce an effect of truth. His *Hans Pfaall* was in the vanguard of a long sequence of hoaxes, anticipating by only a brief space Locke's famous Moon Hoax, which made a great stir in 1835. With its carefully prepared verisimilitude even to effects of costuming, with its intense stress of all outward sensation, *Hans Pfaall* bore a close resemblance to the more elaborate and finished tall tales of the West, which were scrupulous as to detail, and which often gave—as it happened—a particularly keen attention to costume. His *Balloon Hoax* in 1844 had its brief day of acceptance as fact. One of Poe's last stories, *Von Kempelen and His Discovery*, was essentially a hoax; and his talent for comic fantasy was shown in still another form in a topsy-turvy extravaganza, *The Angel of the Odd*.

Poe never used native legends directly except perhaps in *The Gold Bug*; yet in creative bent he was perhaps one of those major writers who instinctively turn toward long-established traditions. Unrooted in any region—if indeed any American of those years could be called rooted—he found no long and substantial accumulation of native materials, even though the comic myth-making faculty was abroad in force during his later youth. None the less Poe followed a course habitually followed by traditional writers and myth-makers: he did not invent, he borrowed and recreated. His *King Pest* was built upon a scene from *Vivian Gray;* he borrowed indeed at every turn.

Even if native legends had been strewn about with unmistakable richness one cannot be sure that Poe would have used them. That restless impulse which had driven other story-tellers farther and farther afield might have moved him. But the patterns, if not the substance of his tales, were those of a native story-telling. The gamut of his moods might have been drawn from the West, plumbing horror, yet turning also to a wild contrived comedy. Because of his own dark fate, and because Poe himself often stressed the *frisson*, terror has overtopped comedy in the general apprehension of his tales. His designations of "grotesque" and "arabesque" and his later "tales of terror" have created a further submergence of the comic. Yet *King Pest*, with its background of the plague and the night, is one of the most brilliant pure burlesques in the language, transmuting terror into gross comedy, as it had often been transmuted in the western tall tales.

According to Poe's original plan for the *Tales of the Folio Club* each member of the Club was to be satirically described; after the telling of each tale they were to criticize it, their comments forming a burlesque of criticism. The tales run through a wide range of humor, from the sheer absurdity of *Lionising* to the hoax of *Hans Pfaall*. The Duc in *The Duc de l'Omelette* bore some relation to those derisive portraits of foreigners which were steadily gaining American favor; he was even given a not inharmonious touch of diabolism. Poe's command of verbal humor was uncertain; his puns often fall below tolerable levels. Yet these too are part of the mode of the time—a time when language was being carelessly and comically turned upside down and even re-created, as if to form a new and native idiom.

His laughter was of a single order: it was inhuman, and mixed with hysteria. His purpose in the hoaxes was to make his readers absurd, to reduce them to an involuntary imbecility. His objective was triumph, the familiar objective of popular comedy. To this end, in his burlesques and extravaganzas, he showed human traits or lineaments in unbelievable distortion, using that grotesquerie which lies midway between the comic and the terrible; with Poe the terrible was always within view. There are touches of chilly barbarity even in *Hans Pfaall*. The fantasy-making of the West had swung from an impinging terror to a gross and often brutal comedy; Poe also stressed black moods and emotions, embracing a dark and ghostly melodrama, employing themes bordering upon those in the romantic tragedy of the day. In the midst of burlesque in *Tales of the Folio Club* he reached an antithetical horror, in *Berenice*.

Western story-telling had often been callous: in callousness

Poe could pass beyond human limits, in the *Facts in the Case of M. Valdemar.* He used the magnified scale in rooms, corridors, draperies, in the accumulation of detail, in sensation. He enjoyed mystification; his tone and level throughout were those of legend; and if his scope in story-telling was brief he verged toward larger forms. His *Tales of the Folio Club* were made to follow in a prismatic sequence, and other stories fall into loosely united cycles.

Poe entered another area marked out by the popular comic tradition: that of the inner mind or consciousness. Not only Emerson approached this, or Thoreau in the delicate exemplification of inner states, or Whitman in his outpourings. Poe— and also Hawthorne, and even Melville—invaded this area and in some measure conquered it. Poe used the first person continually, adopting it in part perhaps to gain an impulse toward an exploration of states of mind or feeling which were often undoubtedly his own. Beyond direct transcriptions, which may have been unconscious, he clearly attempted to explore the character of the inner, even the sub-conscious, mind. In *The Black Cat* he dwelt on "the spirit of PERVERSENESS. . . . Yet I am not more sure that my soul lives than I am that perverseness is one of the primitive impulses of the human heart—one of the indivisible primary faculties or sentiments which give direction to the character of Man. . . ." He mentioned the "unfathomable longing of the soul *to vex itself*—to offer violence to its own nature." He made notations on small crises of the mind, speaking in *Ligeia* of the endeavor to recall to memory something forgotten when "we often find ourselves upon *the very verge* of remembrance, without being able in the end to remember." These fragmentary touches and others like them scattered through Poe's tales culminated in his story of double identity in *William Wilson*, in which memory—its obscure envelopments, its buried treasures—made a recurrent theme. Half symbolical, half factual, filled by intimations of a complex and warring inner state, *William Wilson* stands as a fresh creation in an almost untouched field, a prelude to the so-called psychological novel, and a further revelation of a native bias.

In critical theory the psychological strain has sometimes been linked with the Puritan influences; but surely no tie with the Puritan faith and its habit of introspection can be found for

Poe. By birth and upbringing and sympathy he was wholly alien to the Puritan strain. Nothing remotely moralistic can be found in his observation, no identity with religious feeling, no judgments. Instead, Poe seems near those story-tellers of the West who described wild and perverse actions with blank and undisturbed countenances, and whose insistent use of the first person brought them to the brink of inner revelation.

———————

Since its first publication in 1933 (translated into English in 1949), *The Life and Letters of Edgar Allan Poe: A Psycho-Analytic Interpretation* by Princess MARIE BONAPARTE [1882–1962], a disciple of Freud, has seemed to many readers the ultimate reductio ad absurdum of all such criticism of Poe. "Morella," the subject of the essay that follows, is seen as one of several "Tales of the Mother." As such it exemplifies the psychology of transference and embodies the compulsion to repeat the theme of the "ungratified libido," which dooms the hero to disloyalty and unhappiness.

Morella

MARIE BONAPARTE

Like *Berenice, Morella* forms part of *The Tales of the Folio Club*.

The nameless hero of this story meets a girl named Morella. From the moment they meet, his soul "burned with fires it had never before known." But, says the hero,

> the fires were not of Eros, and bitter and tormenting to my spirit was the gradual conviction that I could in no manner define their unusual meaning, or regulate their vague intensity.

They marry, but—confesses the husband—"I never spoke of passion, nor thought of love."

Morella, the other partner in this strange marriage, is profoundly erudite: "her powers of mind were gigantic." And, indeed, so great is the fascination she exerts over her husband that,

From *The Life and Works of Edgar Allan Poe: A Psycho-Analytic Interpretation*, 1933, translated by John Rodker, 1949.

despite himself, he becomes her pupil in the philosophical and mystic studies in which she is adept. But soon a mysterious malady preys, too, on Morella. She begins to pine and her terror-struck husband grows to regard her with increasing aversion. The nature of her disease is clearer to us than was that of Berenice.

> In time, the crimson spot settled steadily upon the cheek, and the blue veins upon the pale forehead became prominent.

Like Elizabeth Arnold, she is wasting with consumption. And now a morbid eagerness seizes her husband for her death, that seems so slow in coming.

One autumn evening, however, she finally expires, after making the sybilline prophecy: "I am dying, yet I shall live." She then adds:

> her whom in life thou didst abhor, in death thou shalt adore . . . thou shalt bear about with thee thy shroud on the earth. . . .

Then, dying, she gives birth to a daughter.

The child grows in wisdom and stature with disturbing rapidity. At ten, she is already a grown woman, the physical counterpart of her mother, with her mother's smile and eyes; yet, though her father loves her fervently, it is with a love that is soon mingled with fear.

> In the contour of the high forehead, and in the ringlets of the silken hair, and in the wan fingers which buried themselves therein, and in the sad musical tones of her speech, and above all . . . in the phrases and expressions of the dead on the lips of the loved and the living, I found food for consuming thought and horror—for a worm that *would* not die.

For "two lustra" the father watches the child grow under his care, yet never in that time has he named her anything but "my love," or "my child."

But now a mysterious urge takes him to have the child baptised, though even at the font he is unable to decide on a name. Then, however, moved by some unreasoning impulse he suddenly, in the priest's ear, murmurs the name of she who is dead: *Morella*. In that instant the child is convulsed, turns pale and, falling lifeless on the black slabs of the family vault, says, "*I am here!*"

When the father, with his own hands, places his child in the tomb, he finds no trace of the first Morella.

Such, in substance, is this tale. No clearer description of what is known in psycho-analysis as *transference* could be imagined. *Transference* comes about by feelings properly attached to one being, being displaced upon another. Thus, throughout our lives, we all *transfer* our emotions—or, as the psycho-analyst would say, our *libidinal cathexes*—to various objects, insofar as they represent prototypes established, in earliest infancy, by our parents and educators and first loves and hates. All our later loves and hates are but *transferences* from these.

Similarly, the husband and father of both Morellas *transfers* his love from one to the other. It is not difficult to see that the hero is again Poe and that he has here described, under the thinnest of disguises, his own emotional conflict at this time.

Virginia, when Poe was writing *Morella,* was in fact about ten, the age of the second Morella. And it was just at Virginia's age that Morella is baptized with her dead mother's name, whose stature she has reached. Transparent symbols of a real event; for Virginia was about ten when she was elevated by Poe—the stepping-stone being doubtless memories of his sister Rosalie—to the dignity of a *mother-transference* figure.

Such a transference, however, though essentially proof of intense attachment, inevitably involves a certain betrayal of the original object. A doom, therefore, decreed by the dead mother, must thenceforth cloud the destiny of the father who too fondly loved his child. As the first Morella predicted, he must remain faithful to the dead, despite himself and his new love: "Thou shalt bear about with thee thy shroud on the earth," words which might equally have been spoken by Elizabeth Arnold to the little son whom, by her fate, she doomed to eternal mourning. "The hours of thy happiness are over; and joy is not gathered twice in a life." But what "joy" had the father, in fact, known with his wife? He had not loved her with a husband's love—which of Poe's heroes, always a reflection of Poe, was so to do?—but had been spellbound by her "gigantic intellect."

Thus the bonds which once united the tiny boy to his mother are recalled, as also his dependence on her for instruction in the forbidden, "accursed" lore—doubtless sexual knowledge—of which she held the key. Due, however, to the original incest prohibition, which imposed a sex barrier between mother and child, the boy's first resentment is later visited on the wife, with the result that his "joy" fades "into horror." Thus, Poe's ungratified libido, to which normal channels of satisfaction were denied, became changed into the morbid anxiety to which these *Tales* bear witness: tales in which, in fact, "the most beautiful" became "the most hideous."

Nevertheless, the loss of Morella, for the second time, in the person of the beloved daughter, is more than a mere punishment inflicted on him by the dead mother, for this dénouement affords the hero the sombre gratification of once more beholding the corpse on which his love was fixated. Here we find expressed that "repetition-compulsion," which dominates our instinctual life, and impels us always to seek the same emotions in the same forms, whatever the object. Since love, from infancy, for Poe, had worn death's aspect, it was an erotic necessity for him that, in her turn, the second Morella should die, as did the little Virginia some few years later, in the same manner as Elizabeth Arnold.

Before I continue this gruesome survey of Poe's heroines, I must crave the reader's indulgence for the monotony of my theme. Time and again we find the same manifest situation, that of some ideal woman who sickens and dies, yet does not really die, since she lives on in unearthly radiance, putrescent and ethereal at one and the same time. Always and forever it is the same latent theme: that of Elizabeth Arnold's last agony and death—repeated in after years, in the little Virginia's agony and death. Very little else will be found in the next five or six tales and the reader may possibly find their analysis tedious.

And yet, I am unable to spare him. For the very monotony of these tales, their endless repetition, are themselves expressions of Poe's psyche. Since such situations forced themselves on him, we ourselves have no right to ignore them as, at times, I have been tempted to do, or to omit from this analysis one or other of these typical tales, in which the living-dead mother appears and vanishes. For, better perhaps than any single example, the monotonous repetition of the same theme, as of its expression, enables us to feel how crushingly Poe's soul, his life and work, were dominated by the compulsion to repetition.

———————

This critique by YVOR WINTERS [1900–   ], professor of English at Stanford University since 1927, has been called "the most serious, all-out attack" ever made on Poe as a writer. Winters denounces Poe as "a bad writer," a critic who confuses "the manner and the matter" of poetry, a mistaken theorist of poetry and fiction, a writer of little or no taste in language and meter, "an explicit obscurantist," and, finally, a "bad" influence. Though none of these objections and arguments is new, Winters writes as if each were original, as if none, in fact, had been answered before 1937. Documented though it is, much of Winters' argument seems to stem from Neo-Humanist preconceptions, and much from a too-literal reading of Poe—his critical theory as well as his fiction and poetry. Winters fails to make allowance for what Baudelaire neatly identified as an "amusing pride," which often motivated Poe's histrionic overstatements, even in his criticism and social commentary. But as a conscientious and comprehensive statement of the case against Poe, Winters' essay sums up a good deal of what has been and, in some quarters, continues to be, thought about Poe. As such, it deserves careful reading.

Edgar Allan Poe: A Crisis in the History of American Obscurantism

YVOR WINTERS

Men have called me mad; but the question is not yet settled, whether madness is or is not the loftiest intelligence—whether much that is glorious—whether all that is profound—does not spring from disease of thought—from moods of mind exalted at the expense of the general intellect.—*Eleonora*

I

I am about to promulgate a heresy; namely, that E. A. Poe, although he achieved, as his admirers have claimed, a remarkable agreement between his theory and his practice, is exceptionally

From *American Literature,* January 1937.

bad in both. I am somewhat startled, moreover, to awaken to the fact that this is a heresy, that those who object to Poe would do well to establish their position now if ever. Poe has long passed casually with me and with most of my friends as a bad writer accidentally and temporarily popular; the fact of the matter is, of course, that he has been pretty effectually established as a great writer while we have been sleeping. The menace lies not, primarily, in his impressionistic admirers among literary people, of whom he still has some, even in England and in America, where a familiarity with his language ought to render his crudity obvious, for these individuals in the main do not make themselves permanently very effective; it lies rather in the impressive body of scholarship, beginning, perhaps, with Harrison, Woodberry, and Stedman, and continuing down to such writers as Campbell, Stovall, and Una Pope-Hennessy. Much of this scholarship is primarily biographical, historical, and textual; but when a writer is supported by a sufficient body of such scholarship, a very little philosophical elucidation will suffice to establish him in the scholarly world as a writer whose greatness is self-evident. This fact is made especially evident in the work of the two critics who come closest to taking the position which I shall take: W. C. Brownell[1] and especially Norman Foerster.[2] Both approach the essential issue; neither is able, or it may be that because of its absurdity neither is willing, to define it; and both maintain the traditional reverence for Poe as a stylist, a reverence which I believe to be at once unjustified and a source of error in dealing with his theory.

My consternation became acute upon the examination of a recent edition of selections from Poe, prepared, it is true, merely as a classroom text, but prepared with great competence, by a respectable Poe scholar, the late Margaret Alterton, and by an exceptionally distinguished scholar in the field of the English Renaissance, Professor Hardin Craig.[3] The Introduction to this

[1] W. C. Brownell, *American Prose Masters* (New York, 1909).

[2] Norman Foerster, *American Criticism* (Boston and New York, 1928). I should like, if I had time, to examine Professor Foerster's essay on Poe at length, partly because of the similarities and the differences between his position and my own, and partly because of a matter largely irrelevant but none the less astonishing—that is, Professor Foerster's view of the nature and history of music, subjects of which he displays an ignorance nothing less than sweeping.

[3] *Edgar Allan Poe*, edited by Craig and Alterton (New York, 1935).

text, the first and second parts of which were written by Miss Alterton and after her death revised by Professor Craig, the third part of which was written wholly by Professor Craig, offers the best general defense of Poe with which I am acquainted; it is careful and thorough, and it makes as good a case for Poe, I imagine, as can be made. And when one has finished it, one has a perfectly clear idea of why it is wrong.

The problem is a simple one. Most of Poe's essential theory is summarized in three essays: *The Poetic Principle, The Philosophy of Composition,* and *The Rationale of Verse.* Important statements can be found elsewhere, and I shall draw upon other essays, but these essays contain most of the essential ideas. Furthermore the essential statements recur repeatedly in other essays, frequently almost verbatim. By confining oneself largely to these essays, by selecting the crucial statements, by showing as briefly as possible their obvious relations one to another, one can reduce Poe's aesthetic to a very brief and a perfectly accurate statement. In doing this, I shall endeavor in every case to interpret what he says directly, not with the aid of other writers whose theories may have influenced him and by aid of whose theories one may conceivably be able to gloss over some of his confusion; and I shall endeavor to show that this direct approach is fully justified by his own artistic practice.

The passages which I shall quote have all been quoted many times before; I shall have to beg indulgence on that score and ask the reader to examine once and for all their obvious significance.

Any study of Poe should begin with a statement made in connection with Elizabeth Barrett's *A Drama of Exile.* He says: "This is emphatically the thinking age; indeed it may very well be questioned whether man ever substantially thought before."[4] This sentence displays an ignorance at once of thought and of the history of thought so comprehensive as to preclude the possibility of our surprise at any further disclosures. It helps to explain, furthermore, Poe's extraordinary inability to understand even the poetry of ages previous to his own, as well as his subservience in matters of taste to the vulgar sentimentalism which

---

[4] All quotations in this essay are from the edition of Stedman and Woodberry. Quotations from the criticism only are given footnotes. This quotation is from Vol. I, page 294, of the three volumes of criticism.

dominated the more popular poets of his period, such poets as Moore, Hood, and Willis, to mention no others. One seldom encounters a writer so thoroughly at the mercy of contemporaneity. Professor Foerster writes of him: "Of this sustaining power of the past, it must be admitted, Poe himself had but a dim understanding." And he quotes Professor Woodberry (*Life*, I, 132) as follows: "He had, in the narrowest sense, a contemporaneous mind, the instincts of the journalist, the magazine writer."[5]

II

One cannot better introduce the question of Poe's aesthetics than by his well-known remarks about Tennyson, in *The Poetic Principle:* "In perfect sincerity, I regard him as the noblest poet that ever lived. . . . I call him and *think* him, the noblest of poets, not because the impressions he produces are at *all* times the most profound, not because the poetical excitement which he induces is at *all* times the most intense, but because it *is*, at all times the most ethereal,—in other words, the most elevating and the most pure. No poet is so little of the earth, earthy."[6] The italics, of course, here and elsewhere are Poe's; it is seldom necessary to improve upon Poe in this respect. Our task will be primarily to find out what this passage means. I believe that I shall be able to show that it means this: that the poet should not deal with human, that is, moral, experience; that the subject-matter of poetry is of an order essentially supra-human; that the poet has no way of understanding his subject-matter. There will appear certain qualifications to this summary, but they are of very little importance.

In the same essay Poe states: "I hold that a long poem does not exist. I maintain that the phrase, 'a long poem,' is a flat contradiction of terms."[7] And again, thus connecting the last statement with the statement regarding Tennyson: "A poem deserves its title only inasmuch as it elevates by exciting the soul. . . . But all excitements are, through a psychal necessity, transient." "After the lapse of half an hour at the utmost, it [the excitement] flags—fails—a revulsion ensues—and then the poem is in effect,

[5] Foerster, op. cit., pages 1 and 2.
[6] Stedman and Woodberry, op. cit., I, 27.
[7] Ibid., I, 3.

and in fact, no longer such."[8] "This great work [*Paradise Lost*], in fact, is to be regarded as poetical, only when, losing sight of that vital requisite of all works of Art, Unity, we view it merely as a series of minor poems. If, to preserve its Unity,—its totality of effect or impression—we read it (as would be necessary) at a single sitting, the result is but a constant alternation of excitement and depression. . . . It follows from all this that the ultimate, aggregate, or absolute effect of even the best epic under the sun is a nullity:—and this is precisely the fact."[9]

From these passages it follows: first, that Poe's very conception of poetic unity is one of mood, or emotion; and second, that he regards the existence of mood to be governed by narrow mechanical rules—in other words, exaltation of spirit is merely a form of nervous excitement. The word *effect* is used here as elsewhere as a synonym for *impression;* artistic unity is described specifically as totality of effect. There appears to be no awareness whatever of that comprehensive act of the spirit, in part intellectual, whereby we understand and remember *Paradise Lost* as a whole, seize the whole intention with intellect and with memory, and, plunging into any passage, experience that passage in relationship to the whole, an act in which the emotional element, since it is involved in and supported by the rational understanding, rises superior to mechanical necessity.

We should observe further that in these passages Poe begins that process of systematic exclusion, in the course of which he eliminates from the field of English poetry nearly all of the greatest acknowledged masters, reserving the field very largely to Coleridge, Tennyson, Thomas Moore, himself, and R. H. Horne. As we shall see, this process of elimination is not a mere accident of temperament, is not merely a series of accidents of judgment, but is the necessary corollary, in the field of particular judgments, of the general theory which we are now considering.

Poe continues: "On the other hand, it is clear that a poem may be improperly brief. Undue brevity degenerates into mere epigrammatism. A *very* short poem, while now and then producing a brilliant or vivid, never produces a profound or enduring effect."[10] He cites *The Indian Serenade,* by Shelley, a poem

[8] Ibid., I, 4.
[9] Ibid., I, 4.
[10] Ibid., I, 6.

of twenty-four lines, as unduly brief. He regarded one hundred lines as approximately the most effective number for a poem; the length of the lines themselves, he appears never to have considered, though if we compare two of his own poems of nearly the same number of lines, *Ulalume* and *The Raven*, the former, in fact and in effect, is much the shorter.

We may observe in the preceding quotation once more the obliviousness to the function of intellectual content in poetry, and an act of exclusion which deals very shortly, not only with the epigrammatists, but also with every sonneteer in the language, including Shakespeare and Milton, and with all the masters of the short lyric, including so wide a diversity of poets as Herbert, Herrick, Donne, and Landor.

By a further act of exclusion, he eliminates the great satirical and didactic masters. In his essay on Bryant, he says: "A satire is, of course, no poem."[11] And in *The Poetic Principle:* "We find it [the 'epic mania'] succeeded by a heresy too palpably false to be long tolerated. . . . I allude to the heresy of *The Didactic*. It has long been assumed that the end of all poetry is Truth. Every poem, it is said, should inculcate a moral; and by this moral is the poetical merit of the work to be adjudged. We Americans, especially, have patronized this happy idea; and we Bostonians, very especially, have developed it in full. We have taken it into our heads to write a poem simply for the poem's sake, and to acknowledge such to have been our design would be to confess ourselves radically wanting in true poetic dignity and force; but the simple fact is, that, would we but permit ourselves to look into our own souls, we should immediately there discover that under the sun there neither exists nor *can* exist any work more thoroughly dignified, more supremely noble, than this very poem—this poem *per se*—this poem which is a poem and nothing more—this poem written solely for the poem's sake."[12]

Now if Poe had merely intended to exclude some of the unsatisfactory didactic poetry, let us say, of Longfellow or of Lowell, we should have very little complaint to make; however, these poets are bad not because they are didactic, but because they write badly, and because their didacticism is frequently unsound in conception, and because the lesson which they endeavor to

[11] Ibid., I, 111.
[12] Ibid., I, 8.

teach is frequently connected only arbitrarily with their subjects. The didactic close of Bryant's great lyric, *To a Waterfowl,* on the other hand, is merely an explicit statement, and a fine statement, of the idea governing the poem, an idea inherent, but insufficiently obvious, in what has gone before, and it is foolish to object to it; and in the poetry of Samuel Johnson, of Dryden, and of Pope, as in Milton's sonnets, we have yet another form of didacticism, the loss of which would leave us vastly impoverished.[13]

Poe appears never to have grasped the simple and traditional distinction between matter (truth) and manner (beauty); he does not see that beauty is a quality of style instead of its subject-matter, that it is merely the most complete communication possible, through connotation as well as denotation, of the poet's personal realization of a moral (or human) truth, whether that truth be of very great importance or very little, a truth that must be understood primarily in conceptual terms, regardless of whether the poem ultimately embodies it in the form of description, of narration, or of exposition. A sound attitude toward a major problem, communicated with adequacy of detail, is what we ordinarily mean by sublimity. It is through the neglect of these fundamental ideas that Poe runs into difficulty.

"With as deep a reverence for the True as ever inspired the bosom of man," he continues, "I would, nevertheless, limit its modes of inculcation. I would limit to enforce them. I would not enfeeble them by dissipation. The demands of Truth are severe; she has no sympathy with the myrtles. All *that* which is so indispensable in Song, is precisely all *that* with which *she* has nothing whatever to do. . . . In enforcing a truth . . . we must be in that mood which, as nearly as possible, is the exact converse of the poetical."[14]

Poe appears oblivious to the possibility that we may come to a truth with an attitude other than that of the advocate; that we may, in brief, contemplate, with Dante, rather than enforce,

[13] It is instructive to compare *To a Waterfowl* with *The Chambered Nautilus.* Both follow the same rhetorical formula, but in Bryant's poem the "moral" is implicit throughout; in the poem by Holmes, it is a rhetorical imposition. The poem by Holmes is impressively written, notwithstanding; but it illustrates the more vulgar procedure.

[14] Stedman and Woodberry, op. cit., I, 9.

with Aquinas. It follows that he would not recognize the more complex procedure of contemplating the enforcement of truth, the procedure which results, for example, in the didacticism of Pope and of Dryden; nor yet the contemplation of the need of the enforcement of truth, the procedure which results in the satirical poetry of the same writers; nor the contemplation of a discrepancy between personal experience and a standard truth, a procedure which results in much of the poetry of Donne. Yet these are all major human experiences; they all require individual perception and moral adjustment; according to the traditional view, they are thus legitimate material for poetry.

Poe sees truly enough that the enforcement of truth, in itself, does not constitute poetry, and on the basis of that elementary observation he falls into the common romantic error, which may be stated briefly as follows: truth is not poetry; truth should therefore be eliminated from poetry, in the interests of a purer poetry. He would, in short, advise us to retain the attitude, but to discard the object of the attitude. The correct formula, on the other hand, is this: truth is not poetry; poetry is truth and something more. It is the completeness of the poetic experience which makes it valuable. How thoroughly Poe would rob us of all subject matter, how thoroughly he would reduce poetry, from its traditional position, at least when ideally considered, as the act of complete comprehension, to a position of triviality and of charlatanism, we shall presently see.

Poe's passion for exclusion, and the certitude that he has no conception of moral sublimity in poetry, appear very clearly in the essay on Horne's *Orion:* "We shall now be fully understood. If, with Coleridge, who, however erring at times, was precisely the mind fitted to decide such a question as this—if, with him, we reject passion from the true, from the pure poetry—if we reject even passion—if we discard as feeble, as unworthy of the high spirituality of the theme (which has its origin in the Godhead)—if we dismiss even the nearly divine emotion of human *love*, that emotion which merely to name causes the pen to tremble,—with how much greater reason shall we dismiss all else?" [15]

The dismissal appears to be inclusive enough, by this time, in all conscience. There would appear to be some confusion in

[15] Ibid., I, 268.

Poe's mind between a passionate or violent style, which (in spite of the magnificence of *King Lear*) he might reasonably regard as inferior to a style more serene, regardless of subject, as if the poet were to rise superior to his passions in his contemplation of them, and passion as subject-matter. It is his fundamental confusion of matter and manner, to which I have already alluded.

In the same essay, and on the same subject, he writes: "Although we argue, for example, with Coleridge, that poetry and passion are discordant, yet we are willing to permit Tennyson to bring, to the intense passion which prompted his *Locksley Hall*, the aid of that terseness and pungency which are derivable from rhythm and from rhyme. The effect he produces, however, is purely passionate, and not, unless in detached passages of this magnificent philippic, a properly poetic effect. His *Oenone*, on the other hand, exalts the soul not into passion, but into a conception of pure *beauty*, which in its elevation, its calm and intense rapture, has in it a foreshadowing of the future and spiritual life, and as far transcends earthly passion as the holy radiance of the sun does the glimmering and feeble phosphorescence of the glow-worm. His *Morte-d'Arthur* is in the same majestic vein. *The Sensitive Plant* of Shelley is in the same sublime spirit. . . . Readers do exist . . . and always will exist, who, to hearts of maddening fervor, unite in perfection, the sentiment of the beautiful—that divine sixth sense which is yet so faintly understood, that sense which phrenology has attempted to embody in its organ of *ideality*,[16] that sense which speaks of God through His purest, if not His *sole* attribute, which proves, and which alone proves his existence . . . the origin of poetry lies in a thirst for a wilder beauty than earth supplies. . . . Poetry itself is the imperfect effort to quench this immortal thirst by novel combinations of beautiful forms. . . ."[17]

In the remarks on *Oenone*, we may seem at first glance to have the hint that Poe has approached the concept of moral sublimity, but the last sentence quoted brings us back abruptly to the trivial; the exaltation is not a moral exaltation, not the result of the exercise of the intelligence and of character, but is the

[16] See Edward Hungerford, *Poe and Phrenology*, American Literature, II, 209–31 (Nov., 1930).
[17] Stedman and Woodberry, op cit., I, 267–68.

result of manipulation and of trickery. And were we to allow ourselves the luxury of worrying about Poe's minor obscurities, his use of the word *beautiful* in the last sentence would complicate our problem inextricably: that is, it appears that we achieve the beautiful by new combinations of items which are already beautiful; we have again his helpless inability to separate matter from manner, the poem from its subject.

It is obvious, then, that poetry is not, for Poe, a refined and enriched technique of moral comprehension. It can be of no aid to us in understanding ourselves or in ordering our lives, for most of our experience is irrelevant to it. If, indeed, certain human experiences are admitted as legitimate subjects, they are admitted, as we shall see, because the poet cannot write without writing about something—even the most irresponsible use of language involves an inescapable minimum of statement, however incomplete or dismembered; and those experiences are admitted which seem to involve the minimum of complexity. They are admitted, moreover, not as something valuable in themselves, not as something to be understood, but as ingredients in a formula by means of which something outside our experience may be suggested. If Poe moves us most to indignation when defining his exclusions, he perplexes us most profoundly when he endeavors to approximate a definition of what he would include.

He writes in *The Poetic Principle:* "An immortal instinct, deep within the spirit of man, is thus, plainly, a sense of the Beautiful. . . . This thirst belongs to the immortality of man. It is at once a consequence and an indication of his perennial existence. It is the desire of the moth for the star. It is no mere appreciation of the Beauty before us, but a wild effort to reach the Beauty above. Inspired by an ecstatic Prescience of the glories beyond the grave, we struggle by multiform combinations among the things and thoughts of Time to attain a portion of that Loveliness whose very elements, perhaps, appertain to eternity alone. And thus when by Poetry—or when by Music, the most entrancing of the Poetic moods—we find ourselves melted into tears, we weep then, not as the Abbate Gravia supposes through excess of pleasure, but through a certain petulant, impatient sorrow at our inability to grasp now, wholly, here on earth, at once and forever, those divine and rapturous joys, of which *through*

the poem, or *through* the music, we attain to but brief and indeterminate glimpses." [18]

Briefly, Poe implies something like this: the proper subject-
matter of poetry is Beauty, but since true Beauty exists only in
eternity, the poet cannot experience it and is deprived of his
subject-matter; by manipulating the materials of our present life,
we may *suggest that Beauty exists elsewhere,* and this is the best
that we can do.

This is not the same thing as the mysticism of such a writer
as Very, for Very sought to define what he considered a truth,
the experience of mystical beatitude, and the experience of human longing for it; the former experience, though inexpressible,
he strove to express clearly; the latter experience, since it was
clearly expressible, he expressed clearly. Very, moreover, as a
Christian, believed in moral judgment, in poetry and out, in spite
of the fact that as a Calvinist he seems to have believed that his
moral judgments were actually dictated by God. Nor is it the
same thing as the awareness on the part of Emily Dickinson of
the abyss between the human and the supra-human or the extra-
human, for she merely defines the tragic experience of confront-
ing the abyss and communicates her own moral adjustment to
the experience, or at least she does no more than this in her better
poems. Both poets seek to understand and both are as far as
may be successful; Poe seeks a justification for refusing to understand. Poe is no more a mystic than a moralist; he is an excited
sentimentalist.

As we may discover from other passages, especially in *The
Philosophy of Composition,* Poe had certain definite ideas in
regard to which forms of human experience lent themselves best
to this procedure, and also in regard to the rules of the procedure. Having decided, in an astonishing passage to which I
shall presently return, that a melancholy tone most greatly facili-
tated his purpose, he wrote: " 'Of all melancholy topics, what,
according to the universal understanding of mankind is the *most*
melancholy?' Death—was the obvious reply. 'And when,' I said,
'is this most melancholy of topics most poetical?' From what I
have already explained at some length, the answer here also is
obvious—'When it most closely allies itself to Beauty; the death,

[18] Ibid., 10–11.

then, of a beautiful woman is, unquestionably, the most poetical topic in the world. . . .' "[19] In other words, we are not concerned to understand human experience; we are seeking, rather, the isolated elements, or fragments, of experience which may best serve as the ingredients of a formula for the production of a kind of emotional delusion, and our final decision in the matter is determined again by our inability to distinguish between the subject and the style of poetry, by the conviction that beauty is the subject of poetry.

The reader should note carefully what this means; perhaps he will pardon me for restating it: the subject-matter of poetry, properly considered, is by definition incomprehensible and unattainable; the poet, in dealing with something else, toward which he has no intellectual or moral responsibilities whatever ("Unless incidentally," says Poe, "poetry has no concern whatever either with Duty or with Truth"[20]), should merely endeavor to *suggest that a higher meaning exists*—in other words, should endeavor to suggest the presence of a meaning when he is aware of none. The poet has only to write a good description of something physically impressive, with an air of mystery, an air of meaning concealed.

An air of mystery, of strangeness, will then be of necessity, not an adjunct of poetic style, but the very essence of poetic style. In *Ligeia* there occurs the well-known passage which it is now necessary to quote: " 'There is no exquisite beauty,' says Bacon, Lord Verulam, speaking truly of all the forms and genera of beauty, 'without some *strangeness* in the proportion.' " But in Poe's terms, strangeness and beauty, from the standpoint of the practical poet, are identical. Related to this concept is his concept of originality, which I shall take up later and separately.

Poe is, in brief, an explicit obscurantist. Hawthorne, in his four last and unfinished romances, gives us the physical embodiment of allegory without the meaning to be embodied, but he appears to hope for a meaning, to be, somehow, pathetically and unsuccessfully in search of one. Henry James, in many stories, as in *The Spoils of Poynton*, to choose an obvious example, gives us a sequence of facts without being able to pass judgment upon

[19] Ibid., I, 39.
[20] Ibid., I, 12.

them, so that the stories remain almost as inconclusive as Stockton's trivial tour de force, *The Lady or the Tiger?* Both men frequently write in advance of their understanding, the one as an allegorist, the other as a novelist. But in Poe, obscurantism has ceased to be merely an accident of inadequate understanding; it has become the explicit aim of writing and has begun the generation of a method. Poe's aesthetic is an aesthetic of obscurantism. We have that willful dislocation of feeling from understanding, which, growing out of the uncertainty regarding the nature of moral truth in general and its identity in particular situations which produced such writers as Hawthorne and James, was later to result through the exploitation of special techniques in the violent aberrations of the Experimental School of the twentieth century, culminating in the catastrophe of Hart Crane.[21]

Poe speaks a great deal of the need of originality. This quality, as he understands it, appears to be a fairly simple mechanical device, first, for fixing the attention, and second, for heightening the effect of strangeness. We may obtain a fair idea of his concept of originality of theme from his comment on a poem by Amelia Welby, quoted in the series of brief notes entitled *Minor Contemporaries:* "The subject has *nothing* of originality:—A widower muses by the grave of his wife. Here then is a great demerit; for originality of theme, if not absolutely first sought, should be among the first. Nothing is more clear than this proposition, although denied by the chlorine critics (the grass-green). The desire of the new is an element of the soul. The most exquisite pleasures grow dull in repetition. A strain of music enchants. Heard a second time, it pleases. Heard a tenth, it does not displease. We hear it a twentieth, and ask ourselves why we admired. At the fiftieth it produces ennui, at the hundredth disgust."[22]

Now I do not know what music most delighted Poe, unless perchance it may have been the melodies of Thomas Moore, but if I may be permitted to use exact numbers in the same figurative sense in which I conceive that Poe here used them, I am bound to say that my own experience with music differs profoundly. The trouble again is traceable to Poe's failure to under-

---

[21] For a detailed study of these techniques, see a volume by the present writer, *Primitivism and Decadence* (Arrow Editions, New York, 1937).

[22] Stedman and Woodberry, op. cit., III, 284.

stand the moral basis of art, to his view of art as a kind of stimulant, ingeniously concocted, which may, if one is lucky, raise one to a moment of divine delusion. A Bach fugue or a Byrd mass moves us not primarily because of any originality it may display, but because of its sublimity as I have already defined the term. Rehearing can do no more than give us a fuller and more secure awareness of this quality. The same is true of *Paradise Lost*. Poe fails to see that the originality of a poem lies not in the newness of the general theme—for if it did, the possibilities of poetry would have been exhausted long before the time of Poe—but in the quality of the personal intelligence, as that intelligence appears in the minutiae of style, in the defining limits of thought and of feeling, brought to the subject by the poet who writes of it. The originality, from Poe's point of view, of the subjects of such poems as *The Raven, The Sleeper*, and *Ulalume* would reside in the fantastic dramatic and scenic effects by means of which the subject of simple regret is concealed, diffused, and rendered ludicrous. From the same point of view, *Rose Aylmer* would necessarily be lacking in originality.

In *The Philosophy of Composition* Poe gives us a hint as to his conception of originality of style. After a brief discourse on originality of versification, and the unaccountable way in which it has been neglected, he states that he lays no claim to originality as regards the meter or the rhythm of *The Raven*, but only as regards the stanza: "nothing even remotely approaching this combination has ever been attempted." [23] Again we see Poe's tendency to rely upon the mechanically startling, in preference to the inimitable. This fact, coupled with his extraordinary theories of meter, which I shall examine separately, bear a close relationship to the clumsiness and insensitivity of his verse. Read three times, his rhythms disgust, because they are untrained and insensitive and have no individual life within their surprising mechanical frames.

Before turning to the principal poems for a brief examination of them, we should observe at least one remark on the subject of melancholy. In *The Philosophy of Composition*, after stating that, in planning *The Raven*, he had decided upon Beauty as the province of the poem, Poe writes as follows: "Regarding, then, Beauty as my province, my next question referred

[23] Ibid., I, 42.

to the tone of its highest manifestation—and all experience has shown that this tone is one of *sadness*. Beauty, of whatever kind, in its supreme development, invariably excites the sensitive soul to tears. Melancholy is thus the most legitimate of all the poetical tones."[24]

Now if the reader will keep in mind the principles that we have already deduced; namely, that Beauty is unattainable, that the poet can merely suggest its existence, that this suggestion depends upon the ingenious manipulation of the least obstructive elements of normal experience—it will at once be obvious that Poe is here suggesting a reversal of motivation. That is, since Beauty excites to tears (let us assume with Poe, for the moment, that it does), if we begin with tears, we may believe ourselves moved for a moment by Beauty. This interpretation is supported solidly by the last two sentences quoted, particularly when we regard their order.

The Philosophy of Composition thus appears after all to be a singularly shocking document. Were it an examination of the means by which a poet might communicate a comprehensible judgment, were it a plea that such communication be carefully planned in advance, we could do no less than approve. But it is not that; it is rather an effort to establish the rules for a species of incantation, of witchcraft; rules, whereby, through the manipulation of certain substances in certain arbitrary ways, it may be possible to invoke, more or less accidentally, something that appears more or less to be a divine emanation. It is not surprising that Poe expressed more than once a very qualified appreciation of Milton.

We may fairly conclude this phase of the discussion by a passage from *The Poetic Principle*, a passage quoted also by Miss Alterton: "It may be, indeed, that here this sublime end is, now and then, attained in fact. We are often made to feel, with a shivering delight, that from an earthly harp are stricken notes which *cannot* have been unfamiliar to the angels."[25] It should now be clear what Poe had in mind when he referred to Tennyson as the most elevating and the most pure of the poets; what Tennyson might have thought of the attribution is beside the point.

[24] Ibid., I, 36.
[25] Ibid., I, 12.

III

Before turning to the poems themselves, we should examine very briefly Poe's general theory of meter, as it appears primarily in *The Rationale of Verse*. And before doing this we should recall to mind in very general terms the common methods of scansion. They are: first, the classical, in which the measure is based upon quantity, or length of syllable, and in which accent is a source merely of variation and of complication; second, the French, or syllabic, in which the measure is a matter wholly of the number of syllables in the line, and in which the primary source of variation is quantity, if the language be one, like French, which lacks mechanical stress; third, the Anglo-Saxon, or accentual, in which the measure is based purely upon the number of accents, variation being derived from every other source possible; and fourth, the English, or accentual-syllabic, which resembles the classical system in its types of feet, but in which the foot and measure are determined by accent instead of by quantity.

Since it is with English verse, primarily, that we are dealing, we should note one or two other points in connection with it. First, the language is not divided into accented and unaccented syllables; within certain limits, there is an almost infinite variation of accent, and no two syllables are ever accented in exactly the same way. Consequently, for metrical purposes, a syllable is considered accented or unaccented only in relationship to the other syllables in the same foot. For example, let us take Ben Jonson's line:

Drink to/ me on/ly with/ thine eyes.

The accentuation of the first foot is inverted; in each of the other feet the accent falls on the second syllable. Yet the word *with*, which even in normal prose receives more accent than the last syllable of *only*, is less heavily accented than the word *thine*; so that in the last two feet we have a mounting series of four degrees of accent. This variety of accent is one form of variation in English meter; another is quantity; another is the normal procedure of substitution.

We may observe the obvious opposition of quantity to accent in the first foot, a normal iambic one, of this line from Robert Bridges:

Nay, barren are the mountains, and spent the streams.

The first syllable of the foot, *Nay,* is long and unaccented; the second and final syllable, *bar-,* is short and accented. On the other hand, length and accent may be brought to coincide; or there may be immeasurably subtle variations between the two extremes. These sources of variation, when understood and mastered, provide the fluid sensitivity to be found in the best English verse, within even the most rigid of patterns.

But to all this Poe appears oblivious. He says: "Accented syllables are of course always long."[26] This initial confusion is obviously related to Poe's preference for meters dependent upon a heavy, unvaried, and mechanical beat. He makes little use of quantity except as a reinforcement of accent; where it does not reinforce the accent, the failure is an accident and usually results in a clumsy variant rather than a pleasing one.

In *The Rationale of Verse,* Poe offers a new system for marking scansion, based in part upon the heresy which I have just mentioned, in part upon the equally gross concept that all syllables can be grouped into general classes, each class having a fixed and recognizable degree of accent. He is even so rash as to attempt the scansion of Horace on this basis, and to state that French verse is without music because the language is without accent. Poe had an ear for only the crudest of distinctions.

IV

The poems on which Poe's reputation as an important poet must rest are the following: *The City in the Sea, The Haunted Palace, The Conqueror Worm, Ulalume, The Raven,* and *The Sleeper.* These are the ambitious efforts; the others, even if one grant them a high measure of success, are minor. *The City in the Sea* is generally, and I believe rightly, regarded as Poe's best performance. After the first five lines, which are bad enough to have been written by Kipling, the poem displays few gross lapses and some excellent passages. There is admirable description, and there is throughout an intense feeling of meaning withheld. We have, in brief, all of the paraphernalia of allegory except the significance. The poem falls short of being one of the romantic

[26] Ibid., I, 60.

masterpieces of obscure emotionalism chiefly because of weak phrases: it remains Poe's most startling and talented failure.

In *The Haunted Palace*, the physical material has allegorical significance which is perfectly definite. The palace of the monarch Thought is the head; the windows are the eyes; the door is the mouth; the spirits are the thoughts, which issue as words. This, however, is not the real explanation of the poem, for the subject is the change from sanity to insanity. The change occurs in the fifth stanza, suddenly, and without motivation: we have feeling divorced completely from understanding; the change itself is mad, for it is inexplicable.

Ulalume contains very much the same problems as the other poems not yet considered. In examining this poem, we must confine ourselves strictly to what Poe offered us, namely, the poem, and refrain from biographical entanglements, which are both gratuitous and uncertain. If the poem is not self-sufficient, it is obscure; and, as critics of art, we are bound to rest with the assumption that the obscurity was satisfactory to Poe.

The poem opens with allusions to unidentified places, places with dark but unexplained histories: Weir, Auber, ghoul-haunted woodlands; we have, in other words, a good deal of ready-made Gothic mystery. The items are introduced to evoke emotion at small cost: they are familiar romantic devices, but they are none the less deliberately obscure. In the passage opening with the alley Titanic, and ending with Mount Yaanek and the Boreal Pole, we have an explicit reference to a period of violent feeling in the history of the protagonist: the cause and nature of the feeling are alike unexplained at the time, and even the loss of Ulalume, which is a very general sort of datum, is an inadequate account of feelings so grotesquely violent. In lines twenty to twenty-nine, there are dark references to a past event, references which are ultimately cleared up when we learn of the burial of Ulalume, but which, as we come to them, have the effect of gratuitous emotionalizing. Lines thirty to forty are the best in the poem: they hint of the strangeness of the nocturnal turning toward dawn, and then describe the appearance of Astarte, as the rising moon; if this strangeness has any spiritual significance, however, we are given no clue to it. The protagonist wishes to accept Astarte as a guide; Psyche distrusts her; they argue at length but darkly—darkly, in that the purpose of the protagonist and the fears of Psyche alike are not given us, so that the argument is like one in a dream. Psyche yields, but as she does so, they are led by Astarte to the door of the tomb, which brings the protagonist up shortly, with a cold realization of his loss. Lines ninety-five to one hundred and four, omitted by Griswold and by most of the cheap popular editions, but important, it would seem, to the poem, state the possibility that Astarte may have been conjured up to prevent their further irresponsible wandering in the haunted woodlands (which I take to represent the loose feelings through which they have been moving) by recalling them to a sense of definite tragedy.

In other words, the subject of grief is employed as a very general excuse for a good deal of obscure and only vaguely related emotion. This subject is used exactly as we should expect to find it used after examining Poe's aesthetic theory. The poem is as surely an excursion into the incoherencies of dream-consciousness as is the *Larme* of Rimbaud; yet it lacks wholly the fine surface of that poem.

In *The Raven*, that attenuated exercise for elocutionists, and in *The Sleeper*, the general procedure is identical, but the meter in the former and the writing in both are so thoroughly bad that other considerations appear unnecessary. *The Sleeper* is a kind of Gothic parody of Henry King's imperfect but none the less great *Exequy*: a comparison of the two poems will show the difference between moral grandeur and the sensationalism of a poet devoid of moral intelligence. It is noteworthy that King is commonly and justly regarded as one of the smaller poets of his period.

In *The Conqueror Worm*, the desire for inexpensive feeling has led to a piece of writing that is, phrase by phrase, solidly bromidic.

v

In his criticism of Hawthorne's *Tales*, Poe outlines his theory of the short story. He defends the tale, as preferable to the novel, on the same grounds as those on which he defends the short poem in preference to the long. He states the necessity of careful planning and of economy of means.

He says: ". . . having conceived with deliberate care, a

certain unique or single *effect* to be wrought out, he [the skillful literary artist] then invents such incidents—he then combines such events as may best aid him in establishing this preconceived effect." [27] Now the word *effect,* here as elsewhere in Poe, means impression, or mood; it is a word that connotes emotion purely and simply. So that we see the story-teller, like the poet, interested primarily in the creation of an emotion for its own sake, not in the understanding of an experience. It is significant in this connection that most of his heroes are mad or on the verge of madness; a datum which settles his action firmly in the realm of inexplicable feeling from the outset.

Morella begins thus: "With a feeling of deep yet most singular affection I regarded my friend *Morella.* Thrown by accident into her society many years ago, my soul, from our first meeting, burned with fires it had never before known; but the fires were not of Eros, and bitter and tormenting to my spirit was the gradual conviction that I could in no manner define their unusual meaning or regulate their vague intensity." And *Ligeia:* "I cannot, for my soul, remember how, when, or even precisely where, I first became acquainted with the Lady Ligeia. Long years have since elapsed, and my memory is feeble through much suffering." *The Assignation:* "Ill-fated and mysterious man!—bewildered in the brilliancy of thine own imagination, and fallen in the flames of thine own youth." *The Tell-Tale Heart:* "True!—nervous—very, very dreadfully nervous I had been and am! but why *will* you say that I am mad?" *Berenice:* ". . . it *is* wonderful what a stagnation there fell upon the springs of my life—wonderful how total an inversion took place in the character of my commonest thought." *Eleanora:* "I am come of a race noted for vigor of fancy and ardor of passion. Men have called me mad; but the question is not yet settled, whether madness is or is not the loftiest intelligence—whether much that is glorious—whether all that is profound—does not spring from disease of thought—from *moods* of mind exalted at the expense of the general intellect." Roderick Usher, in addition, is mad; *The Black Cat* is a study in madness; *The Masque of the Red Death* is a study in hallucinatory terror. They are all studies in hysteria; they are written for the sake of the hysteria.

[27] Ibid., II, 31.

In discussing Hawthorne, however, Poe suggests other possibilities: "We have said that the tale has a point of superiority even over the poem. In fact, while the rhythm of this latter is an essential aid in the development of the poem's highest idea—the idea of the Beautiful—the artificialities of this rhythm are an inseparable bar to the development of all points of thought or expression which have their basis in *Truth*. But Truth is often, and in very great degree, the aim of the tale. Some of the finest tales are tales of ratiocination. Thus the field of this species of composition, if not in so elevated a region on the mountain of the Mind, is a tableland of far vaster extent than the domain of the mere poem. Its products are never so rich, but infinitely more numerous, and infinitely more appreciable by the mass of mankind. The writers of the prose tale, in short, may bring to his theme a vast variety of modes of inflections of thought and expressions (the ratiocinative, for example, the sarcastic, or the humorous) which are not only antagonistic to the nature of the poem, but absolutely forbidden by one of its most peculiar and indispensable adjuncts; we allude, of course, to rhythm. It may be added here, par parenthèse, that the author who aims at the purely beautiful in a prose tale is laboring at a great disadvantage. For Beauty can be better treated in the poem. Not so with terror, or passion, or horror, or a multitude of other such points." [28]

Poe speaks in this passage, not only of the tale of effect, to which allusion has already been made, but of the tale of ratiocination, that is, of the detective story, such as *The Gold Bug* or *The Murders in the Rue Morgue*. It is noteworthy that this is the only example which he gives of the invasion of the field of fiction by Truth; in other words, his primary conception of intellectual activity in fiction appears to be in the contrivance of a puzzle. Between this childish view of intellectuality, on the one hand, and the unoriented emotionalism of the tale of effect on the other, we have that vast and solid region inhabited by the major literary figures of the world, the region in which human experience is understood in moral terms and emotion is the result of that understanding, or is seen in relationship to that understanding and so judged. This region appears to have been closed to Poe; if we except the highly schematized and crudely melo-

[28] Ibid., II, 31.

dramatic allegory of *William Wilson*, we have no basis for believing that he ever discovered it.

VI

If Poe's chief work is confined to the communication of feeling, what can we say of the quality of that communication? Poe rests his case for art on taste, and though we may disagree with him, yet we are bound to examine his own taste, for if he has no taste, he has nothing. It is my belief that he has little or none.

Every literary critic has a right to a good many errors of judgment; or at least every critic makes a good many. But if we survey Poe's critical opinions we can scarcely fail to be astonished by them. He understood little or nothing that was written before his own age, and though he was not unaware of the virtues, apparently, of some of the better stylists of his period, as for example Coleridge, he at one time or another praised such writers as R. H. Horne, N. P. Willis, Thomas Hood, and Thomas Moore as highly or more highly; in fact, he placed Horne and Moore among the greatest geniuses of all time. He praised Bryant above his American contemporaries, but he based his praise upon poems which did not deserve it. He was able to discover numerous grammatical errors in one of the lesser novels of Cooper, but he was unable to avoid making such errors in large numbers in his own prose; and the faultless, limpid, and unforgettable prose of the seventh chapter of *The Deerslayer*, the profundity of conception of *The Bravo*, the characterization of *Satanstoe* and *The Chainbearer*, were as far beyond his powers of comprehension as beyond his powers of creation.

If we neglect for a moment the underlying defect in all of Poe's work, the absence of theme, and scrutinize carefully the manner in which he communicates feeling, in which alone he is interested, we can scarcely avoid the observation that his work is compounded almost wholly of stereotyped expressions, most of them of a very melodramatic cast. Now one cannot object to a man wholly on the basis of stereotyped expression. There is a measure of stereotyped expression, apparently inadvertent, in many poems and works of prose which sustain themselves notwithstanding by virtue of a fundamental vigor of conception: W. H. Hudson is a writer of prose who sins extensively in this respect, but survives; Henry King is such a poet. On the other hand, the most finished masters of style, and this is perhaps especially true of the poets, have all, in some measure, employed the formulary phrase deliberately to achieve various but precise results: Crashaw, Milton, and Blake are familiar examples of the procedure. Indeed, if we imagine a very precise and solid substructure of theme, as in Crashaw's paraphrase of the *Twenty-third Psalm*, it is possible to see how a passage deliberately stereotyped in a certain measure, yet with a slight but precise admixture of personal perception, may at once define a traditional concept and the relationship of that concept to a personal perception, in fact the entire relationship of personal to traditional feeling—and the perception of such a relationship is in itself and as a whole a profoundly personal or original perception—in a manner more successful than any other conceivable; this procedure, however, presupposes a theme, a sense of history, or tradition, and a recognition of the poetic art as a technique of judgment, and it necessitates incidentally a masterly understanding and control of meter. Poe, on the other hand endeavors as far as may be to escape from a paraphrasable theme; he recognizes no obligation to understand the minimum of theme from which he cannot escape—in fact, he seems to recognize an obligation not to understand it; his historical training and understanding amounted nearly to nothing; so that there is nothing in his work either to justify his formulary expression and to give it content and precison of meaning, on the one hand, or, on the other, to give his work as a whole sufficient force and substance to make us forget the formulary expression—we merely have melodramatic stereotypes in a vacuum. The last instrument which, if well employed, might to some extent have alleviated his phrasing, and which did, in fact, alleviate it in part in a few fragments to which I shall presently allude, the instrument of meter, he was unable to control except occasionally and accidentally. His theory of meter was false. Whether the theory arose from imperception or led to imperception is immaterial, but the fact remains that his meter is almost invariably clumsy and mechanical in a measure perhaps never equalled by another poet who has enjoyed a comparable reputation. His favorite stanzaic and structural device, the device of mechanical repetition, is perhaps equally the result of his untrained and insensitive taste and of his feeling no responsibility to say anything accurately—when there is nothing in particular to be said, every technique is a technique of diffusion, for a technique of concise definition would reduce the poem to nothing.

To illustrate the weakness of detail in his poems and stories is an easy matter; to illustrate the extent of that weakness is impossible, for his work is composed of it. In his poems, one may enumerate the following passages as fairly well·executed, if one grants him temporarily his fundamental assumptions about art: *Ulalume,* lines thirty to thirty-eight, provided one can endure the meter; *The City in the Sea,* lines six to eleven, lines twenty-four to the end; *To One in Paradise,* the first stanza and perhaps the last; the early poem *To Helen,* especially the first three or four lines; *The Spirits of the Dead,* lines five to ten. Perhaps the only passage of his prose which displays comparable ability is the opening of *The Assignation:* the conception is merely that of the typically Byronic man of mystery, and the detail, in its rough identity, is comparably typical, but there is a certain life in the language, especially in the rhythm of the language, that renders the passage memorable.

For the rest, we encounter prose such as the following: "As if in the superhuman energy of his utterance there had been found the potency of a spell, the huge antique panels to which the speaker pointed threw slowly back, upon the instant, their ponderous and ebony jaws." "It was a voluptuous scene, that masquerade. But first let me tell of the rooms in which it was held. They were seven—an imperial suite." "Where were the souls of the haughty family of the bride, when, through thirst of gold, they permitted to pass the threshold of an apartment *so* bedecked, a maiden and a daughter so beloved?" "Morella's erudition was profound. As I hope to live, her talents were of no common order—her powers of mind were gigantic."

We are met on every page of his poetry with resounding puerilities such as "the pallid bust of Pallas," and "the viol, the violet, and the vine." The poetry, in fact, is composed almost wholly of such items as these:

Ah, broken is the golden bowl!—the spirit flown forever!
Let the bell toll! a saintly soul floats on the Stygian river:—
And, Guy de Vere, hast *thou* no tear?—weep now or never more!
See! on yon drear and rigid bier low lies thy love, Lenore!

At midnight in the month of June,
I stand beneath the mystic moon.

For alas! alas! with me
    The light of Life is o'er!
No more—no more—no more—
    (Such language holds the solemn sea
To the sands upon the shore)
    Shall bloom the thunder-blasted tree,
Or the stricken eagle soar!

That motley drama—oh, be sure
    It shall not be forgot!
With its Phantom chased forevermore,
    By a crowd that seize it not,
Through a circle that ever returneth in
    To the self-same spot,
And much of Madness, and more of Sin,
    And horror the soul of the plot.

And the silken, sad, uncertain rustling of each purple curtain
Thrilled me—filled me with fantastic terrors never felt before.

This is an art to delight the soul of a servant girl; it is a matter
for astonishment that mature men can be found to take this kind
of thing seriously. It is small wonder that the claims of Chivers
have been seriously advanced of late years in the face of such
an achievement; they have been fairly advanced, for Chivers is
nearly as admirable a poet. If one is in need of a standard, one
should have recourse to Bridges' *Eros,* to Hardy's *During Wind
and Rain,* or to Arnold's *Dover Beach.* And in making one's
final estimate of the quality of Poe's taste, one should not fail to
consider the style of his critical prose, of which the excerpts
quoted in the present essay are fair, and indeed, as specimens of
taste, are random examples.

VII

On what grounds, if any, can we then defend Poe? We can
obviously defend his taste as long as we honestly like it. The
present writer is willing to leave it, after these few remarks, to

its admirers. As to his critical theory, however, and the structural defects of his work, it appears to me certain that the difficulty which I have raised is the central problem in Poe criticism; yet not only has it never been met, but, so far as one can judge, it has scarcely been recognized.

The attempt to justify Poe on the basis of his place in history can arise only from a confusion of processes: to explain a man's place in history is not the same thing as to judge his value. Poe was largely formed by the same influences which formed other men, both better and worse, Coleridge as well as Chivers; his particular nature resulted in his pushing certain essential romantic notions very nearly as far as they could go. It is unlikely, on the other hand, that the course of romantic literature would have been very different except (perhaps) in America, had Poe never been born; in any event, his influence could only have been a bad one, and to assert that he exerted an influence is not to praise him. His clinical value resides in the fact that as a specimen of late romantic theory and practice he is at once extreme and typical. To understand the nature of his confusion is to come nearer to an understanding not only of his American contemporaries, but of French Symbolism and of American Experimentalism as well.

There are, I believe, two general lines of argument or procedure that may be used more or less in support of Poe's position; one is that of the Alterton-Craig Introduction, the other is that (if I may cite another eminent example) of Professor Floyd Stovall.

The argument of the Introduction appears to be roughly that Poe is an intellectual poet, because: first, he worked out in *Eureka* a theory of cosmic harmony and unity; second, related to this, he held a theory of the harmony and unity of the parts of the poem; and third, he devoted a certain amount of rational effort to working out the rules by which this harmony and unity could be attained.

But this intellectuality, if that is the name for it, is all anterior to the poem, not in the poem; it resides merely in the rules for the practice of the obscurantism which I have defined. The Introduction cites as evidence of Poe's recognition of the intellectual element in poetry, his essay on Drake and Halleck, yet the intellectuality in question here is plainly of the sort which I have just described. As a result, Professor Craig's comparison of Poe to Donne, Dryden, and Aquinas, is, to the present writer at least, profoundly shocking.

The only alternative is that of Professor Stovall, as well as of a good many others: to accept Poe's theory of Beauty as if it were clearly understood and then to examine minor points of Poe criticism with lucidity and with learning. But Poe's theory of Beauty is not understood, and no casual allusion to Plato will ever clarify it.

III. 1949 to Present

In "From Poe to Valéry," his only major essay on Poe, THOMAS STEARNS ELIOT [1888–1965] describes the "immense" though "puzzling" influence of Poe on three successive generations of poets in France, especially the direct impact of Poe's poetic theory and practice on Baudelaire, Mallarmé, and Valéry. Despite Poe's "flavor of provinciality," faults of poetic diction, and dubious notions about the long poem and the creative process, Eliot finds that "by trying to look at Poe through the eyes of Baudelaire, Mallarmé, and most of all Valéry, I become more thoroughly convinced of his importance, of the importance of his *work* as a whole."

From Poe to Valéry

THOMAS STEARNS ELIOT

What I attempt here is not a judicial estimate of Edgar Allan Poe; I am not trying to decide his rank as a poet or to isolate his essential originality. Poe is indeed a stumbling block for the judicial critic. If we examine his work in detail, we seem to find in it nothing but slipshod writing, puerile thinking unsupported by wide reading or profound scholarship, haphazard experiments in various types of writing, chiefly under pressure of financial need, without perfection in any detail. This would not be just. But if, instead of regarding his work analytically, we take a distant view of it as a whole, we see a mass of unique shape and impressive size to which the eye constantly returns. Poe's influence is equally puzzling. In France the influence of his poetry and of his poetic theories has been immense. In England and America it seems almost negligible. Can we point to any poet whose style appears to have been formed by a study of Poe? The only one whose name immediately suggests itself is —Edward Lear. And yet one cannot be sure that one's own writing has *not* been influenced by Poe. I can name positively certain poets whose work has influenced me, I can name others whose work, I am sure, has not; there may be still others of whose influence I am unaware, but whose influence I might be brought to acknowledge; but about Poe I shall never be sure. He wrote very few poems, and of those few only half a dozen

Library of Congress Lecture, November 19, 1948; published in *Hudson Review*, Autumn 1949.

have had a great success: but those few are as well known to as large a number of people, are as well remembered by everybody, as any poems ever written. And some of his tales have had an important influence upon authors, and in types of writing where such influence would hardly be expected.

I shall here make no attempt to explain the enigma. At most, this is a contribution to the study of his influence; and an elucidation, partial as it may be, of one cause of Poe's importance in the light of that influence. I am trying to look at him, for a moment, as nearly as I can, through the eyes of three French poets, Baudelaire, Mallarmé, and especially Paul Valéry. The sequence is itself important. These three French poets represent the beginning, the middle and the end of a particular tradition in poetry. Mallarmé once told a friend of mine that he came to Paris because he wanted to know Baudelaire; that he had once seen him at a bookstall on a quai, but had not had the courage to accost him. As for Valéry, we know from the first letter to Mallarmé, written when he was hardly more than a boy, of his discipleship of the elder poet; and we know of his devotion to Mallarmé until Mallarmé's death. Here are three literary generations, representing almost exactly a century of French poetry. Of course, these are poets very different from each other; of course, the literary progeny of Baudelaire was numerous and important, and there are other lines of descent from him. But I think we can trace the development and descent of one particular theory of the nature of poetry through these three poets and it is a theory which takes its origin in the theory, still more than in the practice, of Edgar Poe. And the impression we get of the influence of Poe is the more impressive, because of the fact that Mallarmé, and Valéry in turn, did not merely derive from Poe through Baudelaire: each of them subjected himself to that influence directly, and has left convincing evidence of the value which he attached to the theory and practice of Poe himself. Now, we all of us like to believe that we understand our own poets better than any foreigner can do; but I think we should be prepared to entertain the possibility that these Frenchmen have seen something in Poe that English-speaking readers have missed.

My subject, then, is not simply Poe but Poe's effect upon three French poets, representing three successive generations;

and my purpose is also to approach an understanding of a peculiar attitude towards poetry, by the poets themselves, which is perhaps the most interesting, possibly the most characteristic, and certainly the most original development of the esthetic of verse made in that period as a whole. It is all the more worthy of examination if, as I incline to believe, this attitude towards poetry represents a phase which has come to an end with the death of Valéry. For our study of it should help towards the understanding of whatever it may be that our generation and the next will find to take its place.

Before concerning myself with Poe, as he appeared in the eyes of these French poets, I think it as well to present my own impression of his status among A.nerican and English readers and critics; for, if I am wrong, you may have to criticise what I say of his influence in France with my errors in mind. It does not seem to me unfair to say that Poe has been regarded as a minor, or secondary, follower of the Romantic Movement: a successor to the so-called "Gothic" novelists in his fiction, and a follower of Byron and Shelley in his verse. This however is to place him in the English tradition; and there certainly he does not belong. English readers sometimes account for that in Poe which is outside of any English tradition, by saying that it is American; but this does not seem to me wholly true either, especially when we consider the other American writers of his own and an earlier generation. There is a certain flavour of provinciality about his work, in a sense in which Whitman is not in the least provincial: it is the provinciality of the person who is not at home where he belongs, but cannot get to anywhere else. Poe is a kind of displaced European; he is attracted to Paris, to Italy and to Spain, to places which he could endow with romantic gloom and grandeur. Although his ambit of movement hardly extended beyond the limits of Richmond and Boston longitudinally, and neither east nor west of these centres, he seems a wanderer with no fixed abode. There can be few authors of such eminence who have drawn so little from their own roots, who have been so isolated from any surroundings.

I believe the view of Poe taken by the ordinary cultivated English or American reader is something like this: Poe is the author of a few, a very few short poems which enchanted him for a time when he was a boy, and which do somehow stick in the memory. I do not think that he re-reads these poems, unless he turns to them in the pages of an anthology; his enjoyment of them is rather the memory of an enjoyment which he may for a moment recapture. They seem to him to belong to a particular period when his interest in poetry had just awakened. Certain images, and still more certain rhythms, abide with him. This reader also remembers certain of the tales—not very many—and holds the opinion that *The Gold Bug* was quite good for its time, but that detective fiction has made great strides since then. And he may sometimes contrast him with Whitman, having frequently re-read Whitman, but not Poe.

As for the prose, it is recognised that Poe's tales had great influence upon some types of popular fiction. So far as detective fiction is concerned, nearly everything can be traced to two authors: Poe and Wilkie Collins. The two influences sometimes concur, but are also responsible for two different types of detective. The efficient professional policeman originates with Collins, the brilliant and eccentric amateur with Poe. Conan Doyle owes much to Poe, and not merely to Monsieur Dupin of *The Murders in the Rue Morgue*. Sherlock Holmes was deceiving Watson when he told him that he had bought his Stradivarius violin for a few shillings at a second-hand shop in the Tottenham Court Road. He found that violin in the ruins of the house of Usher. There is a close similarity between the musical exercises of Holmes and those of Roderick Usher: those wild and irregular improvisations which, although on one occasion they sent Watson off to sleep, must have been excruciating to any ear trained to music. It seems to me probable that the romances of improbable and incredible adventure of Rider Haggard found their inspiration in Poe—and Haggard himself had imitators enough. I think it equally likely that H. G. Wells, in his early romances of scientific exploration and invention, owed much to the stimulus of some of Poe's narratives—*Gordon Pym*, or *A Descent into the Maelström* for example, or *The Facts in the Case of Monsieur Valdemar*. The compilation of evidence I leave to those who are interested to pursue the enquiry. But I fear that nowadays too few readers open *She* or *The War of the Worlds* or *The Time Machine:* fewer still are capable of being thrilled by their predecessors.

What strikes me first, as a general difference between the

way in which the French poets whom I have cited took Poe, and the way of American and English critics of equivalent authority, is the attitude of the former towards Poe's *œuvre,* towards his work as a whole. Anglo-Saxon critics are, I think, more inclined to make separate judgments of the different parts of an author's work. We regard Poe as a man who dabbled in verse and in several kinds of prose, without settling down to make a thoroughly good job of any one *genre.* These French readers were impressed by the variety of form of expression, because they found, or thought they found, an essential unity; while admitting, if necessary, that much of the work is fragmentary or occasional, owing to circumstances of poverty, frailty, and vicissitude, they nevertheless take him as an author of such seriousness that his work must be grasped as a whole. This represents partly a difference between two kinds of critical mind; but we must claim, for our own view, that it is supported by our awareness of the blemishes and imperfections of Poe's actual writing. It is worth while to illustrate these faults, as they strike an English-speaking reader.

Poe had, to an exceptional degree, the feeling for the incantatory element in poetry, of that which may, in the most nearly literal sense, be called "the magic of verse." His versification is not, like that of the greatest masters of prosody, of the kind which yields a richer melody, through study and long habituation, to the maturing sensibility of the reader returning to it at times throughout his life. Its effect is immediate and undeveloping; it is probably much the same for the sensitive schoolboy and for the ripe mind and cultivated ear. In this unchanging immediacy, it partakes perhaps more of the character of very good *verse* than of poetry—but that is to start a hare which I have no intention of following here, for it is, I am sure, "poetry" and not "verse." It has the effect of an incantation which, because of its very crudity, stirs the feelings at a deep and almost primitive level. But, in his choice of the word which has the right *sound,* Poe is by no means careful that it should have also the right *sense.* I will give one comparison of uses of the same word by Poe and by Tennyson—who, of all English poets since Milton, had probably the most accurate and fastidious appreciation of the sound of syllables. In Poe's *Ulalume*— to my mind one of his most successful, as well as typical, poems —we find the lines

> It was night, in the lonesome October
> Of my most immemorial year.

Immemorial, according to the Oxford Dictionary, means: "that is beyond memory or out of mind; ancient beyond memory or record; extremely old." None of these meanings seems applicable to this use of the word by Poe. The year was not beyond memory—the speaker remembers one incident in it very well; at the conclusion he even remembers a funeral in the same place just a year earlier. The line of Tennyson, equally well known, and justly admired because the sound of the line responds so well to the sound which the poet wishes to evoke, may already have come to mind:

> The moan of doves in immemorial elms.

Here *immemorial,* besides having the most felicitous sound value, is exactly the word for trees so old that no one knows just how old they are.

Poetry, of different kinds, may be said to range from that in which the attention of the reader is directed primarily to the sound, to that in which it is directed primarily to the sense. With the former kind, the sense may be apprehended almost unconsciously; with the latter kind—at these two extremes—it is the sound, of the operation of which upon us we are unconscious. But, with either type, sound and sense must cooperate; in even the most purely incantatory poem, the dictionary meaning of words cannot be disregarded with impunity.

An irresponsibility towards the meaning of words is not infrequent with Poe. *The Raven* is, I think, far from being Poe's best poem; though, partly because of the analysis which the author gives in *The Philosophy of Composition,* it is the best known.

> In there stepped a stately Raven of the saintly days of yore.

Since there is nothing particularly saintly about the raven, if indeed the ominous bird is not wholly the reverse, there can be no point in referring his origin to a period of saintliness, even if such a period can be assumed to have existed. We have just heard the raven described as *stately;* but we are told presently that he is *ungainly,* an attribute hardly to be reconciled, without a good deal of explanation, with *stateliness.* Several words in the poem seem to be inserted either merely to fill out the line to the required measure, or for the sake of a rhyme. The bird is addressed as "no craven" quite needlessly, except for the pressing need of a rhyme to "raven"—a surrender to the exigencies of rhyme with which I am sure Malherbe would have had no patience. And there is not always even such schoolboy justification as this: to say that the lamplight "gloated o'er" the sofa cushions is a freak of fancy which, even were it relevant to have a little gloating going on somewhere, would appear forced.

Imperfections in *The Raven* such as these—and one could give others—may serve to explain why *The Philosophy of Composition,* the essay in which Poe professes to reveal his method in composing *The Raven*—has not been taken so seriously in England or America as in France. It is difficult for us to read that essay without reflecting, that if Poe plotted out his poem with such calculation, he might have taken a little more pains over it: the result hardly does credit to the method. Therefore we are likely to draw the conclusion that Poe in analyzing his poem was practising either a hoax, or a piece of self-deception in setting down the way in which he wanted to think that he had written it. Hence the essay has not been taken so seriously as it deserves.

Poe's other essays in poetic esthetic deserve consideration also. No poet, when he writes his own *art poétique,* should hope to do much more than explain, rationalise, defend, or prepare the way for his own practice: that is, for writing his own kind of poetry. He may think that he is establishing laws for all poetry; but what he has to say that is worth saying has its immediate relation to the way in which he himself writes or wants to write: though it may well be equally valid to his immediate juniors, and extremely helpful to them. We are only safe in finding, in his writing about poetry, principles valid for any poetry, so long as we check what he says by the kind of poetry he writes. Poe has a remarkable passage about the impossibility of writing a long poem—for a long poem, he holds, is at best a series of short poems strung together. What we have to bear in mind is that he himself was incapable of writing a long poem. He could conceive only a poem which was a single simple effect: for him, the whole of a poem had to be in one mood. Yet it is only in a poem of some length that a variety of moods can be expressed; for a

variety of moods requires a number of different themes or subjects, related either in themselves or in the mind of the poet.
These parts can form a whole which is more than the sum of the
parts; a whole such that the pleasure we derive from the reading
of any part is enhanced by our grasp of the whole. It follows
also that in a long poem some parts may be deliberately planned
to be less "poetic" than others: these passages may show no
lustre when extracted, but may be intended to elicit, by contrast,
the significance of other parts, and to unite them into a whole
more significant than any of the parts. A long poem may gain
by the widest possible variations of intensity. But Poe wanted
a poem to be of the first intensity throughout: it is questionable
whether he could have appreciated the more philosophical passages in Dante's *Purgatorio.* What Poe had said has proved in
the past of great comfort to other poets equally incapable of
the long poem; and we must recognize that the question of the
possibility of writing a long poem is not simply that of the
strength and staying power of the individual poet, but may have
to do with the conditions of the age in which he finds himself.
And what Poe has to say on the subject is illuminating, in helping us to understand the point of view of poets for whom the
long poem is impossible.

The fact that for Poe a poem had to be the expression of a
single mood—it would here be too long an excursus to try to
demonstrate that *The Bells,* as a deliberate exercise in several
moods, is as much a poem of one mood as any of Poe's—this fact
can better be understood as a manifestation of a more fundamental weakness. Here, what I have to say I put forward only
tentatively: but it is a view which I should like to launch in
order to see what becomes of it. My account may go to explain,
also, why the work of Poe has for many readers appealed at a
particular phase of their growth, at the period of life when they
were just emerging from childhood. That Poe had a powerful
intellect is undeniable: but it seems to me the intellect of a highly
gifted young person before puberty. The forms which his lively
curiosity takes are those in which a pre-adolescent mentality
delights: wonders of nature and of mechanics and of the supernatural, cryptograms and cyphers, puzzles and labyrinths,
mechanical chess-players and wild flights of speculation. The
variety and ardour of his curiosity delight and dazzle; yet in the

end the eccentricity and lack of coherence of his interests tire. There is just that lacking which gives dignity to the mature man: a consistent view of life. An attitude can be mature and consistent, and yet be highly sceptical: but Poe was no sceptic. He appears to yield himself completely to the idea of the moment: the effect is, that all of his ideas seem to be *entertained* rather than believed. What is lacking is not brain power, but that maturity of intellect which comes only with the maturing of the man as a whole, the development and coordination of his various emotions. I am not concerned with any possible psychological or pathological explanation: it is enough for my purpose to record that the work of Poe is such as I should expect of a man of very exceptional mind and sensibility, whose emotional development has been in some respect arrested at an early age. His most vivid imaginative realizations are the realization of a dream: significantly, the ladies in his poems and tales are always ladies lost, or ladies vanishing before they can be embraced. Even in *The Haunted Palace,* where the subject appears to be his own weakness of alcoholism, the disaster has no moral significance; it is treated impersonally as an isolated phenomenon; it has not behind it the terrific force of such lines as those of François Villon when he speaks of his own fallen state.

Having said as much as this about Poe, I must proceed to enquire what it was that three great French poets found in his work to admire, which we have not found. We must first take account of the fact that none of these poets knew the English language very well. Baudelaire must have read a certain amount of English and American poetry: he certainly borrows from Gray, and apparently from Emerson. He was never familiar with England, and there is no reason to believe that he spoke the language at all well. As for Mallarmé, he taught English and there is convincing evidence of his imperfect knowledge, for he committed himself to writing a kind of guide to the use of the language. An examination of this curious treatise, and the strange phrases which he gives under the impression that they are familiar English proverbs, should dispel any rumour of Mallarmé's English scholarship. As for Valéry, I never heard him speak a word of English, even in England. I do not know what he had read in our language: Valéry's second language, the influence of which is perceptible in some of his verse, was Italian.

It is certainly possible, in reading something in a language imperfectly understood, for the reader to find what is not there; and when the reader is himself a man of genius, the foreign poem read may, by a happy accident, elicit something important from the depths of his own mind, which he attributes to what he reads. And it is true that in translating Poe's prose into French, Baudelaire effected a striking improvement: he transformed what is often a slipshod and a shoddy English prose into admirable French. Mallarmé, who translated a number of Poe's poems into French prose, effected a similar improvement: but on the other hand, the rhythms, in which we find so much of the originality of Poe, are lost. The evidence that the French overrated Poe because of their imperfect knowledge of English remains accordingly purely negative: we can venture no farther than saying that they were not disturbed by weaknesses of which we are very much aware. It does not account for their high opinion of Poe's *thought*, for the value which they attached to his philosophical and critical exercises. To understand that we must look elsewhere.

We must, at this point, avoid the error of assuming that Baudelaire, Mallarmé, and Valéry all responded to Poe in exactly the same way. They are great poets, and they are each very different from the other; furthermore, they represent, as I have reminded you, three different generations. It is with Valéry that I am here chiefly concerned. I therefore say only that Baudelaire, to judge by his introduction to his translation of the tales and essays, was the most concerned with the personality of the man. With the accuracy of his portrait I am not concerned: the point is that in Poe, in his life, his isolation and his worldly failure, Baudelaire found the prototype of *le poète maudit*, the poet as the outcast of society—the type which was to realise itself, in different ways, in Verlaine and Rimbaud, the type of which Baudelaire saw himself as a distinguished example. This nineteenth-century archetype, *le poète maudit*, the rebel against society and against middle-class morality (a rebel who descends of course from the continental myth of the figure of Byron) corresponds to a particular social situation. But, in the course of an introduction which is primarily a sketch of the man Poe and his biography, Baudelaire lets fall one remark indicative of an esthetic that brings us to Valéry:

He believed [says Baudelaire], true poet that he was, that the goal of poetry is of the same nature as its principle, and that it should have nothing in view but itself.

"A poem does not say something—it *is* something": that doctrine has been held in more recent times.

The interest for Mallarmé is rather in the technique of verse, though Poe's is, as Mallarmé recognises, a kind of versification which does not lend itself to use in the French language. But when we come to Valéry, it is neither the man nor the poetry, but the *theory* of poetry, that engages his attention. In a very early letter to Mallarmé, written when he was a very young man, introducing himself to the elder poet, he says: "I prize the theories of Poe, so profound and so insidiously learned; I believe in the omnipotence of rhythm, and especially in the suggestive phrase." But I base my opinion, not primarily upon this credo of a very young man, but upon Valéry's subsequent theory and practice. In the same way that Valéry's poetry, and his essays on the art of poetry, are two aspects of the same interest of his mind and complement each other, so for Valéry the poetry of Poe is inseparable from Poe's poetic theories.

This brings me to the point of considering the meaning of the term "la poésie pure": the French phrase has a connotation of discussion and argument which is not altogether rendered by the term "pure poetry."

All poetry may be said to start from the emotions experienced by human beings in their relations to themselves, to each other, to divine beings, and to the world about them; it is therefore concerned also with thought and action, which emotion brings about, and out of which emotion arises. But, at however primitive a stage of expression and appreciation, the function of poetry can never be simply to arouse these same emotions in the audience of the poet. You remember the account of Alexander's feast in the famous ode of Dryden. If the conqueror of Asia was actually transported with the violent emotions which the bard Timotheus, by skillfully varying his music, is said to have aroused in him, then the great Alexander was at the moment suffering from automatism induced by alcohol poisoning, and was in that state completely incapable of appreciating musical or poetic art. In the earliest poetry, or in the most rudimentary enjoyment of poetry, the attention of the listener is directed upon the subject matter; the effect of the poetic art is felt, without the listener's being wholly conscious of this art. With the development of the consciousness of language, there is another stage, at which the auditor, who may by that time have become the reader, is aware of a double interest in a story for its own sake, and in the way in which it is told: that is to say, he becomes aware of style. Then we may take a delight in discrimination between the ways in which different poets will handle the same subject; an appreciation not merely of better or worse, but of differences between styles which are equally admired. At a third stage of development, the subject may recede to the background: instead of being the purpose of the poem, it becomes simply a necessary means for the realization of the poem. At this stage the reader or listener may become as nearly indifferent to the subject matter as the primitive listener was to the style. A complete unconsciousness or indifference to the style at the beginning, or to the subject matter at the end, would however take us outside of poetry altogether: for a complete unconsciousness of anything but subject matter would mean that for that listener poetry had not yet appeared; a complete unconsciousness of anything but style would mean that poetry had vanished.

This process of increasing self-consciousness—or, we may say, of increasing consciousness of language—has as its theoretical goal what we may call *la poésie pure*. I believe it to be a goal that can never be reached, because I think that poetry is only poetry so long as it preserves some "impurity" in this sense: that is to say, so long as the subject matter is valued for its own sake. The Abbé Brémond, if I have understood him, maintains that while the element of *la poésie pure* is necessary to make a poem a poem, no poem can consist of *la poésie pure* solely. But what has happened in the case of Valéry is a change of attitude toward the subject matter. We must be careful to avoid saying that the subject matter becomes "less important." It has rather a different kind of importance: it is important as *means:* the *end* is the poem. The subject exists for the poem, not the poem for the subject. A poem may employ several subjects, combining them in a particular way; and it may be meaningless to ask "What is the subject of the poem?" From the union of several subjects there appears, not another subject, but the poem.

Here I should like to point out the difference between a theory of poetry propounded by a student of esthetics, and the same theory as held by a poet. It is one thing when it is simply an account of how the poet writes, without knowing it, and another thing when the poet himself writes consciously according to that theory. In affecting writing, the theory becomes a different thing from what it was merely as an explanation of how the poet writes. And Valéry was a poet who wrote very consciously and deliberately indeed: perhaps, at his best, not wholly under the guidance of theory; but his theorizing certainly affected the kind of poetry that he wrote. He was the most self-conscious of all poets.

To the extreme self-consciousness of Valéry must be added another trait: his extreme scepticism. It might be thought that such a man, without belief in anything which could be the subject of poetry, would find refuge in a doctrine of "art for art's sake." But Valéry was much too sceptical to believe even in art. It is significant, the number of times that he describes something he has written as an *ébauche*—a rough draft. He had ceased to believe in *ends*, and was only interested in *processes*. It often seems as if he had continued to write poetry, simply because he was interested in the introspective observation of himself engaged in writing it: one has only to read the several essays—sometimes indeed more exciting than his verse, because one suspects that he was more excited in writing them—in which he records his observations. There is a revealing remark in *Variété V*, the last of his books of collected papers: "As for myself, who am, I confess, much more concerned with the formation or the fabrication of works [of art] than with the works themselves," and, a little later in the same volume: "In my opinion the most authentic philosophy is not in the objects of reflection, so much as in the very act of thought and its manipulation."

Here we have, brought to their culmination by Valéry, two notions which can be traced back to Poe. There is first the doctrine, elicited from Poe by Baudelaire, which I have already quoted: "A poem should have nothing in view but itself"; second the notion that the composition of a poem should be as conscious and deliberate as possible, that the poet should observe himself in the act of composition—and this, in a mind as sceptical as Valéry's, leads to the conclusion, so paradoxically inconsistent with the other, that the act of composition is more interesting than the poem which results from it.

First, there is the "purity" of Poe's poetry. In the sense in which we speak of "purity of language" Poe's poetry is very far from pure, for I have commented upon Poe's carelessness and unscrupulousness in the use of words. But in the sense of *la poésie pure*, that kind of purity came easily to Poe. The subject is little, the treatment is everything. He did not have to achieve purity by a process of purification, for his material was already tenuous. Second, there is that defect in Poe to which I alluded when I said that he did not appear to believe, but rather to entertain, theories. And here again, with Poe and Valéry, extremes meet, the immature mind playing with ideas because it had not developed to the point of convictions, and the very adult mind playing with ideas because it was too sceptical to hold convictions. It is by this contrast, I think, that we can account for Valéry's admiration for *Eureka*—that cosmological fantasy which makes no deep impression upon most of us, because we are aware of Poe's lack of qualification in philosophy, theology, or natural science, but which Valéry, after Baudelaire, esteemed highly as a "prose poem." Finally, there is the astonishing result of Poe's analysis of the composition of *The Raven*. It does not matter whether *The Philosophy of Composition* is a hoax, or a piece of self-deception, or a more or less accurate record of Poe's calculations in writing the poem; what matters is that it suggested to Valéry a method and an occupation—that of observing himself write. Of course, a greater than Poe had already studied the poetic process. In the *Biographia Literaria* Coleridge is concerned primarily, of course, with the poetry of Wordsworth; and he did not pursue his philosophical enquiries concurrently with the writing of his poetry; but he does anticipate the question which fascinated Valéry: "What am I doing when I write a poem?" Yet Poe's *Philosophy of Composition* is a *mise au point* of the question which gives it capital importance in relation to this process which ends with Valéry. For the penetration of the poetic by the introspective critical activity is carried to the limit by Valéry, the limit at which the latter begins to destroy the former. M. Louis Bolle, in his admirable study of this poet, observes pertinently: "This intellectual narcissism is not alien to the poet, even though he does not explain the whole of his work:

'why not conceive as a work of art the production of a work of art?' "

Now, as I think I have already hinted, I believe that the *art poétique* of which we find the germ in Poe, and which bore fruit in the work of Valéry, has gone as far as it can go. I do not believe that this esthetic can be of any help to later poets. What will take its place I do not know. An esthetic which merely contradicted it would not do. To insist on the all-importance of subject-matter, to insist that the poet should be spontaneous and irreflective, that he should depend upon inspiration and neglect technique, would be a lapse from what is in any case a highly civilized attitude to a barbarous one. We should have to have an esthetic which somehow comprehended and transcended that of Poe and Valéry. This question does not greatly exercise my mind, since I think that the poet's theories should arise out of his practice rather than his practice out of his theories. But I recognise first that within this tradition from Poe to Valéry are some of those modern poems which I most admire and enjoy; second, I think that the tradition itself represents the most interesting development of poetic consciousness anywhere in that same hundred years; and finally I value this exploration of certain poetic possibilities for its own sake, as we believe that all possibilities should be explored. And I find that by trying to look at Poe through the eyes of Baudelaire, Mallarmé, and most of all Valéry, I become more thoroughly convinced of his importance, of the importance of his *work* as a whole. And, as for the future: it is a tenable hypothesis that this advance of self-consciousness, the extreme awareness of and concern for language which we find in Valéry, is something which must ultimately break down, owing to an increasing strain against which the human mind and nerves will rebel; just as, it may be maintained, the indefinite elaboration of scientific discovery and invention, and of political and social machinery, may reach a point at which there will be an irresistible revulsion of humanity and a readiness to accept the most primitive hardships rather than carry any longer the burden of modern civilization. Upon that I hold no fixed opinion: I leave it to your consideration.

WYSTAN HUGH AUDEN [1907–   ], in this Introduction to *Edgar Allan Poe: Selected Prose and Poetry* (1950), clarifies the "operatic" function of the décor and style in Poe's impressionistic tales. Conventionally rhetorical though it be, to Auden the style is "dramatically right." Most noteworthy are Auden's description and classification of the heroes in the tales and his high estimate of *Eureka* and *The Narrative of Arthur Gordon Pym.*

Introduction

WYSTAN HUGH AUDEN

What every author hopes to receive from posterity—a hope usually disappointed—is justice. Next to oblivion, the two fates which he most fears are becoming the name attached to two or three famous pieces while the rest of his work is unread and becoming the idol of a small circle which reads every word he wrote with the same uncritical reverence. The first fate is unjust because, even if the pieces known are indeed his best work, the reader has not earned the right to say so; the second fate is embarrassing and ridiculous, for no author believes he is that good.

Poe's shade must be more disappointed than most. Certain pieces—how he must hate these old war horses—are probably more familiar to non-Americans than are any pieces by any other American author. I myself cannot remember hearing any poetry before hearing "The Raven" and "The Bells"; and *The Pit and the Pendulum* was one of the first short stories I ever read. At the same time, the known works of no other author of comparable rank and productivity are so few and so invariably the same. In preparing to make this selection, for example, I asked a number of persons whom I knew to be widely read, but not specialists in American letters, if they had read *Gordon Pym* and *Eureka,* which seem to me to rank among Poe's most important works; not one of them had. On the other hand, I was informed by everyone that to omit *The Cask of Amontillado,* which for my taste is an inferior story, would be commercial suicide. Poor Poe! At first so forgotten that his grave went without a tombstone twenty-six years—when one was finally erected the only

From *Edgar Allan Poe: Selected Prose and Poetry,* 1950.

American author to attend the ceremony was Whitman; and to-day in danger of becoming the life study of a few professors. The professors are, of course, very necessary, for it is through their devoted labors that Poe may finally reach the kind of reader every author hopes for, who will read him all, good-humoredly willing to wade through much which is dull or inferior for the delight of discovering something new and admirable.

The Tales

Varied in subject, treatment, style as Poe's stories are, they have one negative characteristic in common. There is no place in any of them for the human individual as he actually exists in space and time, that is, as simultaneously a natural creature subject in his feelings to the influences and limitations of the natural order, and an historical person, creating novelty and relations by his free choice and modified in unforeseen ways by the choices of others.

Poe's major stories fall roughly into two groups. The first group is concerned with states of willful being, the destructive passion of the lonely ego to merge with the ego of another (*Ligeia*), the passion of the conscious ego to be objective, to discover by pure reason the true relationships which sensory appearances and emotions would conceal (*The Purloined Letter*), self-destructive states in which the ego and the self are passionately hostile (*The Imp of the Perverse*), even the state of chimerical passion, that is, the passionate unrest of a self that lacks all passion (*The Man of the Crowd*). The horror tales and the tales of ratiocination belong together, for the heroes of both exist as unitary states—Roderick Usher reasons as little as Auguste Dupin feels. Personages who are the embodiment of such states cannot, of course, change or vary in intensity either through changes in themselves or their environment. The problem in writing stories of this kind is to prevent the reader from ever being reminded of historical existence, for, if he once thinks of real people whose passions are interrupted by a need for lunch or whose beauty can be temporarily and mildly impaired by the common cold, the intensity and timelessness become immediately comic. Poe is sometimes attacked for the operatic quality of the prose and *décor* in his tales, but they are essential

to preserving the illusion. His heroes cannot exist except operat-
ically. Take, for example, the following sentence from *William
Wilson:*

> Let it suffice, that among spendthrifts I out-heroded
> Herod, and that, giving name to a multitude of novel follies,
> I added no brief appendix to the long catalogue of vices
> then usual in the most dissolute university of Europe.

In isolation, as a prose sentence, it is terrible, vague, verbose,
the sense at the mercy of a conventional rhetorical rhythm. But
dramatically, how right; how well it reveals the William Wilson
who narrates the story in his real colors, as the fantastic self who
hates and refuses contact with reality. Some of Poe's successors
in stories about states of being, D. H. Lawrence for example,
have tried to be nonrealistic with fatal results.

In the second group, which includes such tales as *A Descent
into the Maelström* and *Gordon Pym,* the relation of will to environment is reversed. While in the first group everything that
happens is the consequence of a volition upon the freedom of
which there are no natural limits, in these stories of pure adventure the hero is as purely passive as the I in dreams; nothing that
happens is the result of his personal choice, everything happens
to him. What the subject feels—interest, excitement, terror—
are caused by events over which he has no control whatsoever.
The first kind of hero has no history because he refuses to change
with time; this kind has none because he cannot change, he can
only experience.

The problem for the writer of adventure stories is to invent
a succession of events which are both interesting and varied and
to make the order of succession plausible. To secure variety
without sacrificing coherence or vice versa is more difficult than
it looks, and *Gordon Pym,* one of the finest adventure stories ever
written, is an object lesson in the art. Every kind of adventure
occurs—adventures of natural origin like shipwreck; adventures
like mutiny, caused by familiar human beings, or, like the adventures on the island, by strange natives; and, finally, supernatural
nightmare events—yet each leads credibly into the next. While
in the stories of passionate states a certain vagueness of description is essential to the illusion, in the adventure story credibility
is secured by the minutest details, figures, diagrams, and various
other devices, as in Poe's description of the mysterious ravines.

The total length of this chasm, commencing at the opening *a* and proceeding round the corner *b* to the extremity *d,* is five hundred and fifty yards.

Both these types of Poe story have had an extraordinary influence. His portraits of abnormal or self-destructive states contributed much to Dostoevski, his ratiocinating hero is the ancestor of Sherlock Holmes and his many successors, his tales of the future lead to H. G. Wells, his adventure stories to Jules Verne and Stevenson. It is not without interest that the development of such fiction in which the historical individual is missing should have coincided with the development of history as a science, with its own laws, and the appearance of the great nineteenth-century historians; further, that both these developments should accompany the industrialization and urbanization of social life in which the individual seems more and more the creation of historical forces while he himself feels less and less capable of affecting his life by any historical choice of his own.

Poe's minor fiction also falls into two groups. The first is composed, not of narratives, but physical descriptions of Eden, of the Great Good Place *The Domain of Arnheim.* Such descriptions, whoever they may be written by, are bound to be more interesting as revelations of their authors than in themselves, for no one can imagine the ideal place, the ideal home, except in terms of his private fantasies and the good taste of his day. In Poe's case, in particular, his notions of the stylish and luxurious, if they are not to seem slightly vulgar and comic, must be read in the light of his history and the America of the first half of the nineteenth century. And, lastly there is the group of humorous-satiric pieces unrepresented in this selection. Though Poe is not so funny in them as in some of his criticism, at least one story, *A Predicament,* is of interest. A parody of the kind of popular horror story appearing in *Blackwood's,* it is, in a sense, a parody of Poe's serious work in this vein; and it actually uses the same notion of the swinging descending knife which he was later to employ in *The Pit and the Pendulum.*

The Poems

Poe's best poems are not his most typical or original. "To Helen," which could have been written by Landor, and "The City in the Sea," which could have been written by Hood, are more successfully realized than a poem like "Ulalume," which could have been written by none but Poe.

His difficulty as a poet was that he was interested in too many poetic problems and experiments at once for the time he had to give to them. To make the result conform to the intention —and the more experimental the intention, the more this is true —a writer has to keep his hand in by continual practice. The prose writer who must earn his living has this advantage, that even the purest hack work is practice in his craft; for the penniless poet there is no corresponding exercise. Without the leisure to write and rewrite he cannot develop to his full stature. When we find fault with Poe's poems we must never forget his own sad preface to them.

> In defence of my own taste, it is incumbent upon me to say that I think nothing in this volume of much value to the public, or very creditable to myself. Events not to be controlled have prevented me from making, at any time, any serious effort in what, under happier circumstances, would have been the field of my choice.

For faulty they must be admitted to be. The trouble with "The Raven," for example, is that the thematic interest and the prosodic interest, both of which are considerable, do not combine and are even often at odds.

In *The Philosophy of Composition* Poe discusses his difficulties in preventing the poem from becoming absurd and artificial. The artificiality of the lover asking the proper series of questions to which the refrain would be appropriate could be solved by making him a self-torturer. The difficulty of the speaker of the refrain, however, remained insoluble until the poet hit on the notion of something nonhuman. But the effect could still be ruined unless the narration of the story, as distinct from the questions and answers, flowed naturally; and the meter Poe chose, with its frequent feminine rhymes, so rare in English, works against this and at times defeats him.

> Not the least obeisance made he; not a minute stopped or
>   stayed he;
> But with mien of lord or lady, perched above my chamber
>   door.

Here it is the meter alone and nothing in the speaker or the situation which is responsible for the redundant alternatives of "stopped or stayed he" and "lord or lady."

Similarly, "Ulalume" is an interesting experiment in diction but only an experiment, for the poem is about something which never quite gets said because the sense is sacrificed to the vowel sounds. Edward Lear, the only poet, apparently, to be directly influenced by Poe, succeeds with his emotive place names, "The Hills of the Chankly Bore," where Poe fails because he selects a subject where the accidental quality of the name is part of the intended effect. "The Bells," though much less interesting a conception than "Ulalume," is more successful because the subject is nothing but an excuse for onomatopoeic effects.

There remains, however, *Eureka*. The man who had flatly asserted that no poem should much exceed a hundred lines in length—"that music (in its modifications of rhythm and rhyme) is of so vast a moment to Poesy as never to be neglected by him who is truly poetical," that neither Truth, the satisfaction of the Intellect, nor Passion, the excitement of the Heart, are the province of Poetry but only Beauty, and that the most poetical topic in the world is the death of a beautiful woman—this man produces at the end of his life a work which he insists is a poem and commends to posterity as his crowning achievement, though it violates every article in his critical creed. It is many pages in length, it is written in prose, it handles scientific ideas in the truth of which the poet is passionately convinced, and the general subject is the origin and destiny of the universe.

Outside France the poem has been neglected, but I do not think Poe was wrong in the importance he attached to it. In the first place, it was a very daring and original notion to take the oldest of the poetic themes—older even than the story of the epic hero—namely, cosmology, the story of how things came to exist as they do, and treat it in a completely contemporary way, to do in English in the nineteenth century what Hesiod and Lucretius had done in Greek and Latin centuries before. Secondly, it is full of remarkable intuitive guesses that subsequent scientific discoveries have confirmed. As Paul Valéry says:

> It would not be exaggerating its importance to recognise, in his theory of consistency, a fairly definite attempt

to describe the universe by its *intrinsic properties.* The following proposition can be found toward the end of *Eureka:* "Each law of nature depends at all points on all the other laws." This might easily be considered, if not as a formula, at least as the expression of a tendency toward generalized relativity.

That its tendency approaches recent conceptions becomes evident when one discovers, in the poem under discussion, an affirmation of the *symmetrical* and reciprocal relationship of matter, time, space, gravity, and light.

Lastly, it combines in one work nearly all of Poe's characteristic obsessions: the passion for merging in union with the one which is at the root of tales like *Ligeia,* the passion for logic which dominates the detective and cryptographic studies, the passion for a final explanation and reconciliation which informs the melancholy of much of his verse—all are brought together in this poem of which the prose is as lucid, as untheatrical, as the best of his critical prose.

The Critical Writings

Poe's critical work, like that of any significant critic, must be considered in the literary context which provoked it. No critic, however pontifical his tone, is really attempting to lay down eternal truths about art; he is always polemical, fighting a battle against the characteristic misconceptions, stupidities, and weaknesses of his contemporaries. He is always having, on the one hand, to defend tradition against the amateur who is ignorant of it and the crank who thinks it should be scrapped so that real art may begin anew with him and, on the other, to assert the real novelty of the present and to demonstrate, against the academic who imagines that carrying on the tradition means imitation, what modern tasks and achievements are truly analogues to those of the past.

Poe's condemnation of the long poem and of the didactic or true poem is essentially a demand that the poets of his time be themselves and admit that epic themes and intellectual or moral ideas did not in fact excite their poetic faculties and that what really interested them were emotions of melancholy, nostalgia, puzzled yearning, and the like that could find their proper expression in neither epic nor epigram but in lyrics of moderate length. Poe was forced to attack all long poems on principle, to be unfair, for example, to *Paradise Lost* or *An Essay on Criticism*, in order to shake the preconceived notions of poets and public that to be important a poet must write long poems and give bardic advice.

His rejection of passion is really a variation of Wordsworth's observation that, to be capable of embodiment in a poem, emotion must be recollected in tranquility; immediate passion is too obsessive, too attached to the self. Poe's attack is further directed against the popular and amateur notion of poetic inspiration which gives the poet himself no work to do, a reminder that the most inspired poem is also a contraption, a made thing.

> We do not hesitate to say that a man highly endowed with the powers of Causality—that is to say a man of metaphysical acumen—will, even with a very deficient share of Ideality, compose a finer poem than one who without such metaphysical acumen, shall be gifted, in the most extraordinary degree, with the faculty of Ideality. For a poem is not the Poetic faculty, but the *means* of exciting it in mankind.

Through its influence on the French, Poe's general aesthetic is well known. The bulk of his critical writing, and perhaps that which was of the greatest service, is concerned with poetic technique and practical criticism of details. No one in his time put so much energy and insight into trying to make his contemporary poets take their craft seriously, know what they were doing prosodically, and avoid the faults of slovenly diction and inappropriate imagery that can be avoided by vigilance and hard work.

If Poe never developed to his potential full stature as a critic, this was entirely his misfortune, not his fault. Much of his best criticism will never be read widely because it lies buried in reviews of totally uninteresting authors. If he sometimes overpraised the second-rate like Mrs. Osgood or wasted time and energy in demolishing nonentities like Mr. English, such were inevitable consequences when a critical mind, equipped by nature for digesting the toughest of foods, is condemned by circumstances to feed on literary gruel. The first-rate critic needs critical issues of the first importance, and these were denied him. Think of the subjects that Baudelaire was granted—Delacroix,

Constantin Guys, Wagner—and then of the kind of books Poe was assigned to review:

> *Mephistopheles in England, or the Confessions of a Prime Minister*
> *The Christian Florist*
> *Noble Deeds of Women*
> *Ups and Downs in the Life of a Distressed Gentleman*
> *The History of Texas*
> *Sacred Philosophy of the Seasons*
> *Sketches of Conspicuous Living Characters in France*
> *Dashes at Life with a Free Pencil*
> *Alice Day; A Romance in Rhyme*
> *Wakondah; The Master of Life*
> *Poetical Remains of the Late Lucretia Maria Davidson*

One is astounded that he managed to remain a rational critic at all, let alone such a good one.

The Man

If the Muses could lobby for their interest, all biographical research into the lives of artists would probably be prohibited by law, and historians of the individual would have to confine themselves to those who act but do not make—generals, criminals, eccentrics, courtesans, and the like, about whom information is not only more interesting but less misleading. Good artists —the artist *manqué* is another matter—never make satisfactory heroes for novelists, because their life stories, even when interesting in themselves, are peripheral and less significant than their productions.

As a person, for example, Poe is a much less interesting figure than is Griswold. Since Professor Quinn published side by side the original versions of Poe's letters and Griswold's doctored versions, one is left panting with curiosity to know more about the latter. That one man should dislike another and speak maliciously of him after his death would be natural enough, but to take so much trouble, to blacken a reputation so subtly, presupposes a sustained hatred which is always fascinating because the capacity for sustained emotion of any kind is rare, and, in this instance, particularly so since no reasonable cause for it has yet been found.

In his personal reputation, as in so much else, Poe has been singularly unfortunate. Before the true facts were known, he was dismissed by respectable men of letters as a dissolute rake and hailed by the antirespectable as a romantically doomed figure, the Flying Dutchman of Whitman's dream.

> In a dream I once had, I saw a vessel on the sea, at midnight in a storm . . . flying uncontrolled with torn sails and broken spars through the wild sleet and winds and waves of the night. On the deck was a slender, slight, beautiful figure, a dim man, apparently enjoying all the terror, the murk, and the dislocation of which he was the centre and the victim.

Today this portrait has been shown to be false, but the moral climate has changed, and Poe would be more respected if it had been true. Had he been a really bad lot like Villon or Marlowe or Verlaine, someone who drank like a fish and was guilty of spectacular crimes and vices, we should rather admire him; but it turns out that he was only the kind of fellow whom one hesitates to invite to a party because after two drinks he is apt to become tiresome, an unmanly sort of man whose love-life seems to have been largely confined to crying in laps and playing house, that his weaknesses were of that unromantic kind for which our age has least tolerance, perhaps because they are typical of ourselves.

If our present conception of Poe as a person is correct, however, it makes Poe the artist a much odder figure. Nobody has a good word to say for his foster father, John Allan, who certainly does not seem to have been a very attractive gentleman; but if we imagine ourselves in his place in the year 1831, what sort of view would we have taken of Poe's future?

Remembering his behavior at the university, his pointless enlistment in the army, his behavior at West Point, his behavior to ourselves, would he not have seemed to us an obvious case of a certain kind of neurotic with which we are quite familiar—the talented youngster who never comes to anything because he will not or cannot work, whose masterpieces never get beyond the third page, who loses job after job because he cannot get to work on time or meet a date line? We might find psychological excuses for him in his heredity and early childhood—the incompetent, irresponsible father, the death of his mother when he was two—but our prognosis for his future not only as a man but also as a writer would hardly have been sanguine. At the very best we might have hoped that in the course of a lifetime he would produce one or two exquisitely polished lyrics.

But what in fact did happen? While remaining in his personal life just as difficult and self-destructive as we foresaw, he quickly became a very hard-working and conscientious professional writer. None of his colleagues on magazines seems to have had any professional difficulty with him. Indeed, when one compares the quality of most of the books he had to review with the quality of his reviews, one is inclined to wish that, for the sake of his own work, he had been less conscientious. The defects we find in his work are so often just the defects we should have least expected—the errors of a professional who is overtaxed and working against the clock.

As to his private life and personality, had it been more romantically wicked, his work would not have the importance it has as being, in some senses, the first modern work. He was one of the first to suffer *consciously* the impact of the destruction of the traditional community and its values, and he paid the heaviest price for this consciousness. As D. H. Lawrence says in an essay conspicuous for its insights:

> Poe had a pretty bitter doom. Doomed to seethe down his soul in a great continuous convulsion of disintegration, and doomed to register the process. And then doomed to be abused for it, when he had performed some of the bitterest tasks of human experience, that can be asked of a man. Necessary tasks too. For the human soul must suffer its own disintegration, consciously, if ever it is to survive.

To which one might add: "Abused?" No, a worse doom than that. Doomed to be used in school textbooks as a bait to interest the young in good literature, to be a respectable rival to the pulps.

Still, he has had some rewards. Not many authors have been invoked as intercessors with God in an hour of need, as Poe was named by Baudelaire when he felt himself going mad; not many have been celebrated in poems as beautiful as Mallarmé's Sonnet.

GEORGES POULET [1902–   ] obtained his doctorate at the University of Liége in 1927, and has been professor of French at the University of Edinburgh, Johns Hopkins University, and the University of Zurich. The following selection is from the Appendix, "Time and American Writers," in *Studies in Human Time*, translated by Elliott Coleman (The Johns Hopkins Press, 1956). *Études sur le temps humain* received the *Prix Sainte-Beuve* in 1950, and in 1952 the second volume, *La Distance intérieure* (tr. *The Interior Distance*, The University of Michigan Press, 1964), was awarded both the *Grand Prix de la critique littéraire* and the French Academy's *Prix Durchon* in philosophy. As a philosophical literary critic, Poulet defines the vital center of a literary work as the author's sense of time. Poe's dream world, symbolized by the sunken city, has its own time: a perpetual present. The dream ends in death but not in extinction: "the dead-alive person" awakens from unconsciousness into "the pure perception of a time without thought," a "true moment" of consciousness. Out of this awareness comes a final knowledge of the *closed* cycle of time, of the tragic linkage of duration and destiny. In some respects Poulet anticipates Richard Wilbur's study of Poe's hypnagogic dream symbolism.

Poe

GEORGES POULET

> Inspired by an ecstatic prescience of the glories beyond the grave, we struggle by multiform combinations among things and thoughts of Time to attain a portion of that Loveliness whose very elements perhaps appertain to Eternity alone.° [37]

The whole dialectic of time in Poe is involved in this passage. To create a beauty that cannot exist in time, the poet is obliged to recompose the elements of that time and to invent with the help of their multiple combinations a new, imaginary duration, analogous to the divine eternity.

This imaginary duration is that of dream. Cut off from communication with the exterior world, the dream has its own interior place, circumscribed, independent of all other places. It is the "land of dream." In like manner, possessing neither past nor future, existing within itself, unattached to any antecedent or subsequent life, dream has its own time. It is a perpetual present.

From *Studies in Human Time* (pages 330–34), translated by Elliott Coleman, 1956.
° Footnotes in this article start with 37.
[37] "The Poetic Principle," *Works,* Harrison, ed., XIV.

Its symbol is the sunken city:

> No rays from the holy heaven come down
> On the long night-time of that town;
> But light from out the lurid sea
> Streams up the turrets silently . . . . [38]

If time is nocturnal, it is because it does not depend on solar time. The light that streams up the towers comes from the encircling sea, as if the place produced its own illumination. On the other hand if the nocturnal time is long, it is because the hours that comprise it are not differentiated one from another like the hours of solar time. They indefinitely protract themselves into each other, without showing any evidence of a real succession in their passage. Actually they do not pass. They remain. They form an hour that is always the same, a time that is *sheltered* from diurnal duration. This time is effortlessly engendered by an interior diffusion similar to that of light.

But this world is a submarine world. If it exists, it exists beneath the surface. Like the city, the deep time that we have here is a sunken time. Sleep covers it. Between it and waking time a veil is drawn, now half transparent, now opaque. If consciousness perceives it, it is entirely within the depths of itself, not as a part of the present, but as a region infinitely withdrawn from duration. The dreamer who would isolate himself in the exclusive contemplation of his dream is condemned either to bury himself with it in sleep and silence, or to awaken, that is to say to find his way into a present that is entirely different, a momentary present that can only consign to the past this imaginary time that is eternal. Indeed, the poetical work of Poe is less the *presentation* of a dream-universe than the *reminiscence* of it, such as is realized through thicker and thicker layers of distance and oblivion. Thus the work shows itself to be profoundly different from the surrealistic oneirism which, far from recollecting the dream, claims to embody it in an actual world that has become magical. Now the dreams of Poe are never magical. Though once they were, they are so no longer. Thence their unreal, vaporous character, like a thought which in losing its actuality has also lost its consistency. But there is more. In-

[38] "The City in the Sea."

capable of finding a place in the present, these dreams are no less incapable of finding a place in the recognizable past. For dreams have only been dreams. They cannot range themselves, like events of the real past, in chronology or history. Excluded from the known past, they try to locate themselves in the unknown past. They present themselves as the memories of a prenatal epoch. Being of no time, they seem to belong to an epoch that transcends times. Here for example:

> There will occasionally flash across my mind a sensation of familiar things, and there is always mixed up with such indistinct shadows of recollections, an unaccountable memory of old foreign chronicles and ages long ago.[39]

Floating without any anchor in duration, the memories of dreams become more and more fleeting and indistinguishable. They are "a memory like a shadow—vague, variable, indefinite, unsteady . . . ."

Finally there is no memory at all. Everything becomes immemorial. By dint of immersing itself in the depths, of withdrawing into the distance, of dissolving itself in the space of thought, the eternal present is metamorphized into an eternal past. This transformation is impressive, not by reason of its beauty, but, on the contrary, its ugliness. Different from the "fabulous past" of Melville, which energetically unfolds its myths only to collapse all at once through a caprice of the author or of destiny, Poe's oneirous past dies a slow and even nauseated death. A kind of gangrene corrupts it, disintegrates it, transforms it into mental rot. It is nevertheless the greatness of Poe to have fastened his gaze on this spectacle. He wanted to live his dream to the last moment, if not of its eternity, at least of its temporal existence—and, further still, through the charnel house.

Thus, Poe's dream ends in death but not in total extinction. The consciousness of the dreamer survives the death of the dream, a witness of its disappearance. In the *Colloquy of Monos and Una*, Poe describes this posthumous consciousness. In experiencing the death of all his thoughts, the dead-alive person attains to the pure perception of a time without thought:

---

[39] "Ms. Found in a Bottle," *Works*, II, 10.

> Let me term it a mental pendulous pulsation. It was
> the moral embodiment of man's abstract idea of Time . . .
> existing independently of any succession of events . . . .[40]

Thus, at the extremity of dream there is death. And yet at
the extremity of the dream there is also the awakening, that is
to say life.

Sudden passage from death to life, or from the consciousness of death to the consciousness of life.

If the time of dream is an eternal present which degenerates into the past and finally into death or the void, the time of
life is first of all a simple moment of life. It is the moment when
one awakens and there is still no duration, but rather the simple
and immediate feeling of physical existence: "Very suddenly
there came back to my soul motion and sound—the tumultuous
motion of the heart, and, in my ears, the sound of its beating."[41]
All the attention is directed to what is happening, at the instant
it happens. It would be difficult to conceive anything that less
resembles the dream. Life is absorbed with an incomparable
intensity in the mysterious phenomenon of its rising up into
the instant.

But this awakening is not concluded, and as first it places
consciousness in a *true* moment, so thereafter it brings it into a
true time. In other words, having recalled a person to the consciousness of his actual existence, it then recalls him to the consciousness of his nonactual life, that is to say his past and his
future. Now aroused, he can escape neither the past nor the
future. Hence the invariable fright into which, at the end of a
former moment, the awakened sleeper finds himself thrown:

> Then the mere consciousness of existence without
> thought—a condition which lasted long. Then, very sud-
> denly, thought, and shuddering terror, and earnest endeavor
> to comprehend my true state.[42]

Now, to comprehend his true state is to comprehend that
state as it presents itself, not only in the moment but in duration.
There is a knowledge that bears upon the whole ensemble of

[40] "Colloquy of Monos and Una," Ibid., IV, 209.
[41] "The Pit and the Pendulum," Ibid., V, 70.
[42] Loc. cit.

facts which, constituting our past and determining our future, determines as well the precise position in which we find ourselves situated in that ensemble. Almost invariably Poe places his awakened dreamer in such a situation; a situation so tragic that it requires his complete attention to comprehend it. The more threatening the situation, the more the person is forced to manifest that vigilance of the alerted consciousness which is the very contrary of the consciousness of dream. In opposition to the duration of the dream, which is composed of the undefined continuity of long hours, there now appears a mental duration defined with such precision that knowledge of the future is as plain to it as knowledge of the past. Everything constitutes a rigorously comprehensible fatality. By knowing who one has been, one knows who one will be, and when and how one will die. Like the hero of *The Fall of the House of Usher:* "I shall perish," said he, "I *must* perish in this deplorable folly. Thus, thus, and not otherwise, shall I be lost . . . ."[43]

The final knowledge, therefore, is a knowledge of the linkage of the causes which constitute duration and destiny. This linkage necessarily exists in a closed cycle. There can be certain knowledge of our temporal destiny only if that particular time is situated off by itself from the ordinary duration, so that it realizes itself independently of chance. For chance is incalculable. Poe eliminates interventions of chance as much as he can in his stories. It is not only the location of the House of Usher, which is situated apart from all others; it is also the time of Roderick Usher. If the atmosphere of the house has no "affinity with the air of heaven," its inhabitants, on the other hand, descend from a race that has been perpetuated only in a direct line. This particular time, therefore, is a time that cannot be confused with exterior duration. It is an internal fatality, conceived in isolation, and accomplished in isolation. A sort of temporal circle surrounds Poe's characters. A whirlpool envelops them, which, like that of the Maelström, disposes its funnel by degrees from the past in which one has been caught, to the future in which one will be dead. Whether it moves in the limitless eternity of dream or in the limited temporality of awakening, the work of Poe thus always presents a time that is *closed.*

[43] "The Fall of the House of Usher," *Works,* III, 280.

In "The Angelic Imagination" (1952) ALLEN TATE [1899–   ] clarifies the "larger philosophic dimension" implicit in Poe's tales by defining the "philosophic perspective" of the three angelic dialogues—from "the angelic fallacy" of man's godlike intellect divorced from feeling and moral sense ("The Colloquy of Monos and Una") to the fable of man's godlike creativity ("The Power of Words"). But in *Eureka* Poe tried through intellect to reach "God as essence," rather than through "analogy to the natural world"; with the ultimate recovery of unity, God is destroyed. Poe's images of the abyss and of the pit are images of nothingness, and, as Tate puts it, of "that part of our experience which we are least able to face up to: the Dark Night of Sense. . . ." Thus, in "the angelism of the intellect" as one aspect of Poe, Tate has attempted to define "what I think I have seen in Poe that nobody else has seen."

The Angelic Imagination

ALLEN TATE

Poe as God

With some embarrassment I assume the part of amateur theologian and turn to a little-known figure, Edgar Allan Poe, another theologian only less ignorant than myself. How seriously one must take either Poe or his present critic in this new role I prefer not to be qualified to say. Poe will remain a man of letters—I had almost said a poet—whose interest for us is in the best sense historical. He represents that part of our experience which we are least able to face up to: the Dark Night of Sense, the cloud hovering over that edge of the eye which is turned to receive the effluvia of France, whence the literary power of his influence reaches us today. In France, the literary power has been closely studied; I shall not try to estimate it here. Poe's other power, that of the melancholy, heroic life, one must likewise leave to others, those of one's own compatriots who are not interested in literature. All readers of Poe, of the work or of the life, and the rare reader of both, are peculiarly liable to the vanity of discovery. I shall be concerned in the ensuing remarks with what I think I have seen in Poe that nobody else has seen: this undetected quality, or its remote source in Poe's feeling and

Lecture delivered at Boston College during conference, February 10–11, 1951; published in *Kenyon Review*, Summer 1952; *Collected Essays*, 1959.

thought, I believe partly explains an engagement with him that men on both sides of the Atlantic have acknowledged for more than a century.

It was recently acknowledged, with reservations, by Mr. T. S. Eliot, whose estimate must be reckoned with: Poe, he tells us, won a great reputation in Europe because the continental critics habitually view an author's work as a whole; whereas English and American critics view each work separately and, in the case of Poe, have been stopped by its defects. Mr. Eliot's essay[1] is the first attempt by an English-speaking critic to bring to Poe the continental approach and to form a general estimate. I quote from what I take to be Mr. Eliot's summary; Poe, he says,

> appears to yield himself completely to the idea of the moment: the effect is, that all his ideas seem to be entertained rather than believed. What is lacking is not brain-power, but that maturity of intellect which comes only with the maturing of the man as a whole, the development and co-ordination of his various emotions.

What I shall say towards the end of this essay I believe will show that Mr. Eliot is partly wrong, but that on the whole his estimate of Poe's immaturity is right. Does Poe merely "entertain" *all* his ideas? Perhaps all but one; but that one makes all the difference. Its special difference consists in his failure to see what the idea really was, so that he had perpetually to shift his ground—to "entertain," one after another, shabby rhetorics and fantasies that could never quite contain the one great idea. He was a religious man whose Christianity, for reasons that nobody knows anything about, had got short-circuited; he lived among fragments of provincial theologies, in the midst of which "coordination," for a man of his intensity, was difficult if not impossible. There is no evidence that Poe used the word coordination in the sense in which Mr. Eliot finds him deficient in it; but it is justly applied. I am nevertheless surprised that Mr. Eliot seems to assume that *coordination* of the "various emotions" is ever possible: the word gives the case away to Poe. It is a morally neutral term that Poe himself might have used, in his lifelong effort to impose upon experience a mechanical logic;

[1] See the first article of Part III of this anthology.

possibly it came into modern literary psychology from analytic geometry. I take it that the word was not used, if in Mr. Eliot's sense it was known, when considerable numbers of persons were able to experience coordination. I suppose Mr. Eliot means by it a harmony of faculties among different orders of experience; and Poe's failure to harmonize himself cannot be denied.

The failure resulted in a hypertrophy of the three classical faculties: feeling, will, and intellect. The first I have discussed elsewhere.[2] It is the incapacity to represent the human condition in the central tradition of natural feeling. A nightmare of paranoia, schizophrenia, necrophilism, and vampirism supervenes, in which the natural affections are perverted by the will to destroy. Poe's heroines—Berenice, Ligeia, Madeline, Morella, with the curious exception of the abstemious Eleanora—are ill-disguised vampires; his heroes become necromancers (in the root meaning of the word) whose wills, like the heroines' wills, defy the term of life to keep them equivocally "alive." This primary failure in human feeling results in the loss of the entire natural order of experience.

The second hypertrophy is the thrust of the will beyond the human scale of action. The evidence of this is on nearly every page of Poe's serious prose fiction. Poe's readers, especially the young, like the quotation from Glanvill that appears as the epigraph to "Ligeia": "Man does not yield himself to the angels, nor unto Death utterly, save only through the weakness of his feeble will." It is the theme of the major stories. The hero professes an impossibly high love of the heroine that circumvents the body and moves in upon her spiritual essence. All this sounds high and noble, until we begin to look at it more narrowly, when we perceive that the ordinary carnal relationship between man and woman, however sinful, would be preferable to the mutual destruction of soul to which Poe's characters are committed. The carnal act, in which none of them seems to be interested, would witness a commitment to the order of nature, without which the higher knowledge is not possible to man. The Poe-hero tries in self-love to turn the soul of the heroine into something like a physical object which he can know in direct cognition and then possess.

[2] "Our Cousin, Mr. Poe."

Thus we get the third hypertrophy of a human faculty: the intellect moving in isolation from both love and the moral will, whereby it declares itself independent of the human situation in the quest of essential knowledge.

The three perversions necessarily act together, the action of one implying a deflection of the others. But the actual emphases that Poe gives the perversions are richer in philosophical implication than his psychoanalytic critics have been prepared to see. To these ingenious persons, Poe's works have almost no intrinsic meaning; taken together they make up a *dossier* for the analyst to peruse before Mr. Poe steps into his office for an analysis. It is important at this point to observe that Poe takes for granted the old facultative psychology of intellect, will, and feeling. If we do not observe this scheme, and let it point our enquiry, we shall fail to understand two crucial elements in Poe: first, that Poe's symbols refer to a known tradition of thought, an intelligible order, apart from what he was as a man, and are not merely the index to a compulsive neurosis; and, secondly, that the symbols, cast into the framework of the three faculties, point towards this larger philosophical dimension, implicit in the serious stories, but very much at the surface in certain of Poe's works that have been almost completely ignored.

I shall discuss here these neglected works: *The Conversation of Eiros and Charmion, The Colloquy of Monos and Una, The Power of Words,* and *Eureka.* The three first are dialogues between spirits in heaven, after the destruction of the earth; all four set forth a cataclysmic end of the world, modelled on the Christian eschatology. We shall see that *Eureka* goes further, and offers us a semi-rational vision of the final disappearance of the material world into the first spiritual Unity, or God.

It would be folly to try to see in these works the action of a first-rate philosophical mind; there is ingenuity rather than complex thinking. What concerns us is the relation of the semi-philosophical works to Poe's imaginative fiction; that is, a particular relation of the speculative intellect to the work of imagination. I shall have to show that Poe, as a critical mind, had only a distant if impressive insight into the disintegration of the modern personality; and that this insight was not available to him as an imaginative writer, when he had to confront the human situation as a whole man. He was the victim of a disintegration that he seems only intermittently to have understood. Poe is thus a man we must return to: a figure of transition, who retains a traditional insight into a disorder that has since become typical, without being able himself to control it.

Before we examine this insight it will be necessary to fix more clearly in mind than I have yet done the character of Poe as a transitional man. Madame Raïssa Maritain, in a valuable essay, *Magie, Poésie, et Mystique,*[3] says:

> Je ne vois guère de place dans la cosmologie d'Edgar Poe pour des recherches de recettes magiques. Et moins encore dans sa poésie, qui a toujours été parfaitement libre de toute anxiété de ce genre, et dont il n'aurait jamais voulu faire un instrument de pouvoir.

> [I see little place in the cosmology of Edgar Poe for the pursuit of magic recipes. And still less in his poetry, which was always perfectly free of all anxiety of this kind, and of which he never wished to make an instrument of power.]

I am not sure that Madame Maritain is entirely right about the absence of magic, but there is no doubt that Poe *as poet* accepted certain limitations of language. He accepted them in practice. The obscurity of Poe's poetic diction is rather vagueness than the obscurity of complexity; it reflects his uncertain grasp of the relation of language to feeling, and of feeling to nature. But it is never that idolatrous dissolution of language from the grammar of a possible world, which results from the belief that language itself can be reality, or by incantation can create a reality: a superstition that comes down in French from Lautréamont, Rimbaud, and Mallarmé to the Surrealists, and in English to Hart Crane, Wallace Stevens, and Dylan Thomas. (I do not wish it to be understood that I am in any sense "rejecting" these poets, least of all under the rubric "superstition." When men find themselves cut off from reality they will frequently resort to magic rites to recover it—a critical moment of history that has its own relation to reality, from which poetry of great power may emerge.)

Poe, then, accepted his genre *in practice*. If the disorganized, synaesthetic sensibility arrives in the long run at a corre-

---

[3] Jacques et Raïssa Maritain, *Situation de la Poésie* (Paris, 1938), p. 58.

sponding disintegration of the forms of grammar and rhetoric, it must be admitted that Poe stopped short at the mere *doctrine* of synaesthesia. In *The Colloquy of Monos and Una,* the angel Monos describes his passage into the after-life: "The senses were unusually active, although eccentrically so—assuming each other's functions at random. The taste and the smell were inextricably confounded, and became one sentiment, abnormal and intense."[4] But this is not the experience of synaesthesia rendered to our consciousness; to put it as Poe puts it is merely to consider it as a possibility of experience. Eighty years later we find its actuality in the language of an American poet:

> How much I would have bartered! the black gorge
> And all the singular nestings in the hills
> Where beavers learn stitch and tooth.
> The pond I entered once and quickly fled—
> I remember now its singing willow rim.

Rimbaud's "derangement of the senses" is realized. Why did not Poe take the next step and realize it himself? The question is unanswerable, for every writer is who he is, and not somebody else. The discoverer of a new sensibility seldom pushes it as far as language will take it; it largely remains a premonition of something yet to come. Another phase of Poe's disproportion of language and feeling appears in the variations of his prose style, which range from the sobriety and formal elegance of much of his critical writing, to the bathos of stories like *Ligeia* and *Berenice.* When Poe is not involved directly in his own feeling he can be a master of the *ordonnance* of eighteenth century prose; there are passages in *The Narrative of Arthur Gordon Pym* that have the lucidity and intensity of Swift. But when he approaches the full human situation the traditional rhetoric fails him. It becomes in his hands a humorless, insensitive machine whose elaborate motions conceal what it pretends to convey; for without the superimposed order of rhetoric the disorder hidden beneath would explode to the surface, where he would not be able to manage it. Poe is the transitional figure in modern literature because he discovered our great subject, the disintegration of personality, but kept it in a language that had

[4] *Cf.* Baudelaire's *Correspondances:* "Les parfums, les couleurs, et les sons se répondent."

developed in a tradition of unity and order. Madam Maritain is right in saying that he does not *use* language as magic. But he considers its possibility, and he thinks of language as a potential source of quasi-divine power. He is at the parting of the ways; the two terms of his conflict are thus more prominent than they would appear to be in a writer, or in an age, fully committed to either extreme. "When all are bound for disorder," says Pascal, "none seems to go that way."

Of the three dialogues that I shall discuss here, the first, *The Conversation of Eiros and Charmion,* published in 1839, was the earliest written. It is Poe's first essay at a catastrophic version of the disappearance of the earth: a comet passes over the earth, extracting the nitrogen from the atmosphere and replacing it with oxygen, so that the accelerated oxidation ends in world-wide combustion. But in treating the most unpromising materials Poe means what he says, although the occasions of journalism may not allow him to say all that he means. He *means* the destruction of the world. It is not only a serious possibility, it is a moral and logical necessity of the condition to which man has perversely brought himself.

Man's destruction of his relation to nature is the subject of the next dialogue, *The Colloquy of Monos and Una* (1841). From the perversion of man's nature it follows by a kind of Manichean logic that external nature itself must be destroyed: man's surrender to evil is projected symbolically into the world.

This dialogue, the sequel to *The Conversation of Eiros and Charmion,* is a theological fantasy of the destruction of the earth by fire. I call the vision "theological" because the destruction is not, as it was in the preceding dialogue, merely the result of an interstellar collision. Monos says, "That man, as a race, should not become extinct, I saw that he must be *'born again.'* " Rebirth into the after-life is the mystery that Monos undertakes to explain to Una; but first he makes this long digression:

> One word first, my Una, in regard to man's general condition at this epoch. You will remember that one or two of the wise men among our forefathers . . . had ventured to doubt the propriety of the term "improvement" as applied to the progress of our civilization. [They uttered] principles which should have taught our race to submit to

the guidance of the natural laws, rather than attempt their control. Occasionally the poetic intellect—that intellect which we now feel to have been the most exalted of all—since those truths to us were of the most enduring importance and could only be reached by that *analogy* which speaks in proof-tones to the imagination alone, and to the unaided reason bears no weight—occasionally did this poetic intellect proceed a step farther in the evolving of the vaguely philosophic, and find in the mystic parable that tells of the tree of knowledge . . . death-producing, a distinct intimation that knowledge was not meet for man in the infant condition of his soul. . . .

Yet these noble exceptions from the general misrule served but to strengthen it by opposition. The great "movement"—that was the cant term—went on: a diseased commotion, moral and physical. Art—the Arts—rose supreme, and, once enthroned, cast chains upon the intellect which had elevated them to power. Even while he stalked a God in his own fancy, an infantine imbecility came over him. As might be supposed from the origin of his disorder, he grew infected with system, and with abstraction. He enwrapped himself in generalities. Among other odd ideas, that of universal equality gained ground; and in the face of analogy and of God—in spite of the laws of graduation so visibly pervading all things . . . —wild attempts at an omnipresent Democracy were made. Yet this evil sprang necessarily from the leading evil—knowledge. . . . Meanwhile huge smoking cities arose, innumerable. Green leaves shrank before the hot breath of furnaces . . . now it appears that we had worked out *our own destruction in the perversion of our taste* [italics mine] or rather in the blind neglect of its culture in the schools. For in truth it was at this crisis that taste alone—that faculty which, *holding a middle position between the pure intellect and the moral sense* [italics mine], could never safely have been disregarded—it was now that taste alone could have led us gently back to Beauty, to Nature, and to Life.

. . . it is not impossible that the sentiment of the natural, had time permitted it, would have regained its old ascendancy over the harsh mathematical reasoning of the schools. . . . This the mass of mankind saw not, or, living lustily although unhappily, affected not to see.

I have quoted the passage at great length in the hope that a certain number of persons at a certain place and time will have read it. Poe's critics (if he have any critics) have not read it. When they refer to it, it is to inform us that Poe was a reactionary Southerner who disliked democracy and industrialism. It would not be wholly to the purpose but it would be edifying to comment on the passage in detail, for it adumbrates a philosophy of impressive extent and depth. When we remember that it was written in the United States in the early 1840's, an era of the American experiment that tolerated very little dissent, we may well wonder whether it was the result of a flash of insight, or of conscious reliance upon a wider European tradition. (My guess is that Poe's idea of "mathematical reasoning" was derived in part from Pascal's *L'esprit de géométrie,* his "taste" from *L'esprit de finesse.* This is a scholarly question that cannot be investigated here.)

A clue to the connection between Poe's historical and metaphysical insight, on the one hand, and the mode of his literary imagination, on the other, may be found in Paul Valéry's essay, "The Position of Baudelaire," where he says:

. . . the basis of Poe's thoughts is associated with a certain personal metaphysical system. But this system, if it directs and dominates and suggests the [literary] theories . . . *by no means penetrates them* [italics mine.].[5]

His metaphysics was not available to him as experience; it did not *penetrate* his imagination. If we will consider together the "harsh mathematical reasoning of the schools" and the theory of the corruption of taste, we shall get a further clue to the Christian philosophical tradition in which Poe consciously or intuitively found himself. Taste is the discipline of feeling according to the laws of the natural order, a discipline of submission to a permanent limitation of man; this discipline has been abrogated by the "mathematical reasoning" whose purpose is the control of nature. Here we have the Cartesian split—taste,

[5] Paul Valéry, *Variety: Second Series,* trans. from the French by William Aspenwall Bradley (New York, 1938), "The Position of Baudelaire," p. 90.

feeling, respect for the depth of nature, resolved into a sub-
jectivism which denies the sensible world; for nature has become geometrical, at a high level of abstraction, in which "clear
and distinct ideas" only are workable. The sensibility is frustrated, since it is denied its perpetual refreshment in nature:
the operative abstraction replaces the rich perspectives of the
concrete object. Reason is thus detached from feeling, and likewise from the moral sense, the third and executive member of
the psychological triad, moving through the will. Feeling in
this scheme being isolated or—as Mr. Scott Buchanan might put
it—"occulted," it is strictly speaking without content, and man
has lost his access to material forms. We get the hypertrophy
of the intellect and the hypertrophy of the will. When neither
intellect nor will is bound to the human scale, their projection
becomes god-like, and man becomes an angel, in M. Maritain's
sense of the term:

> Cartesian dualism breaks man up into two complete sub-
> stances, joined to one another none knows how: on the one
> hand, the body which is only geometrical extension; on the
> other, the soul which is only thought—an angel inhabiting a
> machine and directing it by means of the pineal gland.
>   . . . for human intellection is living and fresh only
> when it is centered upon the vigilance of sense perception.
> The natural roots of our knowledge being cut, a general dry-
> ing up in philosophy and culture resulted, a drought for
> which romantic tears were later to provide only an insuffi-
> cient remedy. . . . Affectivity will have its revenge.[6]

One cannot fail to see here a resemblance, *up to a point,* between the insights of Poe and of Maritain; but at that point
appears the profound difference between a catastrophic acceptance and a poised estimation, of the Cartesian dualism. *The
Colloquy of Monos and Una* is in the end a romantic tear, and in
Poe's tales of perverted nature "affectivity" takes its terrible
revenge.

We may discern the precise point at which Poe betrays his
surrender to what I shall call the angelic fallacy: it is the point

[6] Jacques Maritain, *The Dream of Descartes* (New York, 1944), Chap. 4, "The
Cartesian Heritage," pp. 179–80. My debt to M. Maritain is so great that I
hardly know how to acknowledge it.

at which his conception of the "poetic intellect" becomes contradictory and obscure. This intellect speaks to us, he says, "by analogy," in "proof tones to the imagination alone." The trap is the adverb *alone,* which contradicts the idea of analogy. He may have meant analogy to the natural world, the higher truths emerging, as they do in Dante, from a rational structure of natural analogy; but he could not have meant all this. And I suppose nobody else in the nineteenth century understood analogy as a mode of knowledge. If the poetic intellect speaks "by analogy" it addresses more than the "imagination alone"; it engages also reason and cognition; for if it alone is addressed there is perhaps a minimum of analogy; if the imagination can work alone, it does so in direct intuition. And in fact in none of the essays and reviews does Poe even consider the idea of analogy. Its single mysterious appearance, in anything like its full historical sense, is in *The Colloquy of Monos and Una.* (It reappears in *Eureka,* where it means simple exemplification or parallelism.) In the "Poetic Principle," the poetic intellect moves independently, with only "incidental" connections with Pure Intellect and the Moral Sense; it is thus committed exclusively to Taste raised to an autonomous faculty. "Imagination is, possibly in man," says Poe in a footnote to his famous review of Halleck and Drake, "a lesser degree of the creative power of God." This is not far from the "esemplastic power" of the Primary Imagination, a Teutonic angel inhabiting a Cartesian machine named Samuel Taylor Coleridge.

Poe's exaltation of the imagination in its Cartesian vacuum foreshadows a critical dilemma of which we have been acutely aware in our own time. His extravagant claims for poetry do not in any particular exceed, except perhaps in their "period" rhetoric, the claims made by two later generations of English critics represented by Arnold and Richards. "Religion," said Arnold, "is morality touched with emotion." But religion, he said elsewhere, has attached itself to the "fact," by which he meant science; so religion has failed us. Therefore "the future of poetry is immense" because it is its own fact; that is to say, poetry is on its own, whatever its own may be—perhaps its own emotion, which now "touches" poetry instead of religion. Therefore poetry will save us, although it has no connection with the Cartesian machine running outside my window, or inside my vascular system. (Mr. Richards' early views I have discussed on several occasions over many years; I am a little embarrassed to find myself adverting to them again.) In Richards' writings, particularly in a small volume entitled *Science and Poetry* (1926), he tells us that the pseudo-statements of poetry—poetry on its own—cannot stand against the "certified scientific statement" about the facts which for Arnold had already failed both religion and poetry. Nevertheless poetry will save us because it "orders our minds"—but with what? For Mr. Richards, twenty-five years ago, the Cartesian machine was doing business as usual. Poetry would have to save us by ordering our minds with something that was not true.

Poe's flash of unsustained insight, in *The Colloquy of Monos and Una*, has, I submit, a greater dignity, a deeper philosophical perspective, and a tougher intellectual fibre, than the academic exercises of either Arnold or Mr. Richards. (I still reserve the right to admire both of these men.) Poe is not so isolated as they, in a provincialism of *time*. He still has access, however roundabout, to the great framework of the Aristotelian psychology to which the literature of Europe had been committed for more than two thousand years: this was, and still is for modern critics, an empirical fact that must be confronted if we are to approach literature with anything better than callow systems of psychological analysis, invented overnight, that put the imaginative work of the past at a distance seriously greater than that of time.

Poe with perfect tact puts his finger upon the particular function, feeling, that has been blighted by the abstraction of the pure intellect into a transcendental order of its own. He will let neither pure intellect nor the pure moral will (both having been purified of "nature") dominate poetry; he sees that poetry must be centered in the disciplined sense-perception which he inadequately calls taste; and he thus quite rightly opposes the "heresy of the didactic" and the "mathematical reasoning of the schools." He opposes both, but he gives in to the latter. Poe's idolatry of reason, ranging from the cryptogram and the detective story to the panlogism of *Eureka,* is too notorious to need pointing out. The autonomy of the will is in part the theme of the greater stories; and the autonomy of poetry, rising contradictorily and mysteriously from the ruin of its source in feeling, reflects "a lesser degree of the creative power of God." It is the creative power of the Word, man's *spoken* word, an extravagant and slippery pun on the Logos.

I now come to the third dialogue, *The Power of Words,* published in 1845, a fable in which the angelic imagination[7] is pushed beyond the limits of the angelic intelligence to the point at which man considers the possibility of creative power through verbal magic. The angels in this dialogue not only know essence directly; they also have the power of physical creation by means of *words.* We may ask here why, if Poe's insight was as profound as I think it was, he succumbed to a force of disintegration that he understood? An answer to this question is difficult. Insights of the critical intelligence, however impressive, will not always correct, they may never wholly rise above, the subtle and elusive implications of the common language to which the writer is born. As Dante well understood, this is the primary fact of his culture that he has got to reckon with. The culture of the imaginative writer is, first of all, the elementary use of language that he must hear and learn in childhood, and, in the end, not much more than a conscious manipulation of what he had received from life before the age of seven. Poe understood the spiritual disunity that had resulted from the rise of the demi-religion of scientism, but by merely opposing its excesses with equally excessive claims for the "poetic intellect," he subtly perpetuated the disunity from another direction. He set up, if we may be allowed the figure, a parallelogram of forces colliding by chance from unpredicted directions, not proceeding from a central unity. Although he was capable of envisaging the unified action of the mind through the three faculties, his own mind acted upon its materials now as intellect, now as feeling, now as will; never as all three together. Had he not been bred in a society committed to the rationalism of Descartes and Locke by that eminent angel of the rationalistic Enlightenment, Thomas Jefferson?[8] Such commitments probably lie so deep in one's sensibility that mere intellectual conviction, Poe's "unaided rea-

---

[7] Strictly speaking, an *angelic imagination* is not possible. Angels by definition have unmediated knowledge of essences.

[8] In the Virginia of Poe's time the subjects of conversation and reading were almost exclusively politics and theology. The educated Virginian was a deist by conviction and an Anglican or a Presbyterian by habit.

son," can scarcely reach them. Perhaps this discrepancy of belief and feeling exists in all ages, and creates the inner conflicts from which poetry comes. If this points to something in the nature of the literary imagination, we are bound to say that it will always lie a little beyond our understanding.

By the time Poe came to write his fable of the power of words, the angels of omnipotent reason could claim a victory. The scene is again the after-life; the characters two angels who meet in interstellar space after the destruction of the earth—a disaster assumed in all three of the dialogues and in *Eureka,* and a possible eventuality in most of Poe's tales. (One scarcely needs to be reminded of the collapse of the world of Roderick Usher.) The probable meaning of this omnivorous symbol I shall try to glance at presently. The climax of the angels' talk will reveal the long way that Poe had come from the philosophic insight of 1841 to the full angelic vision of 1845:

> *Oinos*—But why, Agathos, do you weep—and why, Oh why do your wings droop as we hover over this fair star— which is the greenest and yet most terrible of all we have encountered in our flight. Its brilliant flowers look like a fairy dream—but its fierce volcanoes like the passions of a turbulent heart.
>
> *Agathos*—They *are*—they *are!* This wild star it is now three centuries since, with clasped hands, and with streaming eyes, at the feet of my beloved—I spoke it—with a few passionate sentences—into birth. Its brilliant flowers *are* the dearest of all unfulfilled dreams, and its raging volcanoes *are* the passions of the most turbulent and unhallowed of hearts.

How had Agathos created this beautiful but unhallowed object? By the "physical power of words," he tells Oinos. Madame Maritain is the only critic I have read who has had the perception to take seriously this dialogue; her comment is of great interest:

> Eh bien, ce texte se réfère-t-il vraiment à une conception magique de la poésie et de la parole? Je ne crois pas. Nous avons affaire ici, comme dans *Eureka,* à une philosophie et une cosmologie panthéistiques, où tout mouvement et toute action participent a l'efficicacité d'une action divine.

[Does the text then really refer to a magical conception of poetry and of the word? I do not think so. We have to do here, as in *Eureka*, with a pantheistic philosophy and cosmology, where every movement and every action participates in the efficiency of a divine action.]

There can be no doubt about Poe's pantheism here and in *Eureka*, but in both works we cannot fail to detect special variations in the direction of deism. Madame Maritain quotes Léon Bloy on the eternal consequences of every action of divine grace for the human spirit, an ancient Christian doctrine connected with the belief in the Community of Saints, for which Pascal invented the great natural analogy:

The slightest movement affects the whole of nature; a stone cast into the sea changes the whole face of it. So, in the realm of Grace, the smallest act affects the whole by its results. Therefore everything has its importance.

In every action we must consider, besides the act itself, our present, past, and future conditions, and others whom it touches, and must see the connections of it all. *And so we shall keep ourselves well in check.*[9]

It almost seems as if Poe had just read this passage and had gone at once to his desk to begin *The Power of Words;* as if he had deliberately ignored the moral responsibility, the *check* upon human power, enjoined in the last sentence, and had concentrated upon Pascal's physical analogy for divine grace: "The slightest *movement* affects the whole of nature." One more step, and the "slightest movement," a spoken *word*, will act creatively. A failure of moral responsibility towards the universe would not necessarily issue in an act of physical creation; nor would action undertaken in the state of sanctifying grace produce stars that are both beautiful and hallowed, unless, of course, the *word* is a "magic recipe," incantatory magic, which I believe we undoubtedly get in *The Power of Words*. This is not the same presumption as our own timid, superstitious reverence for an order of poetic language which creates its own reality, but rather a grandiose angelic presumption on the part of man. As usual, Poe is at least partly aware of what he is doing; for Agathos explains:

---

[9] Pascal's *Pensées*, with an English translation, brief notes and Introduction by H. F. Stewart, D.D. (New York, 1950), Adversaria 16; p. 377.

This power of retrogradation [Pascal's "the smallest action affecting the whole by its results"] in its absolute fulness and perfection—this faculty of referring *all* epochs, *all* effects to *all* causes—is of course the prerogative of the Deity alone —but in every variety of degree, short of absolute perfection, is the power itself exercised by the whole host of the Angelic intelligences.

This "power," of course, is not at this stage magical; it represents angelic knowledge rather than power. But when Agathos created his green star he was not yet an angel; he was still man, but man with the creative power, just short of divine perfection, of the angelic intelligences. Wasn't his power on earth actually greater than that of the angels of Christian theology? For they are not primary creators; they are the powerful but uncreative executives of the divine will. Agathos' doctrine transcends the ideal of mere angelic knowledge: it is superangelism. Man is not only an angel, he is God in his aspect of creativity. I remark almost with regret, mingled with uneasiness, that Poe proves my argument, perhaps too well. (When criticism thinks that it has proved anything, it has become angelic itself.) But this is not all: Oinos tells Agathos that he "remembers many successful experiments in what some philosophers were weak enough to denominate animalculae." And Agathos bows to the mathematicians: "Now the mathematicians . . . saw that the results of any given impulse were absolutely endless . . . these men saw, at the same time, that this species of analysis itself had within itself a capacity for indefinite progress. . . ." Mathematicians were about to achieve the omniscience of the Son, and biologists the creative power of the Father.

Are we to conclude that in these fantasies Poe "appears to yield himself completely to the idea of the moment"? I believe that Mr. Eliot's observation is inaccurate. Poe is quite capable of faking his science, and of appearing to take seriously his own wildest inventions; but the invention is the creaking vehicle of something deeper. What he really takes seriously, and what he yields to in the end, is not an *idea* of the moment. He is progressively mastered by one great idea, deeper than any level of conscious belief and developing to the end of his life at an ever increasing rate, until at last he is engulfed by it. It is his own descent into the maelstrom.

He arrives at it, or reaches the bottom of it, in *Eureka,* which he wrote in 1848, the year before his death. I shall not go so far as to connect, symbolically or prophetically, his death and the vision of the pit at the end of *Eureka.* We may only observe that the complete vision, of which the early works represent an approximation, immediately precedes his death. The proposition of which *Eureka* is to provide the "proof," he states at the beginning:

> In the original unity of the first thing lies the secondary cause of all things, with the germ of their inevitable annihilation.

This "nothingness" is a dialectical conversion, not of one symbol into its opposite by analogy, as we see it in Dante, or even in Donne, but of an abstraction into its antithesis. Thesis: the omniscient intellect of man (of Poe as man) achieves a more than angelic knowledge in comprehending the structure and purpose of the created universe. Antithesis: the final purpose of the created universe is the extinction in its own unity of the omniscient intellect of man. There is no Hegelian synthesis. After the original act of divine creation, God withdraws into his deistic aloofness, leaving the separate and local acts of creation to man. This is the sphere of secondary creations which man as angelic delegate of God is empowered to perform. Thus, says Poe at the end of *Eureka,* not only is every man his own God, every man *is* God: every man the non-spatial center into which the universe, by a reverse motion of the atoms, will contract, as into its annihilation. God destroys himself in the eventual recovery of his unity. Unity equals zero. If Poe must at last "yield himself unto Death utterly," there is a lurid sublimity in the spectacle of his taking God along with him into a grave which is not smaller than the universe.

The material universe is in a state of radical disequilibrium, every atom striving to disengage itself from material forms and to return to the original center; but this is not a center in space. It is the Pascalian center which is the everywhere and nowhere, occupied by nothing. Since matter is merely the dialectical movement of attraction and repulsion, it will have ceased to exist when it rejoins the everywhere and nowhere. Space being emptied of matter, there is not even space, for space is that which is occupied by something. We are beyond the topless and bottomless abyss of Pascal.

The image of the abyss is in all of Poe's serious writings: the mirror in "William Wilson"; burial alive; the "tarn" into which the House of Usher plunges; the great white figure towards which Pym is being borne by a current of the sea; the pit over which the pendulum swings; the dead body containing the living soul of M. Valdemar; being walled up alive; the vertigo of the maelstrom.

Poe's most useful biographer, Professor Quinn, exhibits testimonials from modern physicists to bolster up with scientific authority a work in which he probably has little confidence. Let us assume, what may well be false, that *Eureka* from the scientific point of view of any age is nonsense. That would not make *Eureka* nonsense. "The glory of man," says Valéry in his essay on *Eureka*, "and something more than his glory, is to waste his powers on the void. . . . Thus it would seem that the history of thought can be summarized in these words: *It is absurd by what it seeks; great by what it finds*." What did Poe's "absurd" essay in eschatology inadvertently find, if indeed it found anything but nothing? Valéry again (and again the French instruct us in Poe) points, in another context, to the central meaning of *Eureka*, without perhaps quite knowing that he has done so (for Paul Valéry was himself an archangel); he says: "As soon as we leave the bounds of the moment, as soon as we attempt to enlarge and extend our presence outside of itself, our forces are exhausted in our liberty." Is this always and under all conditions necessarily true? I think not; but it was particularly true of Poe.

It was true of him because in *Eureka* he circumvented the natural world and tried to put himself not in the presence of God, but in the seat of God. *The exhaustion of force as a consequence of his intellectual liberation from the sensible world—*that is my reading of Valéry as a gloss upon the angelism of Poe. The intellectual force is exhausted because in the end it has no real object. The human intellect cannot reach God as essence; only God as analogy. Analogy to what? Plainly analogy to the natural world; for there is nothing in the intellect that has not previously reached it through the senses. Had Dante arrived at the vision of God by way of sense? We must answer yes, because Dante's Triune Circle is light, which the finite intelligence can see only in what has already been seen by means of it. But Poe's center is that place—to use Dante's great figure—"where the sun is silent." Since he refuses to see nature, he is doomed to see nothing. He has overleaped and cheated the condition of man. The reach of our imaginative enlargement is perhaps no longer than the ladder of analogy, at the top of which we may see all, if we still wish to *see* anything, that we have brought up with us from the bottom, where lies the sensible world. If we take nothing with us to the top but our emptied, angelic intellects, we shall see nothing when we get there. Poe as God sits silent in darkness. Here the movement of tragedy is reversed: there is no action. Man as angel becomes a demon who cannot initiate the first motion of love, and we can feel only compassion with his suffering, for it is potentially ours.

I have not supposed it necessary to describe in detail the structure of *Eureka,* or to call attention to its great passages of expository prose, which seem to me unsurpassed in their kind in the nineteenth century. I have not discussed Poe from what is commonly known as the literary point of view. I have tried to expound one idea, the angelism of the intellect, as one aspect of one writer. I do not hesitate in conclusion to commit Poe's heresy of the didactic, and to point a moral. We shall be so exhausted in our liberty that we shall have to take our final rest, not in the cool of the evening, but in the dark, if any one of our modes decides to set up in business for itself.

RICHARD WILBUR [1921–   ]. Best known as a poet, Wilbur has taught English at Harvard and, more recently, at Wesleyan University since 1957. While a member of the Society of Fellows at Harvard he began his study of dandyism and Poe. After writing the introductory essay to the Dell Laurel Edition of Poe's poems (March 1959), he delivered the following lecture at the Library of Congress on May 4, 1959. Beginning with a definition of Poe's poetic ideal and of his cosmic myth, Wilbur draws upon his own deep experience with the creative process for an analysis of hypnagogic symbolism in the tales of psychic conflict. "In them, Poe broke wholly new ground, and they remain the best things of their kind in our literature." A long biographical and critical introduction to Poe by Wilbur appears in *Major Writers of America* (New York, 1962).

The House of Poe

RICHARD WILBUR

A few weeks ago, in the *New York Times Book Review*, Mr. Saul
Bellow expressed impatience with the current critical habit of
finding symbols in everything. No self-respecting modern professor, Mr. Bellow observed, would dare to explain Achilles'
dragging of Hector around the walls of Troy by the mere assertion that Achilles was in a bad temper. That would be too
drearily obvious. No, the professor must say that the circular
path of Achilles and Hector relates to the theme of circularity
which pervades *The Iliad*.

In the following week's *Book Review*, a pedantic correspondent corrected Mr. Bellow, pointing out that Achilles did
not, in Homer's *Iliad*, drag Hector's body around the walls of
Troy; this perhaps invalidates the Homeric example, but Mr.
Bellow's complaint remains, nevertheless, a very sensible one.
We are all getting a bit tired, I think, of that laboriously clever
criticism which discovers mandalas in Mark Twain, rebirth
archetypes in Edwin Arlington Robinson, and fertility myths in
everybody.

Still, we must not be carried away by our impatience, to
the point of demanding that no more symbols be reported. The
business of the critic, after all, is to divine the intention of the
work, and to interpret the work in the light of that intention;
and since some writers are intentionally symbolic, there is nothing for it but to talk about their symbols. If we speak of Melville,
we must speak of symbols. If we speak of Hawthorne, we must
speak of symbols. And as for Edgar Allan Poe, whose sesqui-
centennial year we are met to observe, I think we can make no
sense about him until we consider his work—and in particular his
prose fiction—as deliberate and often brilliant allegory.

Not everyone will agree with me that Poe's work has an
accessible allegorical meaning. Some critics, in fact, have refused to see any substance, allegorical or otherwise, in Poe's
fiction, and have regarded his tales as nothing more than complicated machines for saying "boo." Others have intuited undis-
coverable meanings in Poe, generally of an unpleasant kind: I

Library of Congress Anniversary Lecture, May 4, 1959.

recall one Freudian critic declaring that if we find Poe unintelligible we should congratulate ourselves, since if we *could* understand him it would be proof of our abnormality.

It is not really surprising that some critics should think Poe meaningless, or that others should suppose his meaning intelligible only to monsters. Poe was not a wide-open and perspicuous writer; indeed, he was a secretive writer both by temperament and by conviction. He sprinkled his stories with sly references to himself and to his personal history. He gave his own birthday of January 19 to his character William Wilson; he bestowed his own height and color of eye on the captain of the phantom ship in *Ms. Found in a Bottle;* and the name of one of his heroes, Arthur Gordon Pym, is patently a version of his own. He was a maker and solver of puzzles, fascinated by codes, ciphers, anagrams, acrostics, hieroglyphics, and the Kabbala. He invented the detective story. He was fond of aliases; he delighted in accounts of swindles; he perpetrated the famous Balloon Hoax of 1844; and one of his most characteristic stories is entitled *Mystification.* A man so devoted to concealment and deception and unraveling and detection might be expected to have in his work what Poe himself called "undercurrents of meaning."

And that is where Poe, as a critic, said that meaning belongs: not on the surface of the poem or tale, but below the surface as a dark undercurrent. If the meaning of a work is made overly clear—as Poe said in his *Philosophy of Composition*—if the meaning is brought to the surface and made the upper current of the poem or tale, then the work becomes bald and prosaic and ceases to be art. Poe conceived of art, you see, not as a means of giving imaginative order to earthly experience, but as a stimulus to unearthly visions. The work of literary art does not, in Poe's view, present the reader with a provisional arrangement of reality; instead, it seeks to disengage the reader's mind from reality and propel it toward the ideal. Now, since Poe thought the function of art was to set the mind soaring upward in what he called "a wild effort to reach the Beauty above," it was important to him that the poem or tale should not have such definiteness and completeness of meaning as might contain the reader's mind within the work. Therefore Poe's criticism places a positive value on the obscuration of meaning, on a dark suggestiveness, on a deliberate vagueness by means of which the reader's mind may be set adrift toward the beyond.

Poe's criticism, then, assures us that his work does have meaning. And Poe also assures us that this meaning is not on the surface but in the depths. If we accept Poe's invitation to play detective, and commence to read him with an eye for submerged meaning, it is not long before we sense that there *are* meanings to be found, and that in fact many of Poe's stories, though superficially dissimilar, tell the same tale. We begin to have this sense as we notice Poe's repeated use of certain narrative patterns; his repetition of certain words and phrases; his use, in story after story, of certain scenes and properties. We notice, for instance, the recurrence of the *spiral* or *vortex*. In *Ms. Found in a Bottle*, the story ends with a plunge into a whirlpool; the *Descent into the Maelström* also concludes in a watery vortex; the house of Usher, just before it plunges into the tarn, is swaddled in a whirlwind; the hero of *Metzengerstein*, Poe's first published story, perishes in "a whirlwind of chaotic fire"; and at the close of *King Pest*, Hugh Tarpaulin is cast into a puncheon of ale and disappears "amid a whirlpool of foam." That Poe offers us so many spirals or vortices in his fiction, and that they should always appear at the same terminal point in their respective narratives, is a strong indication that the spiral had some symbolic value for Poe. And it did: What the spiral invariably represents in any tale of Poe's is the loss of consciousness, and the descent of the mind into sleep.

I hope you will grant, before I am through, that to find spirals in Poe is not so silly as finding circles in Homer. The professor who finds circles in Homer does so to the neglect of more important and more provable meanings. But the spiral or vortex is a part of that symbolic language in which Poe said his say, and unless we understand it we cannot understand Poe.

But now I have gotten ahead of myself, and before I proceed with my project of exploring one area of Poe's symbolism, I think I had better say something about Poe's conception of poetry and the poet.

Poe conceived of God as a poet. The universe, therefore, was an artistic creation, a poem composed by God. Now, if the universe is a poem, it follows that the one proper response to it is

aesthetic, and that God's creatures are attuned to Him in proportion as their imaginations are ravished by the beauty and
harmony of his creation. Not to worship beauty, not to regard
poetic knowledge as divine, would be to turn one's back on God
and fall from grace.

The planet Earth, according to Poe's myth of the cosmos,
has done just this. It has fallen away from God by exalting the
scientific reason above poetic intuition, and by putting its trust
in material fact rather than in visionary knowledge. The Earth's
inhabitants are thus corrupted by rationalism and materialism;
their souls are diseased; and Poe sees this disease of the human
spirit as having contaminated physical nature. The woods and
fields and waters of Earth have thereby lost their first beauty,
and no longer clearly express God's imagination; the landscape
has lost its original perfection of composition, in proportion as
men have lost their power to perceive the beautiful.

Since Earth is a fallen planet, life upon Earth is necessarily
a torment for the poet: neither in the human sphere nor in the
realm of nature can he find fit objects for contemplation, and
indeed his soul is oppressed by everything around him. The
rationalist mocks at him; the dull, prosaic spirit of the age damps
his imaginative spark; the gross materiality of the world crowds
in upon him. His only recourse is to abandon all concern for
Earthly things, and to devote himself as purely as possible to
unearthly visions, in hopes of glimpsing that heavenly beauty
which is the thought of God.

Poe, then, sees the poetic soul as at war with the mundane
physical world; and that warfare is Poe's fundamental subject.
But the war between soul and world is not the only war. There
is also warfare within the poet's very nature. To be sure, the
poet's nature was not always in conflict with itself. Prior to his
earthly incarnation, and during his dreamy childhood, Poe's poet
enjoyed a serene unity of being; his consciousness was purely
imaginative, and he knew the universe for the divine poem that
it is. But with his entrance into adult life, the poet became involved with a fallen world in which the physical, the factual,
the rational, the prosaic are not escapable. Thus, compromised,
he lost his perfect spirituality, and is now cursed with a divided
nature. Though his imagination still yearns toward ideal beauty,
his mortal body chains him to the physical and temporal and
local; the hungers and passions of his body draw him toward

external objects, and the conflict of conscience and desire degrades and distracts his soul; his mortal senses try to convince him of the reality of a material world which his soul struggles to escape; his reason urges him to acknowledge everyday fact, and to confine his thought within the prison of logic. For all these reasons it is not easy for the poet to detach his soul from earthly things, and regain his lost imaginative power—his power to commune with that supernal beauty which is symbolized, in Poe, by the shadowy and angelic figures of Ligeia, and Helen, and Lenore.

These, then, are Poe's great subjects: first, the war between the poetic soul and the external world; second, the war between the poetic soul and the earthly self to which it is bound. All of Poe's major stories are allegorical presentations of these conflicts, and everything he wrote bore somehow upon them.

How does one wage war against the external world? And how does one release one's visionary soul from the body, and from the constraint of the reason? These may sound like difficult tasks; and yet we all accomplish them every night. In a subjective sense—and Poe's thought is wholly subjective—we destroy the world every time we close our eyes. If *esse est percipi*, as Bishop Berkeley said—if to be is to be perceived—then when we withdraw our attention from the world in somnolence or sleep, the world ceases to be. As our minds move toward sleep, by way of drowsiness and reverie and the hypnagogic state, we escape from consciousness of the world, we escape from awareness of our bodies, and we enter a realm in which reason no longer hampers the play of the imagination: we enter the realm of dream.

Like many romantic poets, Poe identified imagination with dream. Where Poe differed from other romantic poets was in the literalness and absoluteness of the identification, and in the clinical precision with which he observed the phenomena of dream, carefully distinguishing the various states through which the mind passes on its way to sleep. A large number of Poe's stories derive their very structure from this sequence of mental states: *Ms. Found in a Bottle*, to give but one example, is an allegory of the mind's voyage from the waking world into the world of dreams, with each main step of the narrative symbolizing the passage of the mind from one state to another—from wakefulness to reverie, from reverie to the hypnagogic state, from the hypnagogic state to the deep dream. The departure of the narrator's ship from Batavia represents the mind's withdrawal from the waking world; the drowning of the captain and all but one of the crew represents the growing solitude of reverie; when the narrator is transferred by collision from a real ship to a phantom ship, we are to understand that he has passed from reverie, a state in which reality and dream exist in a kind of equilibrium, into the free fantasy of the hypnagogic state. And when the phantom ship makes its final plunge into the whirlpool, we are to understand that the narrator's mind has gone over the brink of sleep and descended into dreams.

What I am saying by means of this example is that the scenes and situations of Poe's tales are always concrete representations of states of mind. If we bear in mind Poe's fundamental plot—the effort of the poetic soul to escape all consciousness of the world in dream—we soon recognize the significance of certain scenic or situational motifs which turn up in story after story. The most important of these recurrent motifs is that of *enclosure* or *circumscription;* perhaps the latter term is preferable, because it is Poe's own word, and because Poe's enclosures are so often more or less circular in form. The heroes of Poe's tales and poems are violently circumscribed by whirlpools, or peacefully circumscribed by cloud-capped Paradisal valleys; they float upon circular pools ringed in by steep flowering hillsides; they dwell on islands, or voyage to them; we find Poe heroes also in coffins, in the cabs of balloons, or hidden away in the holds of ships; and above all we find them sitting alone in the claustral and richly-furnished rooms of remote and mouldering mansions.

Almost never, if you think about it, is one of Poe's heroes to be seen standing in the light of common day; almost never does the Poe hero breathe the air that others breathe; he requires some kind of envelope in order to be what he is; he is always either enclosed or on his way to an enclosure. The narrative of William Wilson conducts the hero from Stoke Newington to Eton, from Eton to Oxford, and then to Rome by way of Paris, Vienna, Berlin, Moscow, Naples, and Egypt: and yet, for all his travels, Wilson seems never to set foot out-of-doors. The story takes place in a series of rooms, the last one locked from the inside.

Sometimes Poe emphasizes the circumscription of his heroes by multiple enclosures. Roderick Usher dwells in a great and crumbling mansion from which, as Poe tells us, he has not ventured forth in many years. This mansion stands islanded in a stagnant lake, which serves it as a defensive moat. And beyond the moat lies the Usher estate, a vast barren tract having its own peculiar and forbidding weather and atmosphere. You might say that Roderick Usher is defended in depth; and yet at the close of the story Poe compounds Roderick's inaccessibility by having the mansion and its occupant swallowed up by the waters of the tarn.

What does it mean that Poe's heroes are invariably enclosed or circumscribed? The answer is simple: circumscription, in Poe's tales, means the exclusion from consciousness of the so-called real world, the world of time and reason and physical fact; it means the isolation of the poetic soul in visionary reverie or trance. When we find one of Poe's characters in a remote valley, or a claustral room, we know that he is in the process of dreaming his way out of the world.

Now, I want to devote the time remaining to the consideration of one kind of enclosure in Poe's tales: the mouldering mansion and its richly-furnished rooms. I want to concentrate on Poe's architecture and decor for two reasons: first, because Poe's use of architecture is so frankly and provably allegorical that I *should* be able to be convincing about it; second, because by concentrating on one area of Poe's symbolism we shall be able to see that his stories are allegorical not only in their broad patterns, but also in their smallest details.

Let us begin with a familiar poem, *The Haunted Palace*. The opening stanzas of this poem, as a number of critics have noted, make a point-by-point comparison between a building and the head of a man. The exterior of the palace represents the man's physical features; the interior represents the man's mind engaged in harmonious imaginative thought.

> In the greenest of our valleys,
>   By good angels tenanted,
> Once a fair and stately palace—
>   Radiant palace—reared its head.

In the monarch Thought's dominion,
    It stood there!
Never seraph spread a pinion
    Over fabric half so fair!

Banners yellow, glorious, golden,
    On its roof did float and flow
(This—all this—was in the olden
    Time long ago),
And every gentle air that dallied,
    In that sweet day,
Along the ramparts plumed and pallid,
    A wingéd odor went away.

Wanderers in that happy valley,
    Through two luminous windows, saw
Spirits moving musically
    To a lute's well-tunéd law,
Round about a throne where, sitting,
    Porphyrogene,
In state his glory well befitting,
    The ruler of the realm was seen.

And all in pearl and ruby glowing
    Was the fair palace door,
Through which came flowing, flowing, flowing,
    And sparkling evermore,
A troop of Echoes, whose sweet duty
    Was but to sing,
In voices of surpassing beauty,
    The wit and wisdom of their king.

I expect you observed that the two luminous windows of
the palace are the eyes of a man, and that the yellow banners on
the roof are his luxuriant blond hair. The "pearl and ruby"
door is the man's mouth—ruby representing red lips, and pearl
representing pearly white teeth. The beautiful Echoes which
issue from the pearl and ruby door are the poetic utterances of
the man's harmonious imagination, here symbolized as an or-
derly dance. The angel-guarded valley in which the palace
stands, and which Poe describes as "the monarch Thought's
dominion," is a symbol of the man's exclusive awareness of ex-

alted and spiritual things. The valley is what Poe elsewhere called "that evergreen and radiant paradise which the true poet knows . . . as the limited realm of his authority, as the circumscribed Eden of his dreams."

As you all remember, the last two stanzas of the poem describe the physical and spiritual corruption of the palace and its domain, and it was to this part of the poem that Poe was referring when he told a correspondent, "By the 'Haunted Palace' I mean to imply a mind haunted by phantoms—a disordered brain." Let me read you the closing lines:

> But evil things, in robes of sorrow,
>   Assailed the monarch's high estate.
> (Ah, let us mourn!—for never morrow
>   Shall dawn upon him, desolate!)
> And round about his home the glory
>   That blushed and bloomed,
> Is but a dim-remembered story
>   Of the old time entombed.
>
> And travellers, now, within that valley,
>   Through the red-litten windows see
> Vast forms that move fantastically
>   To a discordant melody,
> While, like a ghastly rapid river,
>   Through the pale door
> A hideous throng rush out forever,
>   And laugh—but smile no more.

The domain of the monarch Thought, in these final stanzas, is disrupted by civil war, and in consequence everything alters for the worse. The valley becomes barren, like the domain of Roderick Usher; the eye-like windows of the palace are no longer "luminous," but have become "red-litten"—they are like the bloodshot eyes of a madman or a drunkard. As for the mouth of our allegorized man, it is now "pale" rather than "pearl and ruby," and through it come no sweet Echoes, as before, but the wild laughter of a jangling and discordant mind.

The two states of the palace—before and after—are, as we can see, two states of mind. Poe does not make it altogether clear *why* one state of mind has given way to the other, but by recourse to similar tales and poems we can readily find the answer. The palace in its original condition expresses the imaginative harmony which the poet's soul enjoys in early childhood, when all things are viewed with a tyrannical and unchallenged subjectivity. But as the soul passes from childhood into adult life, its consciousness is more and more invaded by the corrupt and corrupting external world: it succumbs to passion, it develops a conscience, it makes concessions to reason and to objective fact. Consequently, there is civil war in the palace of the mind. The imagination must now struggle against the intellect and the moral sense; finding itself no longer able to possess the world through a serene solipsism, it strives to annihilate the outer world by turning in upon itself; it flees into irrationality and dream; and all its dreams are efforts both to recall and to simulate its primal, unfallen state.

The Haunted Palace presents us with a possible key to the general meaning of Poe's architecture; and this key proves, if one tries it, to open every building in Poe's fiction. Roderick Usher, as you will remember, declaims *The Haunted Palace* to the visitor who tells his story, accompanying the poem with wild improvisations on the guitar. We are encouraged, therefore, to compare the palace of the poem with the house of the story; and it is no surprise to find that the Usher mansion has "vacant eye-like windows," and that there are mysterious physical sympathies between Roderick Usher and the house in which he dwells. The House of Usher *is*, in allegorical fact, the physical body of Roderick Usher, and its dim interior *is*, in fact, Roderick Usher's visionary mind.

The House of Usher, like many edifices in Poe, is in a state of extreme decay. The stonework of its facade has so crumbled and decomposed that it reminds the narrator, as he puts it, "of the specious totality of old woodwork which has rotted for long years in some neglected vault." The Usher mansion is so eaten away, so fragile, that it seems a breeze would push it over; it remains standing only because the atmosphere of Usher's domain is perfectly motionless and dead. Such is the case also with the "time-eaten towers that tremble not" in Poe's poem *The City in the Sea;* and likewise the magnificent architecture of *The Domain of Arnheim* is said to "sustain itself by a miracle in mid-air." Even the detective Dupin lives in a perilously decayed structure: the narrator of *The Murders in the Rue Morgue* tells how he and Dupin dwelt in a "time-eaten and grotesque mansion, long deserted through superstitions into which we did not enquire, and tottering to its fall in a retired and desolate portion of the Faubourg St. Germain." (Notice how, even when Poe's buildings are situated in cities, he manages to circumscibe them with a protective desolation.)

We must now ask what Poe means by the extreme and tottering decay of so many of his structures. The answer is best given by reference to *The Fall of the House of Usher*, and in giving the answer we shall arrive, I think, at an understanding of the pattern of that story.

The Fall of the House of Usher is a journey into the depths of the self. I have said that all journeys in Poe are allegories of the process of dreaming, and we must understand *The Fall of the House of Usher* as a dream of the narrator's, in which he leaves behind him the waking, physical world and journeys inward toward his *moi intérieur*, toward his inner and spiritual self. That inner and spiritual self is Roderick Usher.

Roderick Usher, then, is a part of the narrator's self, which the narrator reaches by way of reverie. We may think of Usher, if we like, as the narrator's imagination, or as his visionary soul. Or we may think of him as a *state of mind* which the narrator enters at a certain stage of his progress into dreams. Considered as a state of mind, Roderick Usher is an allegorical figure representing the hypnagogic state.

The hypnagogic state, about which there is strangely little said in the literature of psychology, is a condition of semiconsciousness in which the closed eye beholds a continuous procession of vivid and constantly changing forms. These forms sometimes have color, and are often abstract in character. Poe regarded the hypnagogic state as the visionary condition *par excellence,* and he considered its rapidly shifting abstract images to be—as he put it—"glimpses of the spirit's outer world." These visionary glimpses, Poe says in one of his *Marginalia*, "arise in the soul . . . only . . . at those mere points of time where the confines of the waking world blend with those of the world of dreams." And Poe goes on to say: "I am aware of these 'fancies' only when I am upon the very brink of sleep, with the consciousness that I am so."

Roderick Usher enacts the hypnagogic state in a number of ways. For one thing, the narrator describes Roderick's behavior as inconsistent, and characterized by constant alternation: he is alternately vivacious and sullen; he is alternately communicative and rapt; he speaks at one moment with "tremulous indecison," and at the next with the "energetic concision" of an excited opium-eater. His conduct resembles, in other words, that wavering between consciousness and sub-consciousness which characterizes the hypnagogic state. The trembling of Roderick's body, and the floating of his silken hair, also bring to mind the instability and underwater quality of hypnagogic images. His improvisations on the guitar suggest hypnagogic experience in their rapidity, changeableness, and wild novelty. And as for Usher's paintings, which the narrator describes as "pure abstractions," they quite simply *are* hypnagogic images. The narrator says of Roderick, "From the paintings over which his elaborate fancy brooded, and which grew, touch by touch, into vaguenesses at which I shuddered the more thrillingly because I shuddered without knowing why—from these paintings (vivid as their images now are before me) I would in vain endeavor to educe more than a small portion which should lie within the compass of merely written words." That the narrator finds Roderick's paintings indescribable is interesting, because in that one of the *Marginalia* from which I have quoted, Poe asserts that the only things in human experience which lie "beyond the compass of words" are the visions of the hypnagogic state.

Roderick Usher stands for the hypnagogic state, which as Poe said is a teetering condition of mind occurring "upon the very brink of sleep." Since Roderick is the embodiment of a state of mind in which *falling*—falling asleep—is imminent, it is appropriate that the building which symbolizes his mind should promise at every moment to fall. The House of Usher stares down broodingly at its reflection in the tarn below, as in the hypnagogic state the conscious mind may stare into the subconscious; the house threatens continually to collapse because it is extremely easy for the mind to slip from the hypnagogic state into the depths of sleep; and when the House of Usher *does* fall, the story ends, as it must, because the mind, at the end of its inward journey, has plunged into the darkness of sleep.

We have found one allegorical meaning in the tottering decay of Poe's buildings; there is another meaning, equally important, which may be stated very briefly. I have said that Poe saw the poet as at war with the material world, and with the material or physical aspects of himself; and I have said that Poe identified poetic imagination with the power to escape from the material and the materialistic, to exclude them from consciousness and so subjectively destroy them. Now, if we recall these things, and recall also that the exteriors of Poe's houses or palaces, with their eye-like windows and mouth-like doors, represent the physical features of Poe's dreaming heroes, then the characteristic dilapidation of Poe's architecture takes on sudden significance. The extreme decay of the House of Usher—a decay so extreme as to approach the atmospheric—is quite simply a sign that the narrator, in reaching that state of mind which he calls Roderick Usher, has very nearly dreamt himself free of his physical body, and of the material world with which that body connects him.

This is what decay or decomposition mean everywhere in Poe; and we find them almost everywhere. Poe's preoccupation with decay is not, as some critics have thought, an indication of necrophilia; decay in Poe is a symbol of visionary remoteness from the physical, a sign that the state of mind represented is one of almost pure spirituality. When the House of Usher disintegrates or dematerializes at the close of the story, it does so because Roderick Usher has become all soul. *The Fall of the House of Usher,* then, is not really a horror story; it is a triumphant report by the narrator that it *is* possible for the poetic soul to shake off this temporal, rational, physical world and escape, if only for a moment, to a realm of unfettered vision.

We have now arrived at three notions about Poe's typical building. It is set apart in a valley or a sea or a waste place, and this remoteness is intended to express the retreat of the poet's mind from worldly consciousness into dream. It is a tottery structure, and this indicates that the dreamer within is in that unstable threshold condition called the hypnagogic state. Finally, Poe's typical building is crumbling or decomposing, and this means that the dreamer's mind is moving toward a perfect freedom from his material self and the material world. Let us now open the door—or mouth—of Poe's building and visit the mind inside.

As we enter the palace of the visionary hero of the *Assignation,* or the house of Roderick Usher, we find ourselves approaching the master's private chamber by way of dim and winding passages, or a winding staircase. There is no end to dim windings in Poe's fiction: there are dim and winding woods paths, dim and winding streets, dim and winding watercourses—and, whenever the symbolism is architectural, there are likely to be dim and winding passages or staircases. It is not at all hard to guess what Poe means by this symbol. If we think of waking life as dominated by reason, and if we think of the reason as a daylight faculty which operates in straight lines, then it is proper that reverie should be represented as an obscure and wandering movement of the mind. There are other, and equally obvious meanings in Poe's symbol of dim and winding passages: to grope through such passages is to become confused as to place and direction, just as in reverie we begin to lose any sense of locality, and to have an infinite freedom in regard to space. In his description of the huge old mansion in which William Wilson went to school, Poe makes this meaning of winding passages very plain:

> But the house!—how quaint an old building was this!—
> to me how veritable a palace of enchantment! There was no
> end to its windings—to its incomprehensible subdivisions.
> It was difficult, at any given time, to say with certainty upon
> which of its two stories one happened to be. From each
> room to every other there were sure to be found three or
> four steps either in ascent or descent. Then the lateral
> branches were innumerable—inconceivable—and so returning in upon themselves, that our most exact ideas in regard
> to the whole mansion were not very far different from those
> with which we pondered on infinity.

Dim windings indicate the state of reverie; they point toward that infinite freedom in and from space which the mind achieves in dreams; also, in their curvature and in their occasional doubling-back, they anticipate the mind's final spiralling plunge into unconsciousness. But the immediate goal of reverie's winding passages is that magnificent chamber in which we find the visionary hero slumped in a chair or lolling on an ottoman, occupied in purging his consciousness of everything that is earthly.

Since I have been speaking of geometry—of straight lines and curves and spirals—perhaps the first thing to notice about Poe's dream-rooms is their shape. It has already been said that the enclosures of Poe's tales incline to a curving or circular form. And Poe himself, in certain of his essays and dialogues, explains this inclination by denouncing what he calls "the harsh mathematical reason of the schools," and complaining that practical science has covered the face of the earth with "rectangular obscenities." Poe quite explicitly identifies regular angular forms with everyday reason, and the circle, oval, or fluid arabesque with the otherworldly imagination. Therefore, if we discover that the dream-chambers of Poe's fiction are free of angular regularity, we may be sure that we are noticing a pointed and purposeful consistency in his architecture and décor.

The ball-room of the story *Hop-Frog* is circular. The Devil's apartment in *The Duc de l'Omelette* has its corners "rounded into niches," and we find rounded corners also in Poe's essay *The Philosophy of Furniture*. In *Ligeia*, the bridal chamber is a pentagonal turret-room; however, the angles are concealed by sarcophagi, so that the effect is circular. The corners of Roderick Usher's chamber are likewise concealed, being lost in deep shadow. Other dream-rooms are either irregular or indeterminate in form. For example, there are the seven rooms of Prince Prospero's imperial suite in *The Masque of the Red Death*. As Poe observes, "in many palaces . . . such suites form a long and straight vista"; but in Prince Prospero's palace, as he describes it, "the apartments were so irregularly disposed that the vision embraced but little more than one at a time. There was a sharp turn at every twenty or thirty yards, and at each turn a novel effect." The turret-room of *The Oval Portrait* is not defined as to shape; we are told, however, that it is architecturally "bizarre," and complicated by a quantity of unexpected nooks and niches. Similarly, the visionary's apartment in *The Assignation* is described only as dazzling, astounding and original in its architecture; we are not told in what way its dimensions are peculiar, but it seems safe to assume that it would be a difficult room to measure for wall-to-wall carpeting. The room of *The Assignation*, by the way—like that of *Ligeia*—has its walls enshrouded in rich figured draperies which are continually agitated by some mysterious agency. The fluid shifting of the figures suggests, of course, the behavior of hypnagogic images; but the agitation of the draperies would also produce a perpetual ambiguity of architectural form, and the effect would resemble that which Pevsner ascribes to the interior of San Vitale in Ravenna: "a sensation of uncertainty [and] of a dreamlike floating."

Poe, as you see, is at great pains to avoid depicting the usual squarish sort of room in which we spend much of our waking lives. His chambers of dream either approximate the circle—an infinite form which is, as Poe somewhere observes, "the emblem of Eternity"—or they so lack any apprehensible regularity of shape as to suggest the changeableness and spatial freedom of the dreaming mind. The exceptions to this rule are few and entirely explainable. I will grant, for instance, that the iron-walled torture-chamber of *The Pit and the Pendulum* portrays the very reverse of spatial freedom, and that it is painfully angular in character, the angles growing more acute as the torture intensifies. But there is very good allegorical reason for these things. The rooms of *Ligeia* or *The Assignation* symbolize a triumphantly imaginative state of mind in which the dreamer is all but free of the so-called "real" world. In *The Pit and the Pendulum,* the dream is of quite another kind; it is a nightmare state, in which the dreamer is imaginatively impotent, and can find no refuge from reality, even in dream. Though he lies on the brink of the pit, on the very verge of the plunge into unconsciousness, he is still unable to disengage himself from the physical and temporal world. The physical oppresses him in the shape of lurid graveyard visions; the temporal oppresses him in the form of an enormous and deadly pendulum. It is altogether appropriate, then, that this particular chamber should be constricting and cruelly angular.

But let us return to Poe's typical room, and look now at its furnishings. They are generally weird, magnificent, and suggestive of great wealth. The narrator of *The Assignation,* entering the hero's apartment, feels "blind and dizzy with luxuriousness," and looking about him he confesses, "I could not bring myself to believe that the wealth of any subject in Europe could have supplied the princely magnificence which burned and blazed around." Poe's visionaries are, as a general thing, extremely rich; the hero of *Ligeia* confides that, as for wealth, he possesses "far more, very far more, than ordinarily falls to the lot of mortals";

and Ellison, in *The Domain of Arnheim,* is the fortunate inheritor of 450 million dollars. Legrand, in *The Gold Bug,* with his treasure of 450 *thousand,* is only a poor relation of Mr. Ellison; still, by ordinary standards, he seems sublimely solvent.[1]

Now, we must be careful to take all these riches in an allegorical sense. As we contemplate the splendor of any of Poe's rooms, we must remember that the room is a state of mind, and that everything in it is therefore a thought, a mental image. The allegorical meaning of the costliness of Poe's decor is simply this: that his heroes are richly imaginative. And since imagination is a gift rather than an acquisition, it is appropriate that riches in Poe should be inherited or found, but never earned.

Another thing we notice about Poe's furnishings is that they are eclectic in the extreme. Their richness is not the richness of Tiffany's and Sloan's, but of all periods and all cultures. Here is a partial inventory of the fantastic bridal-chamber in *Ligeia:* Egyptian carvings and sarcophagi; Venetian glass; fretwork of a semi-Gothic, semi-Druidical character; a Saracenic chandelier; Oriental ottomans and candelabra; an Indian couch; and figured draperies with Norman motifs. The same defiance of what interior decorators once called "keeping" is found in the apartment of the visionary hero of *The Assignation,* and one of that hero's speeches hints at the allegorical meaning of his jumbled decor:

> To dream [says the hero of *The Assignation*]—to dream has been the business of my life. I have therefore framed for myself, as you see, a bower of dreams. In the heart of Venice could I have erected a better? You behold around you, it is true, a medley of architectural embellishments. The chastity of Ionia is offended by antediluvian devices, and the sphynxes of Egypt are outstretched upon carpets of gold. Yet the effect is incongruous to the timid alone. Proprieties of place, and especially of time, are the bugbears which terrify mankind from the contemplation of the magnificent.

That last sentence, with its scornful reference to "proprieties of place, and . . . time," should put us in mind of the first stanza of Poe's poem *Dream-Land:*

[1] Actually, Legrand's treasure amounted to "a million and a half of dollars," of which "four hundred and fifty thousand dollars" were in coin.—R. Wilbur.

By a route obscure and lonely,
Haunted by ill angels only,
Where an Eidolon, named NIGHT,
On a black throne reigns upright,
I have reached these lands but newly
From an ultimate dim Thule—
From a wild weird clime that lieth, sublime,
Out of SPACE—out of TIME.

In dream-land, we are "out of SPACE—out of TIME," and the same is true of such apartments or "bowers of dreams" as the hero of *The Assignation* inhabits. His eclectic furnishings, with their wild juxtapositions of Venetian and Indian, Egyptian and Norman, are symbolic of the visionary soul's transcendence of spatial and temporal limitations. When one of Poe's dream-rooms is *not* furnished in the fashion I have been describing, the idea of spatial and temporal freedom is often conveyed in some other manner: Roderick Usher's library, for instance, with its rare and precious volumes belonging to all times and tongues, is another concrete symbol of the timelessness and placelessness of the dreaming mind.

We have spoken of the winding approaches to Poe's dream-chambers, of their curvilinear or indeterminate shape, and of the rich eclecticism of their furnishings. Let us now glance over such matters as lighting, sound-proofing, and ventilation. As regards lighting, the rooms of Poe's tales are never exposed to the naked rays of the sun, because the sun belongs to the waking world and waking consciousness. The narrator of *The Murders in the Rue Morgue* tells how he and his friend Dupin conducted their lives in such a way as to avoid all exposure to sunlight. "At the first dawn of the morning," he writes, "we closed all the massy shutters of our old building; lighting a couple of tapers which, strongly perfumed, threw out only the ghastliest and feeblest of rays. By the aid of these we then busied our souls in dreams. . . ."

In some of Poe's rooms, there simply are no windows. In other cases, the windows are blocked up or shuttered. When the windows are not blocked or shuttered, their panes are tinted with a crimson or leaden hue, so as to transform the light of day into a lurid or ghastly glow. This kind of lighting, in which the sun's rays are admitted but transformed, belongs to the portrayal of those half-states of mind in which dream and reality are blended. Filtered through tinted panes, the sunlight enters certain of Poe's rooms as it might enter the half-closed eyes of a day-dreamer, or the dream-dimmed eyes of someone awakening from sleep. But when Poe wishes to represent that deeper phase of dreaming in which visionary consciousness has all but annihilated any sense of the external world, the lighting is always artificial and the time is always night.

Flickering candles, wavering torches, and censers full of writhing varicolored flames furnish much of the illumination of Poe's rooms, and one can see the appropriateness of such lighting to the vague and shifting perceptions of the hypnagogic state. But undoubtedly the most important lighting-fixture in Poe's rooms—and one which appears in a good half of them—is the chandelier. It hangs from the lofty ceiling by a long chain, generally of gold, and it consists sometimes of a censer, sometimes of a lamp, sometimes of candles, sometimes of a glowing jewel (a ruby or a diamond), and once, in the macabre tale *King Pest*, of a skull containing ignited charcoal. What we must understand about this chandelier, as Poe explains in his poem *Al Aaraaf*, is that its chain does not stop at the ceiling: it goes right on through the ceiling, through the roof, and up to heaven. What comes down the chain from heaven is the divine power of imagination, and it is imagination's purifying fire which flashes or flickers from the chandelier. That is why the immaterial and angelic Ligeia makes her reappearance directly beneath the chandelier; and that is why Hop-Frog makes his departure for dream-land by climbing the chandelier-chain and vanishing through the sky-light.

The dreaming soul, then, has its own light—a light more spiritual, more divine, than that of the sun. And Poe's chamber of dream is autonomous in every other respect. No breath of air enters it from the outside world: either its atmosphere is dead, or its draperies are stirred by magical and intramural air-currents. No earthly sound invades the chamber: either it is deadly still, or it echoes with a sourceless and unearthly music. Nor does any odor of flower or field intrude: instead, as Poe tells in *The Assignation,* the sense of smell is "oppressed by mingled and conflicting perfumes, reeking up from strange convolute censers."

The point of all this is that the dreaming psyche separates itself wholly from the bodily senses—the "rudimental senses," as Poe called them. The bodily senses are dependent on objective stimuli—on the lights and sounds and odors of the physical world. But the sensuous life of dream is self-sufficient and immaterial, and consists in the imagination's Godlike enjoyment of its own creations.

I am reminded, at this point, of a paragraph of Santayana's, in which he describes the human soul as it was conceived by the philosopher Leibniz. Leibniz, says Santayana, assigned

> a mental seat to all sensible objects. The soul, he said, had no windows and, he might have added, no doors; no light could come to it from without; and it could not exert any transitive force or make any difference beyond its own insulated chamber. It was a *camera obscura,* with a universe painted on its impenetrable walls. The changes which went on in it were like those in a dream, due to the discharge of pent-up energies and fecundities within it. . . .

Leibniz' chamber of the soul is identical with Poe's chamber of dream: but the solipsism which Leibniz saw as the normal human condition was for Poe an ideal state, a blessed state, which we may enjoy as children or as preexistent souls, but can reclaim in adult life only by a flight from everyday consciousness into hypnagogic trance.

The one thing which remains to be said about Poe's buildings is that cellars or catacombs, whenever they appear, stand for the irrational part of the mind; and that is so conventional an equation in symbolic literature that I think I need not be persuasive or illustrative about it. I had hoped, at this point, to discuss in a leisurely way some of the stories in which Poe makes use of his architectural properties, treating those stories as narrative wholes. But I have spoken too long about other things; and so, if you will allow me a few minutes more, I shall close by commenting briskly on two or three stories only.

The typical Poe story occurs *within* the mind of a poet; and its characters are not independent personalities, but allegorical figures representing the warring principles of the poet's divided nature. The lady Ligeia, for example, stands for that heavenly beauty which the poet's soul desires; while Rowena stands for that earthly, physical beauty which tempts the poet's passions. The action of the story is the dreaming soul's gradual emancipation from earthly attachments—which is allegorically expressed in the slow dissolution of Rowena. The result of this process is the soul's final, momentary vision of the heavenly Ligeia. Poe's typical story presents some such struggle between the visionary and the mundane; and the duration of Poe's typical story is the duration of a dream.

There are two tales in which Poe makes an especially clear and simple use of his architectural symbolism. The first is an unfamiliar tale called *The System of Dr. Tarr and Prof. Fether,* and the edifice of that tale is a remote and dilapidated madhouse in southern France. What happens, in brief, is that the inmates of the madhouse escape from their cells in the basement of the building, overpower their keepers, and lock them up in their own cells. Having done this, the lunatics take possession of the upper reaches of the house. They shutter all the windows, put on odd costumes, and proceed to hold an uproarious and discordant feast, during which there is much eating and drinking of a disgusting kind, and a degraded version of Ligeia or Helen does a strip-tease. At the height of these festivities, the keepers escape from their cells, break in through the barred and shuttered windows of the dining-room, and restore order.

Well: the madhouse, like all of Poe's houses, is a mind. The keepers are the rational part of that mind, and the inmates are its irrational part. As you noticed, the irrational is suitably assigned to the cellar. The uprising of the inmates, and the suppression of the keepers, symbolizes the beginning of a dream, and the mad banquet which follows is perhaps Poe's least spiritual portrayal of the dream-state: *this* dream, far from being an escape from the physical, consists exclusively of the release of animal appetites—as dreams sometimes do. When the keepers break in the windows, and subdue the revellers, they bring with them reason and the light of day, and the wild dream is over.

The Masque of the Red Death is a better-known and even more obvious example of architectural allegory. You will recall how Prince Prospero, when his dominions are being ravaged by the plague, withdraws with a thousand of his knights and ladies into a secluded, impregnable and windowless abbey, where after a time he entertains his friends with a costume ball. The weird decor of the seven ballrooms expresses the Prince's own taste, and in strange costumes of the Prince's own design the company dances far into the night, looking, as Poe says, like "a multitude of dreams." The festivities are interrupted only by the hourly striking of a gigantic ebony clock which stands in the westernmost room; and the striking of this clock has invariably a sobering effect on the revellers. Upon the last stroke of twelve, as you will remember, there appears amid the throng a figure attired in the blood-dabbled grave-clothes of a plague-victim. The dancers shrink from him in terror. But the Prince, infuriated at what he takes to be an insolent practical joke, draws his dagger and pursues the figure through all of the seven rooms. In the last and westernmost room, the figure suddenly turns and confronts Prince Prospero, who gives a cry of despair and falls upon his own dagger. The Prince's friends rush forward to seize the intruder, who stands now within the shadow of the ebony clock; but they find nothing there. And then, one after the other, the thousand revellers fall dead of the Red Death, and the lights flicker out, and Prince Prospero's ball is at an end.

In spite of its cast of one thousand and two, *The Masque of the Red Death* has only one character. Prince Prospero is one-half of that character, the visionary half; the nameless figure in grave-clothes is the other, as we shall see in a moment.

More than once, in his dialogues or critical writings, Poe describes the earth-bound, time-bound rationalism of his age as a *disease*. And that is what the Red Death signifies. Prince Prospero's flight from the Red Death is the poetic imagination's flight from temporal and worldly consciousness into dream. The thousand dancers of Prince Prospero's costume ball are just what Poe says they are—"dreams" or "phantasms," veiled and vivid creatures of Prince Prospero's rapt imagination. Whenever there is a feast, or carnival, or costume ball in Poe, we may be sure that a dream is in progress.

But what is the gigantic ebony clock? For the answer to that, one need only consult a dictionary of slang: we call the human heart a *ticker*, meaning that it is the clock of the body;

and that is what Poe means here. In sleep, our minds may roam beyond the temporal world, but our hearts tick on, binding us to time and mortality. Whenever the ebony clock strikes, the dancers of Prince Prospero's dream grow momentarily pale and still, in half-awareness that they and their revel must have an end; it is as if a sleeper should half-awaken, and know that he has been dreaming, and then sink back into dreams again.

The figure in blood-dabbled grave-clothes, who stalks through the terrified company and vanishes in the shadow of the clock, is waking, temporal consciousness, and his coming means the death of dreams. He breaks up Prince Prospero's ball as the keepers in *Dr. Tarr and Prof. Fether* break up the revels of the lunatics. The final confrontation between Prince Prospero and the shrouded figure is like the terrible final meeting between William Wilson and his double. Recognizing his adversary as his own worldly and mortal self, Prince Prospero gives a cry of despair which is also Poe's cry of despair: despair at the realization that only by self-destruction could the poet fully free his soul from the trammels of this world.

Poe's aesthetic, Poe's theory of the nature of art, seems to me insane. To say that art should repudiate everything human and earthly, and find its subject-matter at the flickering end of dreams, is hopelessly to narrow the scope and function of art. Poe's aesthetic points toward such impoverishments as *poésie pure* and the abstract expressionist movement in painting. And yet, despite his aesthetic, Poe is a great artist, and I would rest my case for him on his prose allegories of psychic conflict. In them, Poe broke wholly new ground, and they remain the best things of their kind in our literature. Poe's mind may have been a strange one; yet all minds are alike in their general structure; therefore we can understand him, and I think that he will have something to say to us as long as there is civil war in the palaces of men's minds.

Born in Alabama, STEPHEN L. MOONEY [1913–   ] studied at Howard
College, Trinity College (Dublin), and the University of Tennessee. He
has taught English at the University of Alabama, the University of Ten-
nessee (where he did his dissertation on Poe), and is now professor of
English at the University of South Alabama. In addition to "Poe's Gothic
Waste Land," Professor Mooney has published poetry, and two essays on
Poe's comic tales, "Comic Intent in Poe's Tales" (1961) and "The Comic
in Poe's Fiction" (1962). For Mooney, as for Wilbur, Poe is not "merely
Gothic." "In a sense he is still waiting to be read. . . ." Poe's "fatal
drama of cognition" exploits the Gothic as "a Gestalt of psychic states"
symbolized by the House, the Double, the Abyss, and the Waste Land.
Poe's remark about the "philosophical lynxeye" is seen as the angle of Poe's
serio-comic vision, a vision which makes Poe "the proving ground for the
modern consciousness."

Poe's Gothic Waste Land

STEPHEN L. MOONEY

> I make no exception even in Dante's favor;—the only thing well said
> of Purgatory is that a man may go farther and fare worse.—*Marginalia*

The Gothic in fiction may be defined as a Gestalt of psychic
states produced from architectural images, including the grotesque. Gothic is heightening of sense perception, sublimity of
mind; secrecy; terror of soul. It is Cartesian and Biblical: the
physical as container for the spiritual, but separated from it—
the soul in the body, the spirit in the temple, the Ghost in the
Machine, the Family in the House. Two tales of Poe, "Metzengerstein" and "Usher," are parables of Gothic. Each tale is a
family, a castle, a display of human perversity, and a gathering
of all these self-destructive forces into their own annihilation.
The House is Man personified. Body and soul, having desecrated
their humanity, deserve to die. The rise of the House of Metzengerstein in fire and smoke, the fall of the House of Usher into
water, each to its own destruction, are fatal dramas of cognition.
The imagination of the writer, the lives of his characters, and
the comprehension of the reader are caught up in one symbolic
action, a psycho-architectural or psychosomatic gesture, in which
mind and body, dying together, become one.

In Poe the psychic life of the character produces events that

From *Sewanee Review,* January–March 1962.

harmonize metaphysically with the setting and the general atmosphere. The doctrine of effect, which he made the primum mobile of his theory, thus becomes one with the doctrine of organic unity—that there shall be no integer that does not mathematically belong to the whole. Whatever the character needs in order to feel real to himself emerges around him in the form of persons, places, and actions designed to fulfill his expectations of anxiety. For the reader the unity of the tale becomes a mode of social, artistic, and cultural insight through such images of man's interior nature as Poe was able to construct for his own time and, as he no doubt expected, for ours.

A good deal of Poe's historical importance depends upon his special adaptation of the dehumanizing forces of his day, exploited in terms of the Gothic mode then fashionable. His achievement was to describe, by Gothic means, states of consciousness that picture modern man's distress in his search for values. The thing that needs to be affirmed about Poe is that he is the literary axis on which a certain kind of cycle involving the eighteenth and the twentieth centuries turns. It will be the thesis of this essay to maintain that, from plot-ruses and character-disguises, secret crimes and immolations, pseudo-science and reincarnation theories, Poe fashioned ironic images of man in a nineteenth century age of anxiety which derive from Gothicism and forecast the twentieth century waste land as a theme for literature.

The dominance of the Gothic in the tales may be said to proceed from the kind of character that Poe found it desirable to create: typically, a man beset by a sense of anxiety that rises at times to the pitch of fear and terror, but is seldom subdued to pity or compassion. The recreation of these ancient emotions has been the concern, in some degree, of all literary artists; something of the "Gothic" has always been present in European literature. It might not be wrong to say, in fact, that the Gothic is an over-specialization, an over-emphasis, of what had earlier been an assimilable part of the literature. The difference between the earlier and the later mode is one of degree, rather than of kind. Poe inherited a world of exquisitely calculated nightmare from that species of novel whose composers chose to be specialists in their field, subordinating other human emotions, desirably or undesirably, to the one theme of terror.

We may quickly discriminate between two varieties of the Gothic that depend upon the writer's point-of-view: *supernatural Gothic* and *rational Gothic*. The former view regards the events of the fiction as ultimately beyond the reach of human understanding and therefore admits inexplicable and fantastic details into the design; the latter, while admitting many of the same details and perhaps even more horrible ones, reserves an explanation that, in the end, by subterfuge and ingenious devices, clears away the mystery altogether and accounts for it on rational grounds. Brockden Brown characteristically preferred rational Gothic, just as Poe (who may have been influenced by him) chooses to do in such tales as "Thou Art the Man" and "The Sphinx," both of which depend on a comic turn for their effect.

Another useful distinction for the student of Poe is to be found in Nathan Drake's terms *terrible Gothic* and *sportive Gothic*. The "vulgar Gothic superstition," as Drake points out in his *Literary Hours* [London, 1804], is almost as old as the mind of man.

> Even in the present polished period of society [he says], there are thousands who are yet alive to all the horrors of witchcraft, to all the solemn and terrible graces of the appalling spectre. The most enlightened mind, the mind free from all taint of superstition, involuntarily acknowledges the power of Gothic fancy. . . . The enchanted forest of Tasso, the spectre of Camoens, and the apparitions of Shakespeare, are to this day highly pleasing, striking, and sublime features in these delightful compositions. . . . The vulgar Gothic . . . turns chiefly on the ministration of the Spectre, or the innocent gambols of the Fairy, the former, perhaps, partly derived from the Platonic Christianity, the latter from the fictions of the East, as imported into Europe during the period of the Crusades.

Poe's own terms, *grotesque* and *arabesque*, are suggested in Drake's *terrible* and *sportive*, a distinction that does not contradict the rational and the supernatural, but rather complements it. Poe's typical theme is alienation; his plot, survival; and his character, anxiety personified. In certain tales, the setting—and hence the mind of the character of whom it is the manifestation —is beatified, an idyllic moment of respite from the tragi-comedy of a purgatorial world. More characteristically, however, the fictional technique of the tales is turned toward the satiric, the grotesquely comic, and the genuinely terrible, at least from the present-day readers's point-of-view. Yet the reader must beware. Behind all of Poe's doors lurks the ghost of the hoaxer, secretly working toward the construction of fantastic ironies with which to plague the literalist.

Among the Poesque motifs that recur throughout modern literature, the idea of the double, the *Doppelgänger*, the *semblable*, is one of the most common. Frequently interpreted in our time as a correlative of the alienated consciousness, the motif is at least as old as Ovid's *Metamorphoses;* it may be associated with the combination of Dante and Vergil in *The Divine Comedy;* but for our purposes, it begins with Poe, is found again in Dostoevski and Conrad, and recurs as a major feature in Eliot. The doubles in Poe's *Pym* and "William Wilson," Dostoevski's *The Double,* and Conrad's *The Secret Sharer* all have affinities with some of the characters in *The Waste Land* and *Four Quartets.* All, it may be observed, are carried away, as was Narcissus himself, by the image of an alter-ego whose presence determines a fatal commitment of the self to the other, whether for salvation or destruction. As an aspect of dehumanization, this motif points to a division of the soul and the body—of the moral and the physical—that recalls Peter Schlemihl's loss of his shadow in Chamisso's story, a work well known in Poe's day and one which Poe commented upon.

More directly, the motif of the double may be related to Poe's adaptation of *The Rime of the Ancient Mariner* of Coleridge to the fictional use in the "MS. Found in a Bottle." The fact that in this tale he may have been satirizing what he regarded as Gothic excess need not proscribe any interpretation of the tale for ultimately serious purposes. Indeed, the possibility of satiric intent opens up for explication another dimension of Kierkegaardian absurdity as a factor in the modern literary theme of anxiety.

Floyd Stovall long ago pointed out the similarity of certain features of Poe's tale to Coleridge's ramparts of ice, to the two hurricanes, and to the two ocean currents leading toward the South Pole. These hazards may be related thematically to "the end of the *Inferno* when Vergil and Dante pass through the ice at the dead center of hell," in John Senior's words, "and find themselves instantaneously climbing up." More recently, Florence Marsh has observed in her article "The Ocean-Desert . . ." that *The Waste Land* and *The Ancient Mariner* are mutually illuminating if read together. Both, she maintains, are religious poems describing the need "to recover from a living death, from spiritual dryness" and from the inability to love. Though the techniques of the two poems are completely different, the presence of thematic affinities links them. Coleridge's mariner, by his experience on the ocean-desert, forecasts the twentieth century waste land of the spirit, and, one may add, emphasizes Poe's representation of this personal purgatory. For the history of ideas in literature, both Poe's and Coleridge's visions were forecast by Dante's.

Allen Tate has described Poe as "a religious man whose Christianity . . . had got short-circuited" through trying to reach God as essence. That is to say, Poe desired something resembling an existence among Platonic forms, an impossibility in a world where knowledge of God is limited to knowledge by analogy, which is to say the knowledge of the senses. The "angelic" imagination, as Mr. Tate suggests, is that which in the absence of essence sets itself up as God and is inevitably defeated, in spite of any "bibles" that it may construct, as for example Poe's *Eureka*. Yeats, to bring in another view, did not care for Poe's approach to mysticism through science. His own approach was through the occult, a way which Poe well understood but generally derogated as a serious pursuit.

Both Yeats and Eliot, to suggest a point of agreement, entertained reincarnation theory as a way of comprehending the soul's successive efforts toward perfection. Yeats apparently believed in the theory. Eliot's poetry is full of "comparative religion" and occultism, just as Poe's was full of the Gothic; but this is not a reason for saying that Eliot himself is merely an occultist, or that Poe was merely Gothic. Poe in his tales entertains occult views; Ligeia is reborn as Rowena; the second Morella appears as a re-embodiment of the first; Bedlo[e] discovers himself living in a previous incarnation as Oldeb (the name itself forming a palindrome, mechanical evidence of the two existences reversed).

Among the possible accountings for such events is the interpretation that unknowable reality is unfolded in schizoid hallucinations producing Doppelgänger images; or as literal representations of a truly existing supernatural world. In any event, they are not far from Shelley's Zoroaster-episode in *Prometheus Unbound*, which Mr. Eliot has taken over as one of the speeches for his priest-psychiatrist, Harcourt-Reilly, in *The Cocktail Party* —another version, and a way out, of the waste land:

> Ere Babylon was dust
> The magus Zoroaster, my dead child,
> Met his own image walking in the garden.
> That apparition, sole of men, he saw.
> For know there are two worlds of life and death:
> One which thou beholdest; but the other
> Is underneath the grave, where do inhabit
> The shadows of all forms that think and live
> Till death unite them and they part no more.

"The shadows of forms" in Poe are discoverable in "Eiros and Charmion," "Monos and Una," "The Power of Words," and "Shadow: a Parable," to name some of the philosophic tales; and in "Some Words with a Mummy" and "The Facts in the Case of M. Valdemar," among tales which may be regarded as comic. The alter-ego tales "William Wilson" and "The Man of the Crowd," as well as "A Tale of the Ragged Mountains," are likewise dialogues between the Self and the Soul divided from one another by the necessity of inhabiting two different bodies. The question of intent, whether comic or serious, in another story of this species, "Mesmeric Revelation," Poe has himself perhaps decided, as a reference in *Marginalia*, which will be noticed later on, reveals.

"Shadow," to choose one tale for brief review, is one of Poe's earliest ventures of its kind (*Southern Literary Messenger*, September 1835). The speaker is the Greek Oinos, who with six of his friends sat drinking wine "in the city of the Ptolemais" (his name signifies wine; the city is perhaps Poe's disguise for Charlottesville, Virginia, so designated to please those readers who rejoiced in scenes of distant strangeness, or to mask contemporary references that may well be present). They sang the songs of Anacreon (perhaps identifiable as Tom Moore, whose anacreontics had for some time enjoyed a vogue and who was referred to as "Anacreon" Moore). The spirit of Zoilus—his corpse is nearby, and the symposium is a wake in his honor—was soon perceived to dominate the revels, and from the darkness *Shadow* appeared. Upon the request of Oinos that Shadow speak, there came an answer, "not of one, but of a multitude of beings— the well remembered and familiar accents of many thousand departed friends."

If this tale, like its companion-piece "Silence," is a comedy, Poe's concealment is so exquisitely accomplished as to make the humor almost perfectly esoteric for many modern readers. The fact that it is an early tale, possibly one of the Folio group, does suggest comic intent; we know that Poe, early and late, was not above satirizing ideas and topics that he appeared at times to take seriously. Again it is suggested that for him, as for the Greeks, comedy and tragedy were sometimes interchangeable masks for the human spirit in its drama of existence. The ambiguity, if it produces a wavering between two worlds of interpretation, adds thereby a structural accompaniment to Poe's essential theme.

The uniting of visible forms with their shadows in death, "where they part no more," is an adaptation of the kind of Oriental idea commonly entertained for literary purposes in the nineteenth century, by Poe, as well as by Emerson, Thoreau, and others. Not infrequently such ideas can be traced back to the *Bhagavad Gita*. It is interesting to note that ten years after the publication of "Shadow," Poe's "M. Valdemar" appeared in the *American (Whig) Review* (December 1845) in the same issue with an unsigned essay, "The Bhagvat Geeta—Doctrine of Immortality." The Orientals, as this essay observed,

> . . . held, as a very general thing, the Abyss to be God. The visible universe is nothing other than the Abyss itself, proceeding from the potential state into actual relations— proceeding from invisibility to visibility. Hence the invisible world, if it have a substantial existence . . . is the *substance* of the visible, so that there would be but one substance or being in the universe; for the Abyss . . . is *one* [and] consists in this, that all which distinguishes one thing from another is swallowed up, destroyed.

Regardless of Poe's announced opinions of the Swedenborgians and the Transcendentalists, parts of the essay just noted are harmonious with his description of cosmological unity in *Eureka:*

Space and Duration are one; . . . with the very idea of God, omnipotent, omniscient, we entertain the idea of *the infallibility* of his law. With Him there being neither Past nor Future—with Him all being *Now*—do we not insult Him in supposing his laws so contrived as not to provide for every possible contingency?

The literary overtones of this passage are strong, if we make a few simple substitutions: *setting* for space, *time* for duration, *omniscient author* for God, and *unity* for law. Whether such substitutions are quite justifiable, it is still worth considering that Poe has derived his theology from his literary insights. The skillful literary artist in constructing a tale, like Poe's God, sees no past or future as he ordains events in the lives of his characters; all to him is *Now*, but he sets up for his characters the illusion of time, to cause an apparent separation between space and duration. And certainly he must "provide for every possible contingency," every detail of unity which may be made to engage in the total working of the story.

Approaching the matter from a slightly different view, Allen Tate describes the conclusion of *Eureka* in this way:

Thus, says Poe . . . , not only is every man his own God, every man *is* God: every man the non-spatial center into which the universe, by a reverse action of the atoms, will contract, as into its annihilation. God destroys himself in the eventual recovery of his unity. Unity equals zero. If Poe must at last "yield himself unto Death utterly," there is a lurid sublimity in his taking God along with him into a grave which is not smaller than the universe.[1]

Whether Universe or Abyss, this place—or condition—is the destination of the characters in Poe's fictional world. And yet (whether because they are literary reincarnations of Gothic romances of the past or because they were the ancestors of ideas that Poe was to bring over into *Eureka*) the dead will not keep still. They materialize again and again on earth to bring news of the unknowable and strange tidings of their experiences among the dead. They are the dehumanized messengers of "the spirit's outer world" whose words are intended for a living audience that Poe deems scarcely less dehumanized than they. To illus-

[1] See Tate's "The Angelic Imagination" in this section.—Editor's note.

trate: The mechanical, stereotyped restlessness of some of Poe's comic social groups, as they flee from one party to another in search of diversion, suggests a world of moral counterfeiters who are best described in Eliot's finely tautological line

> Distracted from distraction by distraction.

This is the endless continuity of a despair unable to recognize itself: an infinity as reduplicative as that in Shakespeare's

> Tomorrow and tomorrow and tomorrow

or in Hopkins's circular formulation

> Do what you may do, what, do what you may.

Existence in flux produces acute anxiety when the vacant repetitions of stereotyped action are the standard operations of the mind. In Greece and the Middle Ages, as Ortega y Gasset says in *The Dehumanization of Art,*

> . . . it was believed that *operari sequitur esse*—actions follow, and derive from, being. The nineteenth century may be said to have established the opposite principle: *esse sequitur operari*—the being of a thing is nothing else than the sum total of its actions and functions.

It is this movement and instability that Poe employs to represent the anxiety of characters who, impelled by their almost unconquerable wills to communicate with living men, find it so difficult to die utterly. Motion, an endless dance of *becoming*, is their mode of life, as of death, in the tales: Vertical, horizontal, spiral, serpentine motion is the existential correlative of flux. Ascent is escape; descent, capture. An awesome realization of space-time as one realm opens upon the consciousness of man as he journeys over water or through forests to discover his own image rising to meet him. The vertical journey upward, the migration into futurity, is no less a revelation than the journey down into the buried psychic past, the grave of experience. Poe's characters are frequently sent out to meet their fate on such journeys and to suffer the realization that all points of time may exist simultaneously as knowledge held in one mind.

Eliot's *The Waste Land*, in a similar depiction of experience, proposes to show

> . . . something different from either
> Your shadow at morning striding behind you
> Or your shadow at evening rising to meet you:
> I will show you fear in a handful of dust.

A token of this fear emerges in the unreal city, when the speaker engages in a moment of dialogue with an apparition for whom Space and Duration are one: the ghostly migration of persons and ideas from ancient time is cognitively manifested in phrases and whole lines brought over into the new literary context.

> Then I saw one I knew, and stopped him,
>   crying, "Stetson!
> You who were with me in the ships at Mylae!
> That corpse you planted last year in your garden,
> Has it begun to sprout? Will it bloom this year? . . .
> You! hypocrite lecteur!—mon semblable,—mon frère!"

This encounter, if interpreted as the self meeting the self, is illuminating when placed beside Poe's "William Wilson" and "Eiros and Charmion." The theme of both tales is self-destruction and catastrophe. The consequences of pursuing illusory visions of life are presented on a scale that ranges from the personal to the cosmic: William Wilson in one sense dies, and the earth of "Eiros and Charmion" explodes. Both tales present to us the picture of a personal purgatory: the one a waste land of the self, guilty of self-murder, with its consequent aridity and sense of anguish; the other a cosmic purgatory in which intellectual entities face the dilemma of existing without bodies because all physical things have been destroyed; for whom there is only the brief, final moment of cognition by which their dilemma can be explained and comprehended.

William Wilson's "death" defines the nature of his life; knowledge—communicable only through words, the most human of all inventions—persists in spite of the eradication of human values and of words as we are accustomed to understand them, and "Eiros and Charmion" maintains a similar illusion. The dialectic movement of mental states within the minds of the two William Wilsons has its parallel in the dialogue between Eiros and Charmion who, like Monos and Una, are two aspects of a single intelligence. The unity of character thus depends upon an irremediable division of the self which nevertheless is meta-physically bonded into a single entity.

The proof of purgatorial anxiety lies in the very fact that the self-murderer still must suffer knowing what he has done. William Wilson, as the speaker of his own story, demonstrates dramatically the degree of self-knowledge he has achieved through self-inflicted suffering. His articulateness is the measure of his recognition that the wages of self-murder are spiritual death. Poe turns the Wordsworthian maxim, "The child is father of the man," to the purposes of Gothic horror when he reveals that from such children as William Wilson emerge such men as the one Wilson ultimately becomes.

The exchange of identity in several such tales prefigures the modern *déjà-vu* of the psychologists and the karmic encounter of the occultists: the meeting of the double of oneself, to give a picture of two incarnations at once. As a way of presenting this kind of encounter Eliot in *Four Quartets* follows the design that Poe earlier made famous. His "familiar compound ghost/Both intimate and unidentifiable," though the same person as the speaker, is still another, and speaks in another's voice. The young man in Poe's "The Man of the Crowd" sees, or thinks he sees, his double, a disreputable old man whom he follows about the streets to determine their common identity. Eliot's speaker and his double

> . . . at this intersection time
> Of meeting nowhere, no before and after,

tread the pavement "in a dead patrol." In Poe's tale there is no exchange of words. In Eliot, there is. So, the double says, he finds words he "never thought to speak"

> In streets I never thought I should revisit
> When I left my body on a distant shore.

The "rending pain of re-enactment" of conscience returns to punish him for the unpurified motives of the past and for ill deeds once mistaken "for exercise of virtue." The whole passage is reminiscent of Hamlet's meeting with the ghost of his father, who may indeed be regarded as the double of Hamlet, his conscience that will not die. It is thus that conscience, the moral, indestructible part, is the dominant presence for certain of Poe's characters when they are alive, and a force that impels them, when dead or condemned to suffer death-in-life, to go on speaking of the nature of reality they have newly discovered. The literary purpose of picturing such illusory states is to induce in the reader a discovery of that reality which is the province of art. Explicated, the revelation may run somewhat as follows: If everything, even ultimate catastrophe, is illusory, one can only suppose the creation itself to be a phantasy of God's mind; or, conversely, a phantasm of man's mind imagining itself in the act of god-like creation and destruction. This act would come into being through God as a divine agent, performing as the counterpart of the artist of fiction himself. Thus knowledge of God might be inferred from a knowledge of art. If what is known in this way shows itself finally to be a cosmic illusion, the dilemma so produced is at least a human dilemma which it is the business of art to make real.

The artist is of course not required to solve the philosophic mysteries of creation, but rather to represent them imaginatively and effectively. Illusion is his subject, the evocation of reality his object. He is not required to communicate "beliefs" or moral attitudes, though—if his work is unified—a view of life will emerge in his fictional world that will be seen as a constant, panoramic movement of scenes, people, and actions. Never didactic (except perhaps in the footnotes that he attaches to certain tales), Poe allows the individual tale to dramatize its own part in the general theme. In the true comedies, such as "The Man That Was Used Up" and "Lionizing," the success of the protagonist follows the tendency of comic writing to produce "happy endings," and all the comic heroes escape from their predicaments to practise their frauds and delusions another day. But this is just the feature that, considered in the light of the theme of degradation in the life of the waste land, renders the comic as an ironical illustration of and commentary on the seriously philosophic tales.

Poe in "Monos and Una" expresses concern for the effects of the Industrial Revolution on humanity and on the earth as a habitable place. These, and other, effects are seen in the disintegration of personality ("Ligeia"), the pretensions of science ("Hans Pfaall"), the failure of valid social life in the community

("Lionizing" and "The Man That Was Used Up"), the fraudulence of business practices ("The Business Man" and "A Tale of Jerusalem"), the failure of ethics in everyday life ("Diddling"), the decay of technique in literature ("How to Write a Blackwood Article," illustrated by "A Predicament" and indirectly by "Loss of Breath"), and the deterioration of government ("Four Beasts in One").

To illustrate the theme of the waste land from Poe's work in later years, we may consider in some detail the parvenu characters of "Diddling" and "The Business Man" in conjunction with "Monos and Una." The modes of Poe's parvenu are brash trickery and improvisation, again aspects of the ratiocinative determination to control life. The shallow opportunism exhibited here emphasizes Poe's picture of the tendency of democratic man to make himself cheap in thought and action. Appearing to instruct the reader in the finer points of cheating and winning one's way by fraudulent means, the parvenu displays an almost total amorality that becomes the more offensive as it becomes more bold. The protagonists of "Diddling" and "The Business Man" are glib, shifty, trivial, and grossly witty—evidence, at least, of Poe's facility in conceiving unsympathetic characters dramatically and contriving for them situations conducive to self-revelation. Though the parvenu in Poe's tales is in no way admirable, he nevertheless rounds out the picture of nineteenth century Babbittry by constructing variants on the general theme of the fiction: that of human degradation in a naïvely democratic society, where economic roguery and questionable ethics are permitted to flourish unretarded.

The conduct which the parvenu describes is a source of concrete illustration for the mystical tales of destruction: "Monos and Una," an account of the judgment passed upon a world laid waste by getting and spending, is never so clear as when it is read side by side with "Diddling" and "The Business Man." The voice of the parvenu gives evidence for the truth of the mystical dialogue of "Monos and Una."

> Among other old ideas [Monos says], that of universal equality gained ground. . . . Huge smoking cities arose, innumerable. Green leaves shrank before the hot breath of furnaces. . . . We worked out our own destruction in the

perversion of taste . . . that faculty which, holding a middle position between the pure intellect and the moral sense, could never safely have been disregarded.

The activities of the Business Man, who engages in Assault and Battery, Cur-Spattering and Cat-Growing, and of the Diddler are evidences for the indictments of Monos, essential to the picture of mankind on trial for the desecration of his humanity. The emphasis is upon mundane survival and economic gain, where man is treated as a means for achieving questionable aims, rather than as a philosophic end in himself. The important feature to consider here is that Monos as speaker demonstrates his author's search for oneness in the universe and its revelation as an embodiment of language appropriate to fiction. The overtone of wistfulness that rises out of his speech has its source in the love of words for themselves—the love of earthly things, of their history, of their existence in time—which can be known only in a state of transience and mutability: *Monos, Una,* and *One* embody in their etymologies a symbol for Greek, Latin, and Saxon history which becomes a single thought at an abstract point, beyond language, where knowledge—as Monos suggests—can exist without physical incarnation and without words.

"It is only the philosophical lynxeye," Poe tells us, "that, through the indignity-mist of Man's life, can still discern the dignity of man." The lynxeye was, for Poe, the serio-comic vision that could penetrate the American scene of the early nineteenth century, even when it was most densely shrouded in ideological darkness, to discover where it failed as a community in its lack of power to nourish the individual consciousness. It was from this vision that he created a fictional world in which the symbol of the lynx became the ratiocinative private eye that silently prowls the darkest haunts of criminals to find out guilt, and ventures into the best-lighted drawing rooms and morgues to note down the comic relationships of ghosts who have not yet realized that they are quite dead.

The "indignity-mist"—etymologically the Mist of Unworthiness—is exhibited in the elaborate camouflage of the burlesque tales, the illusions of the mystical, and the ingenious ruses of the ratiocinative. The mist itself has a tragic shadowing, but Poe's way of penetrating it is frequently comic. The exposure of illusion and the lighting up of reality in the tales, serious though the theme may ultimately be, is the deliberate calculation of an artist who himself stands aside from his materials, watching the effect that he may bring about in the responses of his reader. The frequent linking of both comic and serious themes in one context is a means of guaranteeing continuity in diversity.

The supernal comedy of "Silence" and the compelling ratiocination of "A Descent into the Maelström" are projections of the symbolic lynxeye. "Lionizing" and "King Pest" are his sportive forays into surrealism, where the literal data of life are set into the motion of a fantastic dance. Very little dignity remains to man as protagonist in some of these tales; his proneness to debase himself socially, politically, and intellectually remains Poe's all-absorbing theme.

Unwilling to commit himself to the fads of philosophy and pseudo-religion that he found all around him, Poe in his detach ment confirms his artistic integrity. He asserts in *Marginalia* that

> The Swedenborgians inform me that they have discovered all that I said in a magazine article, entitled 'Mesmeric Revelation,' to be absolutely true, although at first they were strongly inclined to doubt my veracity—a thing which, in that particular instance, I never dreamed of not doubting myself. The story is a pure fiction from beginning to end.

Unless this commentary is regarded again as the prompting of the Imp of the Perverse to confuse us, we shall best accept the statement at face value: It is a fiction, and Poe's role as creator was to sacrifice everything, including "truth," to fictional effectiveness. This view need not blind us to his having entertained the theory *as* theory. But even his disposition to return again and again to a particular theory, even when masked in apparent sincerity, reveals nothing in the nature of belief genuinely held. What is revealed, however, is the perpetual searching to distinguish reality from illusion on the ocean-waste-land: the fear that resides in a handful of dust, whether of the corpse that was planted last year in the garden, or of the familiar compound ghost who returns to explain the nature of evil, at the "intersection time of meeting nowhere," or in the Abyss which is God.

It quickly becomes evident to anyone who attempts to comprehend Poe's total achievement in fiction that to describe him definitely in his artistic intentions is to put oneself in the position of the Swedenborgians who decided, after all, that "Mesmeric Revelation" was true. Poe will already have gone on record somewhere to imply that it may be a hoax and at any rate it is a fictional construction, made by a professional who cares very little about satisfying the world's need for definiteness; he only writes its fiction. If the artist can manage to exist in a world of flux, the critic may be expected to take care of himself. One gradually learns to accept the possibility that perhaps Poe was never "serious"; he never committed himself to any belief except the Artist's Credo, and all that we have to work with are his assorted fictions and criticisms, contradictory as these frequently are.

The error that many of his readers and critics have made, time after time, is to attribute to him an autobiographical, quasi-Wordsworthian theory of composition—the very reverse of what he set forth in his critical pieces. It is largely because of this error that a consideration of the total meaning of his tales has been delayed. Except in certain poems and in private letters, Poe is rarely interested in expressing his own emotions, as such. The tales are noteworthy for their attitude of dramatic objectivity, a fact that should have discouraged autobiographical interpretation, although it has not done so. Poe is detached. Even in the letters he is capable sometimes of playing skillfully upon the emotions of his correspondents (for example, John Pendleton Kennedy and Maria Clemm), who are treated as an audience that will respond to studied effects; he is aware of needing to turn the most subtle lights upon himself to project the desired image. To note the fact is not to accuse him of being insincere. Rather, it is to acknowledge that he was an artist, first and last, and his sincerity had to consist in creating effects. Anything less would have been a betrayal of his philosophy of composition, which may very nearly be read as his philosophy of life.

Least of all is he interested in the spontaneous overflow of powerful emotions recollected in tranquillity. Overflow was exactly the thing that he denounced; it was the *controlled* flow, carefully foreseen and regulated by deliberate calculation, that excited his imagination. He was not out to exploit his own emotions. He was scarcely interested in them. He was out to exercise the power of the artist over the reader's attention, and thereby to master and to manipulate the reader's responses. The naïve reader always assumes that he is in control of the words before him. The experienced reader of Poe knows better. Poe is in control.

Concerning such matters, he has been remarkably frank. He made certain observations in *Marginalia*, after finishing *The Mysteries of Paris* of Eugène Sue, that recall the protests of Milton's offended critics, objecting to the conscious manipulation of emotion for literary effect, even when this is necessary in fulfilling the requirements of a literary genre; Milton's detachment in "Lycidas" has been held against him. Like Milton, Poe in addressing his Muse—who no doubt would have to be some incarnation of the Imp of the Perverse—would not be ashamed to recommend to the Muse that she "somewhat loudly sweep the string." The professional is not carried away by his own performance. He carries his audience away. As Poe says,

> In effect, the writer is always saying to the reader, 'Now— in a moment—you shall see what you shall see. I am about to produce upon you a remarkable impression. Prepare to have your imagination, or your pity, greatly excited.'

This is the tone of the magician whose sleight-of-hand will astonish the crowd in a profusion, an extravagant flourish, of skill. Whether Poe in his tales is presenting a Grand Guignol performance of the utmost grotesquerie, or an idyllic tableau of Landor's cottage miraculously transposed into the forests of New York State, or a picture of dead souls struggling to come alive, there is always the possibility that he is standing urbanely to the side, so as to say in the tones of a perfect gentleman, "Entrez, mesdames, messieurs; everything you see around you is false."

"In perusing a . . . pathetic chapter in 'The Mysteries of Paris,'" Poe declares, "we say to ourselves, without shedding a tear—'Now here is something that will move every reader to tears.'" Here, in short, is a perfectly achieved effect. Poe warns interpreters, however, against "over-reading":

> The philosophic motives attributed to Sue are absurd in the extreme. His first, and in fact his sole object, is to make an exciting book and therefore a saleable book. The cant (im-

plied or direct) about the amelioration of society, etc., is but a very usual trick among authors, whereby they hope to add such a tone of dignity or utilitarianism to their pages as shall gild the pill of their licentiousness.

Poe's art is the art of those literalists of the imagination who, in Marianne Moore's over-famous picture, are capable of conjuring up real toads in imaginary gardens; or, in Coomaraswamy's terms, of demonstrating to the audience the grotesque immorality of casting false pearls before real swine. All that Poe ever said of simplicity as a literary doctrine, or of continuity and unity, or of appropriate brevity, was encompassed within the doctrine of effect: the calculation of the artist to involve the reader in the life of the fiction, so that an experience of reality would be forged in the consciousness, fully and permanently. Poe never says with Whitman, "Who are you now, holding me by the hand?" He is not so attractively ingenuous nor so ardently in love with the physical body of posterity. Poe is a spiritual aggressor. He moves in upon consciousness like an invading army. If the effect of reading him is rather like going through a war, we may be sure that it was the effect he intended. The reader does not forget. He knows that Poe has been there, arranging patterns of seriocomic destruction with the utmost *sang-froid*.

Poe, as Mr. Tate has said, "is the transitional figure in modern literature because he discovered our great subject, the disintegration of personality." One must not suppose that in history personalities had never disintegrated before Poe's discovery of the state. Rather, it was that he perceived the modern personality in the youngest nation on earth to be undergoing a change from what had been traditionally understood in Europe. Poe, like the nation that produced him, was in many ways an advance-guard spokesman for varieties of personal and political experience that were not to become common in Europe for many decades. He was the proving-ground for the modern consciousness; what he experienced as an artist has had the profoundest effect on the literature of the twentieth century.

His mode is irony. The serious disguises of so many of the tales that are comic in origin, and the comic disguises of the serious, are his ratiocinative discovery of himself as Eiron. Like his forebear in Greek comedy, Poe's Eiron (whether self or character) is required to use his wits as his chief means of survival.

Poe found this to be dependent upon catering to an immensely stupid but necessary antagonist, that Alazon, his audience, who never realized how profoundly they had been manipulated, or perhaps even hoaxed. Like those readers who impute a personally believed occultism and "comparative religionism" to Eliot because these things appear in his work, or those who similarly misread Baudelaire's depiction of evil, Poe's audience has always insisted a little too rashly that his life was as Gothic as his work. Evidence, imagined, speculated on, wishfully invented, and even forged, has from time to time been brought forward to prove the imperfections of the life. But the biographical facts are still at variance with the image of the work. The intellect of man is forced to choose, as Yeats said, and Poe chose to perfect the work as well as he could.

He was a good editor and writer of fiction and a fine critic. There is actually nothing to show that he did not love his wife or that he was impotent. The fact that readers have made so much of his drinking and his so-called drug-addiction is far more a criticism of and a commentary on them than it is, from the evidence we certainly have, on Poe. What may be so simply explained away can only be taken as the average reader's way of confirming, after all, his fine appreciation of his own "common sense," which supplies him with plenty of literary gossip but not much gossip about the quality of the poet's imagination. Relishing the image of Poe as the drunken dope-fiend of American literature, the gossiping reader is saved by his common-sense notion that a writer is always his own most important character. This notion makes very little room for art and comes to the general rescue when men glimpse the darker recesses of themselves—the very recesses that Poe pointed to when he said that his exploitation of terror was "not of Germany, but of the soul." This may well be his denunciation of the *merely* Gothic, the stereotype that deadens definition; it is certainly a claim staked out on a large literary ambition. In a sense, he is still waiting to be read, but he is still with us.

His especial contribution to serio-comedy is the syncopated paradox, the earnestly calculated hoax, the ironic discovery that existence actually does precede essence. Like Emily Dickinson he received

Bulletins all day
From Immortality.

His mortal disguises of the immortal news are everywhere in
the tales; he believed in a technique that would require the
reader to discover for himself where the meaning lies. If the
final meaning is fairly close to the doctrines of those Millerites,
catastrophists, and apocalyptists who flourished in his day, he
has at least left Monos and Una, Eiros and Charmion, and the
Power of Words to describe things for us.

———————

CHARLES L. SANFORD [1920–   ], a graduate of Middlebury, Brown, and
Harvard, has taught at Middlebury, Amherst, and since 1955, at Rensse-
laer Polytechnic Institute. In 1961–62 he served as Fulbright lecturer in
American studies at Clermont-Ferrand and Strasbourg, France. His *Quest
for Paradise* appeared in 1961. The following essay places Poe squarely
within the anti-European culture-pattern of the "American Adam" and the
American "quest for paradise."

Edgar Allan Poe

CHARLES L. SANFORD

Recent studies of Edgar Allan Poe have rightfully stressed his
relationship to a total Western sensibility called "the Romantic
Imagination." Indeed, his writing has had a greater seminal
influence on French literature than on American literature.
Nevertheless, the frequent charge of certain American critics
that in his "flight from reality" he lived too narrowly and failed
to respond to the vivid explorations of his countrymen needs
to be re-examined.[1]

From *Rives*, Spring 1962.

[1] See, for instance, Edward H. Davidson, *Poe: A Critical Study* (Cambridge,
Mass.: Harvard University Press, 1957), 265; Haldeen Braddy, "Poe's Flight
From Reality," *Texas Studies in Literature and Language,* I (Autumn 1959),
394–400.

Such a re-examination would reveal, I believe, an important affinity with the cult of the American Adam.[2]

From this point of view, the cycles of aspiration and disillusionment which shape Poe's work would relate to the cultural drive for a paradisiac fulfillment in the New World. Dispossessed from the earthly paradise by the lateness of the hour, Poe acted out in the strangely transmuted symbols of his art the anguish of his loss and his dreams of a restoration. The pain of loss is contained in images of diseased nature, poisoned gardens, ruined castles, depraved humanity, and above all, in the image of a mysterious blight moving across the landscape and rotting the seed of all lovely, young life. This blight, as will be seen, was often associated in Poe's mind with the progress in America of the scientific, industrial revolution. The dream of a restoration to paradise, on the other hand, is contained in the many images of the reincarnation of his dead heroines, forever isolated out of the world with him in some "great good place" like the Valley of the Many-Colored Grass. Significantly, in invoking this "great good place," Poe likened his role to that of the landscape gardener, who labored in fulfillment "not only of his own destiny as poet, but of the august purposes for which the Deity had implanted the poetic sentiment in man."[3]

His elevation of art to a position more "real" than sensible reality itself helped to compensate for his sense of impotence and inadequacy in the imperfect world around him. Repeating the original act of creation made him feel god-like, and hence, with other Romantics, he stressed the supreme virtue of originality. But his neurotic quest for originality was also inspired by American Adamic individualism; indeed, it constitutes his first, and perhaps most basic, point of contact with the visceral, quotidian experience of being an American. Ever since the Revolution, Americans have individually made a fetish of

[2] The recent book of R. W. B. Lewis, *The American Adam* (Chicago: The University of Chicago Press, 1955), does not include a study of Poe. But see a suggestive article by R. D. Jacobs, "Poe's Earthly Paradise," *American Quarterly*, XII (Fall 1960), 404–13. My own analysis here is the revision of a chapter on Poe which I did not have space to include in my *Quest for Paradise: Europe and the American Moral Imagination* (Urbana: University of Illinois Press, 1961).

[3] *The Complete Works of Edgar Allan Poe.* Virginia edition, James A. Harrison, ed. 17 vols. (New York: Thomas Y. Crowell Co., 1902), VI, 182.

declaring their independence of the past, of Europe, of the advantages of wealth and birth and have sought to begin life anew, often asserting themselves in novel ways and craving new sensations by which to satisfy Edenic expectations. As Tocqueville pointed out, they often spoke as if they belonged to a distinct and separate race of mankind.

Poe's lonely pursuit of originality owed much to a cultural nationalism which abhorred imitating Old World conventions. If, as a literary nationalist, he sometimes sought to curb "the most egregious national vanity," refusing to applaud inferior works merely because they were American, nevertheless he reserved his highest critical praise for "native *invention, novelty, originality.*" Thus he wrote that the cosmopolitan literati who contributed to the *Knickerbocker* magazine lacked "that absolutely indispensable element, individuality." Longfellow, he felt, was wedded to conventionality by didacticism, was frequently imitative, and wasted on translations time which might better have been spent in original creation. On the other hand, he hailed the genius of Hawthorne, whose most distinctive note was "invention, creation, imagination, originality—a trait which, in the literature of fiction, is positively worth all the rest."[4] In his own work, Poe strained against mortal flesh and blood to achieve, as he said, "an absoluteness of novelty," and he considered that he derived the terror of his Gothic tales not from Germany, but from the lonely depths of his own soul.

Because he wanted so badly to succeed in the American game and on American terms, he was not always able to be sincere. He would have us believe that he wrote his poem "The Raven" backward from his conception of its total effect "keeping originality always in view." His prose-poem *Eureka,* which handed down from on high a master plan of the universe, waved a magisterial finger. He often exploited the novelties of horror in his tales of the grotesque and, when this source of cerebral excitement failed, invented crude hoaxes. Like P. T. Barnum, he paraded before the American public much that was merely cheap and sensational: what could be more in offensive bad taste than the hideous disclosures of his story "Berenice." Neverthe-

---

[4] "Hawthorne's *Twice-Told Tales*," *Complete Works*, XI, 102–13; "Longfellow's *Ballads*," Ibid., XI, 64–85; "Lewis Gaylord Clark," Ibid., XV, 114–16.

less, his resolute pioneering in novel experience beyond the reach of average men left a record of exploration quite as vivid and more profound, even "truer," than the myriad, shallow delineations of frontier life in the wake of James Fenimore Cooper or the many evocations of an idyllic plantation life in the South such as George Tucker's *Valley of the Shenandoah.*

Only an original genius like Poe could have persisted in observing the condition of "pleasurable ecstasy" between sleeping and waking until he was able to transfer the point into conscious memory. Only Poe, of all American writers, would then have constructed a useful, and even novel, aesthetic theory based upon his study of the strange sensations evoked by such experience. He found, for instance, a certain identity in the sensations created by the orange ray of the spectrum, the buzz of a gnat, and an odor in the air. He could hear grass grow. This condition of synaesthesia could not be rendered directly, but only suggested or intimated in language which approached the indefiniteness and the disciplined form of music. His recommendation for poetry of a rational process of creation after the precise mathematical pattern of music thus broke sharply with the "fine frenzy," the "ecstatic intuition" of Romantic theory. His success in evoking subtly undifferentiated overtones and shades of feeling by means of sharp, particularized images in musical juxtaposition endeared him to French symbolists.

Although Poe's retreat into imagination was destructive of the real world of the senses, his sublimations of experience mirrored the deeper, mythic meaning of America. What could be more true about the Southland, for instance, than its fatal fascination with the aristocratic ideal, a fascination which Poe inverted into incestuous horror twenty years before the Civil War and a hundred years before William Faulkner's tangled genealogies of fallen pride? Indeed, Poe's aesthetic theories have much in common with the gentlemanly code of the Southern cavalier and his lady. The Southern planter argued in defense of slavery that cultivation of the finer things of life depended on a leisure class free of manual labor and coarse material considerations. To the habit of authority as a mark of his class he added the external embellishments of the gentleman: polite learning, elegance, grace, form, refinement of dress and manners. Thus, in his art, Poe tended to concentrate on *form* almost to the exclusion of *matter.* His poetic principles implied that poetry, like music, should be a *graceful* accomplishment, quite remote from harsh realities, didactic considerations, and even coarse passion. And the central position given to the death of beautiful women as the subject matter best fitted to "elevate the Soul" in both poetry and fiction was almost a parody of the South's deification of womanhood.

In the main, Poe inverted the South'and's aristocratic ideal, investing it with the alien trappings of that feudal European culture which the American Adam has traditionally associated with Hell. It has been said in this respect that Poe's stories with their medieval European settings could have been written if he had never set foot in America. This charge, besides being irrelevant to the question of artistic merit, is certainly untrue. The furniture for Poe's stories comes straight out of the Southern mind. The more the South was put to defend its shaky institutions, that is, the more frantically the plantation gentry sought to trace their aristocratic lineage back to Europe, the more enamoured they became with the ancient example of European privilege. Just prior to the Civil War, the Southern mind became so saturated with Sir Walter Scott's romantic idealizations of chivalry that Mark Twain half-facetiously attributed the Civil War to Sir Walter Scott. Poe rearranged the furniture of Sir Walter Scott for the scenario of an American "Frankenstein." Thus he converted the Southland's flattering self-image into the American Adam's familiar stereotype of the hellish Old World.

The American Adam was a child of virgin forests and prairies who liked to contrast the natural virtues and beauty of his native land with effete Old World civilization. But Poe, Perry Miller has written in *The Raven and the Whale,* summoned only evil out of the land of nature. This charge also is not quite true. Rather to the contrary, the lurking, insidious malevolence of Poe's stories is most often connected with the infiltration of the Gardenland by ancient European wrongs and precedents. It can be argued, in fact, that Poe's impossible dreams of supernal beauty and ineffable bliss were part of his cultural inheritance as an American Adam. Like Emerson and Cooper—and, of course, Jefferson, whose University of Virginia he once attended —Poe was attracted to the pole of ideality represented by the American West. His realistically written, though fictitious, account of the first passage across the Rockies by a white man "The Journal of Julius Rodman," surveyed both the actuality of "howling wilderness" and the romantic West of fabulous promise.

The narrator in it confessed that he pursued the ideal rather than profit: "I was anxious to *go on*—to get, if possible, beyond the extreme bounds of civilization. . . ."[5] A similar sentiment attached to the poem "Eldorado," and almost all of Poe's evocations of supernal beauty merge in some way with the details of a luxurious garden setting far from civilization. A classic example is the tale "Eleonora," which re-enacts the story of Adam and Eve. "The loveliness of Eleonora," Poe writes, "was that of the Seraphim; but she was a maiden artless and innocent as the brief life she had led among the flowers." Of course, the grass, the streams, the flowers spoke to the young lovers "in loud tones of the love and of the glory of God."[6]

Poe's favorite subject was the death of a beautiful woman, a preference which suggests that his own experience of the inevitable fall from Paradise was intimately connected with failure in love. But he habitually enveloped the sympathy of a woman in the beauty of nature. Thus, he compared the garden of Arnheim to a lady fair, "that lay as if she slumbered in delight." In this sketch, "The Domain of Arnheim," Ellison devoted his whole enormous fortune to the "one master passion of his soul, the thirst for beauty; above all, it was in the sympathy of a woman, not unwomanly, whose loveliness and love enveloped his existence in the purple atmosphere of Paradise, that Ellison thought to find, *and found,* exemption from the ordinary cases of humanity. . . ."[7] Similarly, in the poem "To One in Paradise," Poe finds his highest bliss in a woman whose beauty he rendered in the imagery of a green isle, a fountain, and a shrine wreathed about with fruits and flowers. Conversely, he frequently rendered the features of the natural landscape in feminine form. But Poe's master image for Eden was not rank wilderness; it was the landscape garden, wherein the creativity of man completed the primitive intention of nature. This was Poe's poetic counterpart for Thomas Jefferson's agrarian conception of transforming a wilderness into a rural utopia.

[5] "The Journal of Julius Rodman," *Complete Works*, IV, 77.
[6] *Complete Works*, IV, 238–39.
[7] Ibid., VI, 188.

In expressing their sense of the cultural midpoint between savagery and sophistication, Jefferson thought on the plane of national destiny, Poe of personal destiny. The one envisioned a nation of yeoman farmers; the other the more gentlemanly "bower of love." Yet Poe shared Jefferson's agrarian prejudices against manufacturing, industry, and urban centers; and both feared the encroachment of European civilization on the Eastern seaboard. Although Poe revered the methods of science, at least to the point where logic broke down, he felt intuitively that the wedding of science to commerce and technological progress was wreaking havoc. With Thoreau, he symbolized science as a vulture preying upon the human heart. In his story "The Purloined Letter," the microscope aptly suggested "all this boring, and probing, and sounding, and scrutinizing" in the interest of mere utility. Like Hawthorne, he sometimes depicted diabolical machines of torture imported from Europe. His story "The Business Man" satirized the success formula. He once wrote from harsh personal experience that in no country were the poor more despised.

In his essay on the "Philosophy of Furniture" he deplored the new American monied aristocracy's degraded rage for glitter and glare. He overlooked the same extravagance in his own nature. Society's vain attempts to mirror European aristocracy, concentrating in Eastern cities, became the subject of two allegories, both with settings in Europe. The first was "The Masque of the Red Death," which summed up in the image of the princely revellers the futility of all pretension. The second, "The Man of the Crowd," located the ancestral home of human crime in the city of London. The old man in this story was "the type and the genius of deep crime. He refuses to be alone. *He is the man of the crowd*."[8] Thus, Poe's fascination with crime, which dates from this story, was from the beginning vaguely associated with the transit of European civilization to the New World, bringing with it a mysterious blight. This fascination with ancestral depravity, joined to his interest in the methods of science, produced the detective story. But his stories of detection have in common with his tales of the supernatural the fact that they are equally concerned, though in different ways, with images of diseased nature. In this respect, the murdering orangutan is one

[8] Ibid., IV, 145.

with the revenge of Montresor, the incestuous fixation of Usher, the terrible intensities of the ladies Madeline and Ligeia, and such fissures in nature as the Maelström of Moskoe or the cataclysmic storm which tumbled the House of Usher into the haunted tarn.

If this reading is accurate, Poe summoned evil not out of the land of nature, but, more traditionally, out of the fallen garden of Europe. He understood instinctively that this process of corruption began on the Eastern seaboard and spread westward. Thus, in a tale entitled "The Island of the Fay," he attached a symbolic significance to the geography of east and west. The western end of the island "was all one radiant harem of garden beauties. It glowed and blushed beneath the eye of the slant sunlight, and fairly laughed with flowers. . . . The other or eastern end of the isle was whelmed in the blackest shade."[9]

This island sanctuary from the "wreck of the race" was finally invaded from the east by blight and death. This image of blight moving over the face of the land represented long before the desperate pilgrimages of F. Scott Fitzgerald's heroes a profound displacement of the American dream. It exposes, too, the callow optimism of those classic American refugees from civilization: Daniel Boone, Cooper's Natty Bumppo, and Twain's Huck Finn.

> And o'er his heart a shadow
> Fell as he found
> No spot of ground
> That looked like Eldorado.

That the coming of the industrial revolution was largely responsible for Poe's disillusionment is suggested by the fact that he described it in the same imagery of mysterious blight which surrounded the deaths of his many lovely heroines. "Meantime," he wrote, "huge smoking cities arose, innumerable. Green leaves shrank before the hot breath of furnaces. The fair face of Nature was deformed as with the ravages of some loathsome disease." He recalled Adam and Eve's fall from Paradise, finding in "the mystic parable that tells of the tree of knowledge, and of its forbidden fruit, death-producing, a distinct intimation that

[9] Ibid., IV, 197.

knowledge was not meet for man in the infant condition of his soul." For him, as for Henry James later, Europe had written large the remedial lessons of worldly experience: "The Earth's records had taught me to look for widest ruin as the price of highest civilization."[10] His mind recoiled before the swift and unaccustomed changes wrought by industrialism, and he delivered himself over to the romantic preoccupation with the passage of time. In "Tamerlane" he wrote:

> . . . boyhood is a summer sun
> Whose waning is the dreariest one.
> For all we live to know is known,
> And all we seek to keep hath flown.
> Let life, then, as the day-flower, fall
> With the noon-day beauty—which is all.

Everywhere in his writing, the short seasons of human life pass in swift review to the sound of tolling bells or the ticking of the symbolic clock which finally ended the gruesome "Masque of the Red Death."

Poe's belief that too much knowledge brings destruction and death is in the tradition of the American Adam. It reminds one of the theoretical anti-intellectualism of Jefferson and Emerson and even, at times, of the emotional anti-intellectualism of frontier preachers and pioneers. But it also established another link between his premonitions of industrial doom and his fear of death and personal extinction. The loved ones of his stories are commonly destroyed by too much knowledge, victims of psychic probing and analysis. His intuitionism, on the other hand, supplied the basis for a belief in the persistence of personal identity after death. He argued in *Eureka* that both Aristotelian deduction and Baconian induction, being inadequate, must give way to *intuition*. In his story "The Gold Bug" he wrote "The mind struggles to establish a connection, a sequence of cause and effect, and, being unable to do so, suffers a species of temporary paralysis." Yet too vainly intelligent to be caught flat-footed in an anti-intellectual stance, he sometimes argued that by intuition he meant a higher faculty of human intelligence: human reason, which has exhausted itself for man's improvement. Only then

[10] Ibid., IV, 204.

would man's "natural state be ultimately reached, or thoroughly determined."[11]

What he probably meant was a state of disinterested intelligence beyond carnal knowledge, as in his almost religious adoration of Woman as Diana, goddess of chastity. His deification of such women gave them access to a life beyond the grave, from which his own sexual guilt and knowledge barred him. The theme of spiritual rebirth appears in such stories as "Eleonora," "Ligeia," "The Assignation," "The Fall of the House of Usher," and "Morella," as well as in many poems. In "Morella," for instance, this theme is related to that of incest. A radiantly lovely woman who dies in childbirth is spiritually reincarnated in the person of her daughter. The husband then falls in love with his daughter, destroying her with his incestuous knowledge. Here, as elsewhere, the tragic rhythm of hope alternating with despair is manifest. The important thing to note, however, is that, whatever the form of sublimation, Poe shared the American Adam's hope for a life renewal—and even a social reformation.

His hope for a social reformation rested on the total extinction of the present industrial society. If mankind were to survive, the society must undergo the same throes of disease, death, and rebirth as his many heroines. "That man, as a race, should not become extinct, I saw that he must be 'born again.'" He has his characters, Monos and Una, discourse of the days to come after the Apocalypse: [12]

> when the Art-scarred surface of the Earth, having undergone that purification which alone could efface its rectangular obscenities, should clothe itself anew in the verdure and the mountain-slopes and the smiling waters of Paradise, and be rendered at length a fit dwelling-place for man:—for man the Death-purged—for man to whose now exalted intellect there should be the poison in knowledge no more—for the redeemed, regenerated, blissful, and now immortal, but still for the *material*, man.

[11] Cf. "Marginalia," *Complete Works*, XVI, 7; "The Colloquy of Monos and Una," Ibid., IV, 201–6, 208; *Eureka*, Ibid., XVI, 204, 314–15.

The role of intuition is also treated in "The Gold Bug," Ibid., V, 123; "Murders in the Rue Morgue," Ibid., IV, 149–50; "The Purloined Letter," Ibid., VI, 28–52.

[12] *Complete Works*, IV, 205.

Poe's thinking thus followed the traditional pattern of Christian millennialism. A similar millennialism had become a central article of faith of those early settlers and colonists who sought a restoration to Paradise in the New World and who periodically read the signs of their coming bliss in the rapid deterioration of the present. One wonders how Poe would have confronted the apocalyptic image of the mushroom cloud, which certainly hastens the day of the total extinction of our present industrial civilization without promising a rebirth of the material man.

Poe's more intimately personal image of life renewal, however, was his poetry, which he also clothed in paradisiac raiment. "If, indeed, there be any one circle of thought distinctly and palpably marked out from amid the jarring and tumultuous chaos of human intelligence," he once wrote, "it is that evergreen and radiant Paradise which the true poet knows, and knows alone, as the limited realm of his authority—as the circumscribed Eden of his dreams."[13] His main statement of poetic faith, "The Poetic Principle," expresses a similar sentiment. Here he wrote that only poetry was capable of speaking to the inner man with the force of waving grain-fields, slanting tall trees, gleaming silver streams, voluptuous hyacinth perfume, singing birds, and the beauty of woman. Nor did he forget to pay his respects to the master metaphor of his poetic calling, the landscape garden:[14]

> The poetic sentiment, of course, may develop itself in various modes: in painting, in sculpture, in architecture, in the dance, very especially in music, and very peculiarly and with a wide field, in the composition of the landscape garden.

One concludes that Poe embraced poetry as an image of transcendent ideality which isolated him with his landscape garden out of an imperfect world in which he could only bewail the lateness of the hour. He early experienced that profound displacement of the American Dream which is proving to be so very disturbing to the new generation of Americans.

[13] Ibid., VIII, 281.
[14] Ibid., XIV, 274.

In 1963–64 JAMES W. GARGANO [1917–   ], professor of English at Washington and Jefferson College, served as Fulbright lecturer at the University of Caen. He has published articles on James, Whitman, and Hawthorne; and the following articles on Poe: "Poe's 'To Helen'" (1960); "'The Black Cat': Perverseness Reconsidered" (1960); and "'Ligeia': Dream and Destruction" (1962). In the following essay, Professor Gargano concentrates on a relatively neglected aspect of Poe's impressionistic tales: the psychology of the narrator as *persona* determined by elements of dramatic irony, structure, and function.

The Question of Poe's Narrators

JAMES W. GARGANO

Part of the widespread critical condescension toward Edgar Allan Poe's short stories undoubtedly stems from impatience with what is taken to be his "cheap" or embarrassing Gothic style. Finding turgidity, hysteria, and crudely poetic overemphasis in Poe's works, many critics refuse to accept him as a really serious writer. Lowell's flashy indictment of Poe as "two-fifths sheer fudge"[1] agrees essentially with Henry James's magisterial declaration that an "enthusiasm for Poe is the mark of a decidedly primitive stage of reflection."[2] T. S. Eliot seems to be echoing James when he attributes to Poe "the intellect of a highly gifted young person before puberty."[3] Discovering in Poe one of the fountainheads of American obscurantism, Yvor Winters condemns the incoherence, puerility, and histrionics of his style. Moreover, Huxley's charge that Poe's poetry suffers from "vulgarity" of spirit, has colored the views of critics of Poe's prose style.[4]

Certainly, Poe has always had his defenders. One of the most brilliant of modern critics, Allen Tate finds a variety of styles in Poe's works; although Tate makes no high claims for

From *College English*, December 1963.

[1] "A Fable for Critics," *The Complete Poetical Works of James Russell Lowell* (Cambridge, 1896), p. 140.

[2] Henry James, "Charles Baudelaire," *French Poets and Novelists* (London, 1878).

[3] T. S. Eliot, "From Poe to Valéry," p. 28.

[4] Aldous Huxley, "Vulgarity in Literature," *Music at Night and Other Essays* (London, 1949), pp. 297–309.

Poe as stylist, he nevertheless points out that Poe could, and often did, write with lucidity and without Gothic mannerisms.[5] Floyd Stovall, a long-time and more enthusiastic admirer of Poe, has recently paid his critical respects to "the conscious art of Edgar Allan Poe."[6] Though he says little about Poe's style, he seems to me to suggest that the elements of Poe's stories, style for example, should be analyzed in terms of Poe's larger artistic intentions. Of course, other writers, notably Edward H. Davidson, have done much to demonstrate that an intelligible rationale informs Poe's best work.[7]

It goes without saying that Poe, like other creative men, is sometimes at the mercy of his own worst qualities. Yet the contention that he is fundamentally a bad or tawdry stylist appears to me to be rather facile and sophistical. It is based, ultimately, on the untenable and often unanalyzed assumption that Poe and his narrators are identical literary twins and that he must be held responsible for all their wild or perfervid utterances; their shrieks and groans are too often conceived as emanating from Poe himself. I believe, on the contrary, that Poe's narrators possess a character and consciousness distinct from those of their creator. These protagonists, I am convinced, speak their own thoughts and are the dupes of their own passions. In short, Poe understands them far better than they can possibly understand themselves. Indeed, he often so designs his tales as to show his narrators' limited comprehension of their own problems and states of mind; the structure of many of Poe's stories clearly reveals an ironical and comprehensive intelligence critically and artistically ordering events so as to establish a vision of life and character which the narrator's very inadequacies help to "prove."

What I am saying is simply that the total organization or completed form of a work of art tells more about the author's sensibility than does the report or confession of one of its characters. Only the most naive reader, for example, will credit as the "whole truth" what the narrators of *Barry Lyndon, Huckleberry Finn,* and *The Aspern Papers* will divulge about themselves and

---

[5] Allen Tate, "Our Cousin, Mr. Poe," *The Man of Letters in the Modern World,* Meridian Books, pp. 132–45.

[6] Floyd Stovall, "The Conscious Art of Edgar Allan Poe," *College English,* 24 (March 1963), 417–21.

[7] Edward H. Davidson, *Poe: A Critical Study* (Cambridge, 1957).

their experiences. In other words, the "meaning" of a literary work (even when it has no narrator) is to be found in its fully realized form; for only the entire work achieves the resolution of the tensions, heterogeneities, and individual visions which make up the parts. The Romantic apologists for Milton's Satan afford a notorious example of the fallacy of interpreting a brilliantly integrated poem from the point of view of its most brilliant character.

The structure of Poe's stories compels realization that they are more than the effusions of their narrators' often disordered mentalities. Through the irony of his characters' self-betrayal and through the development and arrangement of his dramatic actions, Poe suggests to his readers ideas never entertained by the narrators. Poe intends his readers to keep their powers of analysis and judgment ever alert; he does not require or desire complete surrender to the experience of the sensations being felt by his characters. The point of Poe's technique, then, is not to enable us to lose ourselves in strange or outrageous emotions, but to see these emotions and those obsessed by them from a rich and thoughtful perspective. I do not mean to advocate that, while reading Poe, we should cease to feel; but feeling should be "simultaneous" with an analysis carried on with the composure and logic of Poe's great detective, Dupin. For Poe is not merely a Romanticist; he is also a chronicler of the consequences of the Romantic excesses which lead to psychic disorder, pain, and disintegration.

Once Poe's narrative method is understood, the question of Poe's style and serious artistry returns in a new guise. Clearly, there is often an aesthetic compatibility between his narrators' hypertrophic language and their psychic derangement; surely, the narrator in "Ligeia," whose life is consumed in a blind rage against his human limitations, cannot be expected to consider his dilemma in cooly rational prose. The language of men reaching futilely towards the ineffable always runs the risk of appearing more flatulent than inspired. Indeed, in the very breakdown of their visions into lurid and purple rhetoric, Poe's characters enforce the message of failure that permeates their aspirations and actions. The narrator in "Ligeia" blurts out, in attempting to explain his wife's beauty in terms of its "expression": "Ah,

words of no meaning!" He rants about "incomprehensible anomalies," "words that are impotent to convey," and his inability to
capture the "inexpressible." He raves because he cannot explain. His feverish futility of expression, however, cannot be
attributed to Poe, who with an artistic "control," documents the
stages of frustration and fantastic desire which end in the narrator's madness. The completed action of "Ligeia," then, comments on the narrator's career of self-delusion and exonerates
Poe from the charge of lapsing into self-indulgent, sentimental
rodomontade.

In "The Tell-Tale Heart" the cleavage between author and
narrator is perfectly apparent. The sharp exclamations, nervous
questions, and broken sentences almost too blatantly advertise
Poe's conscious intention; the protagonist's painful insistence in
"proving" himself sane only serves to intensify the idea of his
madness. Once again Poe presides with precision of perception
at the psychological drama he describes. He makes us understand that the voluble murderer has been tortured by the nightmarish terrors he attributes to his victim: "He was sitting up in
bed listening;—just as I have done, night after night, harkening
to the death watches in the wall"; further the narrator interprets
the old man's groan in terms of his own persistent anguish:
"Many a night, just at midnight, when all the world slept, it has
welled up from my own bosom, deepening, with its dreadful
echo, the terrors that distracted me." Thus, Poe, in allowing his
narrator to disburden himself of his tale, skillfully contrives to
show also that he lives in a haunted and eerie world of his own
demented making.

Poe assuredly knows what the narrator never suspects and
what, by the controlled conditions of the tale, he is not meant
to suspect—that the narrator is a victim of his own self-torturing
obsessions. Poe so manipulates the action that the murder, instead of freeing the narrator, is shown to heighten his agony
and intensify his delusions. The watches in the wall become the
ominously beating heart of the old man, and the narrator's
vaunted self-control explodes into a frenzy that leads to self-
betrayal. I find it almost impossible to believe that Poe has no
serious artistic motive in "The Tell-Tale Heart," that he merely
revels in horror and only inadvertently illuminates the depths of

the human soul. I find it equally difficult to accept the view that Poe's style should be assailed because of the ejaculatory and crazy confession of his narrator.

For all of its strident passages, "William Wilson" once again exhibits in its well-defined structure a sense of authorial poise which contrasts markedly with the narrator's confusion and blindness. Wilson's story is organized in six parts: a rather "over-written" *apologia* for his life; a long account of his early student days at Dr. Bransby's grammar school, where he is initiated into evil and encounters the second Wilson; a brief section on his wild behavior at Eton; an episode showing his blackguardly conduct at Oxford; a nondramatic description of his flight from his namesake-pursuer; and a final, climactic scene in which he confronts and kills his "double." The incidents are so arranged as to trace the "development" of Wilson's wickedness and moral blindness. Moreover, Poe's conscious artistic purpose is evident in the effective functioning of many details of symbolism and setting. "Bright rays" from a lamp enable Wilson to see his nemesis "vividly" at Dr. Bransby's; at the critical appearance of his double at Eton, Wilson's perception is obscured by a "faint light"; and in the scene dealing with Wilson's exposé at Oxford, the darkness becomes almost total and the intruder's presence is "felt" rather than seen. Surely, this gradual extinction of light serves to point up the darkening of the narrator's vision. The setting at Dr. Bransby's school, where it was impossible to determine "upon which of its two stories one happened to be," cleverly enforces Poe's theme of the split consciousness plaguing Wilson. So, too, does the portrait of the preacher-pastor: "This reverend man, with countenance so demurely benign, with robes so glossy and so clerically flowing, with wig so minutely powdered, so rigid and so vast,—could this be he who, of late, with sour visage and in snuffy habiliments, administered, ferule in hand, the Draconian laws of the academy? Oh, gigantic paradox, too utterly monstrous for solution!" Finally, the masquerade setting in the closing scene of the tale ingeniously reveals that Wilson's whole life is a disguise from his own identity.

To maintain that Poe has stumbled into so much organization as can be discovered in "William Wilson" and his other tales requires the support of strong prejudice. There seems little reason for resisting the conclusion that Poe knows what ails Wilson and sees through his narrator's lurid self-characterization as a "victim to the horror and the mystery of the wildest of all sublunary visions." Assuredly, a feeling for the design and subtlety of Poe's "William Wilson" should exorcise the idea that he is as immature and "desperate" as his protagonist. After all, Poe created the situations in which Wilson confronts and is confronted by his *alter ego;* it is Wilson who refuses to meet, welcome, and be restrained by him.

Evidence of Poe's "seriousness" seems to me indisputable in "The Cask of Amontillado," a tale which W. H. Auden has belittled.[8] Far from being his author's mouthpiece, the narrator, Montresor, is one of the supreme examples in fiction of a deluded rationalist who cannot glimpse the moral implications of his planned folly. Poe's fine ironic sense makes clear that Montresor, the stalker of Fortunato, is both a compulsive and pursued man; for in committing a flawless crime against another human being, he really (like Wilson and the protagonist in "The Tell-Tale Heart") commits the worst of crimes against himself. His reasoned, "cool" intelligence weaves an intricate plot which, while ostensibly satisfying his revenge, despoils him of humanity. His impeccably contrived murder, his weird mask of goodness in an enterprise of evil, and his abandonment of all his life-energies in one pet project of hate convict him of a madness which he mistakes for the inspiration of genius. The brilliant masquerade setting of Poe's tale intensifies the theme of Montresor's apparently successful duplicity; Montresor's ironic appreciation of his own deviousness seems further to justify his arrogance of intellect. But the greatest irony of all, to which Montresor is never sensitive, is that the "injuries" supposedly perpetrated by Fortunato are illusory and that the vengeance meant for the victim recoils upon Montresor himself. In immolating Fortunato, the narrator unconsciously calls him the "noble" Fortunato and confesses that his own "heart grew sick." Though Montresor attributes this sickness to "the dampness of the catacombs," it is clear that his crime has begun to "possess" him.

[8] Auden, "Introduction" to *Edgar Allan Poe: Selected Prose and Poetry,* Rinehart editions, p. v.

We see that, after fifty years, it remains the obsession of his life; the meaning of his existence resides in the tomb in which he has, symbolically, buried himself. In other words, Poe leaves little doubt that the narrator has violated his own mind and humanity, that the external act has had its destructive inner consequences.

The same artistic integrity and seriousness of purpose evident in "The Cask of Amontillado" can be discovered in "The Black Cat." No matter what covert meanings one may find in this much-discussed story, it can hardly be denied that the nameless narrator does not speak for Poe. Whereas the narrator, at the beginning of his "confession," admits that he cannot explain the events which overwhelmed him, Poe's organization of his episodes provides an unmistakable clue to his protagonist's psychic deterioration. The tale has two distinct, almost parallel parts: in the first, the narrator's inner moral collapse is presented in largely symbolic narrative; in the second part, the consequences of his self-violation precipitate an act of murder, punishable by society. Each section of the story deals with an ominous cat, an atrocity, and an exposé of a "crime." In the first section, the narrator's house is consumed by fire after he has mutilated and subsequently hanged Pluto, his pet cat. Blindly, he refuses to grant any connection between his violence and the fire; yet the image of a hanged cat on the one remaining wall indicates that he will be haunted and hag-ridden by his deed. The sinister figure of Pluto, seen by a crowd of neighbors, is symbolically both an accusation and a portent, an enigma to the spectators but an infallible sign to the reader.

In the second section of "The Black Cat," the reincarnated cat goads the narrator into the murder of his wife. As in "William Wilson," "The Tell-Tale Heart," and "The Cask of Amontillado," the narrator cannot understand that his assault upon another person derives from his own moral sickness and unbalance. Like his confreres, too, he seeks psychic release and freedom in a crime which completes his torture. To the end of his life, he is incapable of locating the origin of his evil and damnation within himself.

The theme of "The Black Cat" is complicated for many critics by the narrator's dogged assertion that he was pushed into evil and self-betrayal by the "imp of the perverse." This imp is explained, by a man who, it must be remembered, eschews explanation, as a radical, motiveless, and irresistible impulse within the human soul. Consequently, if his self-analysis is accepted, his responsibility for his evil life vanishes. Yet, it must be asked if it is necessary to give credence to the words of the narrator. William Wilson, too, regarded himself as a "victim" of a force outside himself and Montresor speaks as if he has been coërced into his crime by Fortunato. The narrator in "The Black Cat" differs from Wilson in bringing to his defense a well-reasoned theory with perhaps a strong appeal to many readers. Still, the narrator's pat explanation is contradicted by the development of the tale, for instead of being pushed into crime, he pursues a life which makes crime inevitable. He cherishes the intemperate self-indulgence which blunts his powers of self-analysis; he is guided by his delusions to the climax of damnation. Clearly, Poe does not espouse his protagonist's theory any more than he approves of the specious rationalizations of his other narrators. Just as the narrator's well constructed house has a fatal flaw, so the theory of perverseness is flawed because it really explains nothing. Moreover, even the most cursory reader must be struck by the fact that the narrator is most "possessed and maddened" when he most proudly boasts of his self-control. If the narrator obviously cannot be believed at the end of the tale, what argument is there for assuming that he must be telling the truth when he earlier tries to evade responsibility for his "sin" by slippery rationalizations?

A close analysis of "The Black Cat" must certainly exonerate Poe of the charge of merely sensational writing. The final frenzy of the narrator, with its accumulation of superlatives, cannot be ridiculed as an example of Poe's style. The breakdown of the shrieking criminal does not reflect a similar breakdown in the author. Poe, I maintain, is a serious artist who explores the neuroses of his characters with probing intelligence. He permits his narrator to revel and flounder into torment, but he sees beyond the torment to its causes.

In conclusion, then, the five tales I have commented on display Poe's deliberate craftsmanship and penetrating sense of irony. If my thesis is correct, Poe's narrators should not be construed as his mouthpieces; instead they should be regarded as expressing, in "charged" language indicative of their internal disturbances, their own peculiarly nightmarish visions. Poe, I contend, is conscious of the abnormalities of his narrators and does not condone the intellectual ruses through which they strive, only too earnestly, to justify themselves. In short, though his narrators are often febrile or demented, Poe is conspicuously "sane." They may be "decidedly primitive" or "wildly incoherent," but Poe, in his stories at least, is mature and lucid.

Selected Ann Arbor Paperbacks
Works of enduring merit

For a complete list of Ann Arbor Paperback titles write:
THE UNIVERSITY OF MICHIGAN PRESS ANN ARBOR